Praise for Dr. Nicole LePera and *How to Do the Work*

"The world needs this book! No matter where you are on your healing journey, *How to Do the Work* will guide you to stronger relationships, more joy, and a clearer path for your future. We can't always control what happens to us, but Nicole gives us a road map on how to respond from a place of healing and inner peace."

—Lewis Howes, *New York Times* bestselling author of *The School of Greatness*

"In her book *How to Do the Work*, Nicole LePera brilliantly demystifies life-changing therapeutic principles in a way that is easy to digest. This book is a must-read for anyone on a path of personal growth."

—Gabby Bernstein, #1 *New York Times* bestselling author

"*How to Do the Work* is an invitation to do the work with the inner tools we all carry within ourselves. The invitation is yours if you choose to accept it. Wherever you are on your path, Dr. LePera meets you with open arms; your current level of self-mastery is the only prerequisite. This is a guide for your journey of becoming. The world needs your gifts, now more than ever."

—Karlyn Percil-Mercieca, CEO of KDPM Consulting Group, Inc., certified emotional strategist, and neuro-life coach

"On the surface, Dr. LePera's book appears to be a 'how to' manual, but, at its fundament, it's a book about *understanding* the self. For it is only when we deeply understand that we're able to heal."

—The Minimalists

"Want more from life? Looking for answers? *How to Do the Work* will teach you how to find them within yourself. A masterpiece of empowerment—this book changed my life, and trust me, it'll change yours, too."

—Mel Robbins, author of the international bestseller *The 5 Second Rule*

How to Be the Love You Seek

Also by Dr. Nicole LePera

How to Do the Work
How to Meet Your Self

How to Be the Love You Seek

Break Cycles, Find Peace +
Heal Your Relationships

Dr. Nicole LePera

HARPER WAVE
An Imprint of HarperCollins*Publishers*

HOW TO BE THE LOVE YOU SEEK. Copyright © 2023 by Nicole LePera. All rights reserved. Printed in the United States of America. No part of this book may be used or reproduced in any manner whatsoever without written permission except in the case of brief quotations embodied in critical articles and reviews. For information, address HarperCollins Publishers, 195 Broadway, New York, NY 10007.

HarperCollins books may be purchased for educational, business, or sales promotional use. For information, please email the Special Markets Department at SPsales@harpercollins.com.

FIRST EDITION

Art by Leah Carlson-Stanisic; Alfmaler/Shutterstock, Inc.; and first vector trend/Shutterstock, Inc.

Library of Congress Cataloging-in-Publication Data
Names: LePera, Nicole, author.
Title: How to be the love you seek / Dr. Nicole LePera.
Identifiers: LCCN 2023015277 (print) | LCCN 2023015278 (ebook) | ISBN 9780063267749 (hardcover) | ISBN 9780063267756 (ebook)
Subjects: LCSH: Interpersonal relations. | Self-acceptance. | Mind and body. | Healing—Psychological aspects.
Classification: LCC HM1106 .L47 2023 (print) | LCC HM1106 (ebook) | DDC 158.2—dc23/eng/20230413
LC record available at https://lccn.loc.gov/2023015277
LC ebook record available at https://lccn.loc.gov/2023015278

23 24 25 26 27 LBC 5 4 3 2 1

To my mom, and all those who have gone before,
may they rest in the infinite peace of love.

To all of us who remain, may we alchemize
our pain and heal our hearts.

CONTENTS

How to Be
the Love
You Seek

INTRODUCTION

YOU CREATE CHANGE

You're probably reading this book because there's a relationship in your life that's causing you stress. Whether it's with a romantic partner, parent, sibling, child, friend, or colleague, you'd like your dynamic with another person to change—and if you're like most of us, you'd like this change to happen as quickly as possible. Some of you may even be on the fence about continuing to work on a particular relationship, unsure if it's worth the effort or if repair is even possible. Others may be having difficulty finding or sustaining relationships, fearing a future of isolation or loneliness.

I get it. Over the course of a decade working as a clinical psychologist, I had many clients who deeply desired to find a lasting love, resolve repeated conflicts, or break dysfunctional habits. During sessions with individuals, couples, and families, I witnessed a similar pattern again and again: despite their best intentions and efforts, most people were unable to create or maintain the relationships they wanted, and many had grown frustrated and often resentful in the process.

The majority of my clients read relationship books and had, over time, tried all of the latest strategies and tools, hoping something, anything, would help. Many had heard about the concept of "love languages," made popular by Dr. Gary Chapman's 1992 book *The Five Love Languages: The Secret to Love That Lasts*. Dr. Chapman's theory suggests that asking our partner to demonstrate their love in different ways—through physical touch, quality time together, gift giving, words of affirmation, or acts of service (like making the bed or cooking dinner)—can deepen our connection.

This larger approach of implementing external change—expecting others to adapt their behaviors to meet our needs—is a common thread in most relationship-based therapy. Though the practices and tools differ across therapists, books, and ideologies, in general, the core message is generally the same: we must change ourselves in some ways to better meet another's needs and vice versa.

In theory, if you don't feel supported or connected in your relationship, asking the other person to modify their behavior probably sounds like a good plan. But when we take this approach in real life, it often backfires. We can't change others, and relying on them to change their ingrained relational patterns doesn't usually work, at least not for very long. Instead, seeking external change often increases the tension between people, causing reactivity or discontent, and perpetuating conflict or disconnection. It can actually be a recipe for a lifetime of resentment and contempt.

You might (rightly) be wondering, *So what am I supposed to do?* If expecting others to adapt who they are to better accommodate who we are doesn't work, then what does? For years, I asked this question, too.

Early in my adult life, I struggled to create the bonds I craved. Though I had numerous therapeutic tools at my disposal, I continued to feel dissatisfied in most of my relationships, despite my best efforts to increase my self-reflection, self-awareness, and communication. I felt constantly alone, even when surrounded by others, whether it was my family during holiday time, a group of friends who had gathered to celebrate my birthday, or a romantic partner on an intimate vacation. In those moments when I wanted (or even expected) to feel a deep connection, I often found myself feeling lonely and unloved. No matter what I said, how I said it, or what others did or tried to do for me, I still felt disconnected and alone. The more desperately I tried to get close to others, the farther away I felt and the deeper my ache grew.

One Christmas, stuck in these unfulfilling yet familiar cycles, my relationship patterns became clearer to me. At the time, I was dating Sara, a relationship you'll read more about in chapter 1. We had been together for several years and were living in a shared East Village apartment. Because we both went home to our respective families for Christmas Day, we had a tradition of celebrating the holiday together a few days early. That particular year, Sara had asked if we could hang out as a couple, just the two of us. That was a significant departure from our normal dynamic. Sara was a very social person, and our relationship for years had revolved around parties and group dinners. I was touched that she wanted to spend the day with me, and I hoped this special gesture would help deepen our bond.

That morning, we woke up in our decorated apartment, and I cooked us a special breakfast before we sat down to exchange gifts. I was thrilled when I opened an envelope from Sara that included two tickets to see a Cirque du Soleil show—my favorite!—later that day. *She wants to spend more time alone with me! She remembered how much I like Cirque du Soleil! She loves me!* I thought. It was the ultimate romantic gesture. But as we got ready to leave, I started to feel the same gnawing sense of disconnection.

Several hours later, as I sat next to her in a dark, crowded theater, I didn't feel any differently; in fact, I felt even more alone than I had earlier in the day. We weren't speaking or making eye contact, and instead of feeling connected by some invisible band of love that I expected to flow silently between us, I felt as though I were sitting next to a stranger. To deal with the discomfort, I ordered a beer and continued to drink throughout the performance, hoping it would break down whatever wall existed between us.

At the time, I was in the second year of my clinical psychology program and seeing my own therapist. I was working on myself and becoming more self-aware—or so I thought—and communicating my learned insights to others. That only compounded my belief that the problem in my relationship with Sara must be *her* unwillingness or inability to connect.

The longer I stewed in my familiar loneliness and increasing feelings of disconnection, the more I began to think that maybe I had something to do with my unhappiness after all. As I had many times before with many other people, maybe I felt alone with Sara because, emotionally, I was alone. Though it pained me to recognize that I might be unknowingly creating my deepest suffering, it also sparked hope that, as the one responsible, I might also have the power to break these repeated cycles.

Like many of the relational patterns we repeat as adults, my emotional loneliness began when I was young, as a result of my earliest relationships within my family. In childhood, I never learned how to emotionally connect with anyone because no one around me was emotionally connected, either—they didn't learn how. In order to emotionally connect with another person, as I discovered years later, you have to be emotionally connected with yourself. And to be emotionally connected with yourself, you have to be able to authentically feel and express your emotions. Authentically expressing our emotions allows us to feel truly seen, known, and supported by others—core emotional needs we all share.

Because I continually held others responsible for my relationship problems and expected them to change for me, I couldn't see the role I was playing in my own unhappiness. I couldn't see how disconnected I was from my own wants and needs. Though I was working to understand myself better, I wasn't fully aware of how I was showing up in my relationships. Like many of my clients, I expected others to tend to my emotions or make me feel better, without knowing how to do so myself. Believing that the "right" person would "just know" how to ease or take away my deep-rooted feelings of loneliness, I felt disappointed when they didn't, no matter what they did or who they were. Looking to others to meet my needs was sabotaging my relationship satisfaction, yet I continued to repeat the same behaviors, not just in my romantic partnerships but in all of my other relationships, too.

Slowly, as I started to see that I was the one constant in all my relationships, I began to realize that I could never really control what others would or wouldn't do, let alone how quickly, effectively, or comprehensively they could or would support my needs. And, I started to understand that expecting or demanding someone else to change who they were or how they authentically expressed themselves would only leave us both feeling unloved. To be loved for who we are is a universal human need—and one that I definitely didn't want to deny my loved ones.

What I hadn't been taught by my family or in my clinical training was that in order to change how we relate to others and experience our relationships, we have to first change how we relate to and experience ourselves. How we relate to and experience ourselves as adults is directly impacted by how others related to and experienced us in our earliest relationships. Whenever our care was unpredictable, inconsistent, or neglectful when we were young, we formed the core belief that we were unworthy of being cared for or getting our needs met. Feeling intrinsically unworthy, we then began to modify how we expressed ourselves and related to others. Over time, we started to show others only our "acceptable" parts by playing certain roles—what I call *conditioned selves* in this book—to protect ourselves and fit into our earliest environments. As adults, we're still driven by our deep-rooted fears of unworthiness and continue to repeat these habitual patterns within our relationships.

Playing these familiar roles disconnects us from our unique essence, or our individual way of being with others, inevitably leaving us to feel undervalued in our relationships. In order to authentically express ourselves with others, we need to feel safe and secure enough to do so. And in order to feel safe and secure, we first have to feel truly safe and secure in our own body. Many of us, however, can't actually access this sense of safety, because our body can't access it. With chronically unmet needs, our nervous system remains chronically stressed. We get stuck in survival mode, physiologically unable to *feel* safe in the presence of others.

That realization opened my eyes. If I never felt truly safe in my own body, how could I be open to feeling safe enough to experience the moments of joy, ease, and connection that authentic love can provide? If I'm constantly focused on how I measure up to others or to society's standards, suppressing my authentic needs and desires in the process, how can anyone around me have the opportunity to connect with the real *me*? If I don't know and love *all* of me, how can I expect myself to allow someone else to know and love all of me?

I'm sharing my story with you because it's a common one. Regardless of the unique aspects of your story, few of us feel worthy or lovable on our own, without receiving another's validation or approval. As we did when we were children, we constantly look to others to make us feel safe and secure. We continue to suppress the parts of ourselves we once learned were shameful, confirming our deep-rooted fears that those parts are as unworthy as we were originally led to believe. Our stress level increases as we avoid, deny, or modify our authentic expression alongside our resentment toward others. Feeling overwhelmed, we often end up yelling at our loved ones when they don't ask about our day, avoiding difficult but important conversations with our family, or shutting down when our friends try to support us—common habits many of us have as we continue to reenact our childhood coping strategies, even if they only continue to cause us pain and suffering today.

When we reconnect with who we really are and our inherent worthiness, something beautiful happens—and not just to us. The more safe and secure we become in our own Self-expression, the more readily we can create safety and security for others to vulnerably and authentically express themselves, too. It wasn't until I became more connected to what I needed and wanted that I was able to truly *be* my authentic Self with others, allowing me to offer the love I thought I'd been giving them all along. And, to understand what I needed and wanted, I had to connect with my physical body, exploring how it felt in that moment.

As I began to reconnect with my physical body and feel more comfortable curiously exploring its sensations, I became better able to handle stressful or upsetting experiences and share my feelings rather than checking out or shutting down, as I'd done for years. Feeling more comfortable with my emotions and more confident in my growing ability to express myself, I found myself better able to tolerate the discomfort I felt when being emotionally vulnerable around others. Over time, I found myself sharing more honestly with others, even with those I had just met. Opening myself up to my own emotional experiences in relationships allowed me to then be more present to, or to empathize with, the emotional experiences of another.

The reality was, I had to teach myself how to feel safe and secure enough in my own physical body to open my heart and be able to both give and receive the love I craved. Embarking on this life-changing journey has shown me how deep, fulfilling, and expansive love can be, and has taught me that the goal is not only to find love, but also to find and remove all the protective barriers that have been built against it. Love, I have learned, is not about showing up in any particular way but about embodying the feeling itself, offering others the support and opportunity to *be* themselves, exactly as they are.

In this book, I'll share the information and tools I've learned to help guide you on your own journey back to your heart. Throughout these pages, you'll discover how to reconnect with all of you: body, mind, and soul. You'll learn how to recognize the different conditioned selves you play in your relationships, how to identify and meet your needs, how to soothe overwhelming emotions, and ultimately how to reconnect with your heart's innate and limitless capacity to love. Your journey, and this book itself, is about healing your connection to and relationship with your own heart as much as it is about healing your connection to and relationship with the hearts of those around you. As you too will come to learn, it is not until we are connected to and in care of our own hearts that we can truly connect with and tend to the heart of another.

Reconnecting with the infinite wisdom and intuition that lives in your own heart will guide you to make choices that will bring you joy and fulfillment, both within and outside your relationships. Your journey will help you spread love to the spaces between and around you, granting you access to your deepest potential as individuals, partners, and families, and will ultimately benefit all of our shared communities. *Being* the love we seek is the greatest and most healing gift we can give to ourselves, those around us, and the world we all share.

Within your heart is the power to change your relationships, as well as the environment around you. It's the love that lives inside each of you that is the true source of all healing.

1

THE POWER OF YOUR RELATIONSHIPS

Most of us view relationships as happening *to* us rather than *with* or even *because of* us. We "fall in love," getting swept up in another person's passion or power. We pick the wrong people over and over again, missing the "red flags" repeatedly, even if we think we know better. When a relationship falls apart or ends, we often blame the other person, believing that they were unwilling or incapable of making us happy.

It's often difficult to recognize the active role we play in our relationships, including the fact that we may instinctively choose certain people for specific reasons. Many of us "fall in love" with someone not because they've awakened our heart's desire, but rather because that person satisfies unconscious needs we're not even aware we have. And most of us unconsciously choose to surround ourselves with people who enable us to reenact familiar interpersonal habits and patterns from our earliest relationships.

We often feel powerless in our relationships because we spend most of our time and energy focusing on the things we can't control: other people. Though you may currently feel helpless or hopeless to change your relationships, it's empowering to realize that you can, in fact, have agency. We all can. We can all find and create healthy and happy relationships. We can all *be* the love we seek, regardless of what others are doing or what's happening around us.

MY ROLE IN MY RELATIONSHIPS

Until my early thirties, I often felt powerless and passive in my romantic relationships. I jumped from partner to partner, blaming each one for the dissatisfaction I inevitably felt and believing that I could remedy the situation by finding someone who was a "better match" for me. That pattern started when I was sixteen years old and started dating Billy. He was my first romantic relationship, and I was in love—or so I thought.

As in any typical teen romance, we spent most of our time together on the weekends watching TV, hanging out with friends, and going to movies. My family knew about Billy and were supportive of us spending time together. Even so, I never talked about him with my family, only grumbling a short response if my mom or sister happened to ask about him or complaining if he had recently done something to upset me. I didn't talk about our relationship in detail with my friends, either, not because I didn't like him or have strong feelings for him; quite the opposite, I thought I was *in love* with him. But in my family, we didn't share our feelings unless we were upset or worried about something. And I continued that pattern, feeling comfortable talking (or really complaining) about Billy only if he'd hurt or bothered me.

A year and a half into our relationship, Billy and I broke up. I was devastated. One reason was that we were going to go to different colleges the following fall, two universities that were separated by thirteen hours of interstate highway. But another reason was that I was, in Billy's words, "emotionally unavailable," a description that has stuck with me to this day. At the time, I was shocked: I didn't feel emotionally unavailable. I felt very loving toward Billy. From a young age, I had always prided myself on worrying about others and being a good, caring person.

A year into college, I was surprised to find myself attracted to the possibility of dating women. Suddenly I saw the whole Billy incident in a completely different light. *Of course I was emotionally unavailable!* I thought. *I'm gay!* I met my first girlfriend, Katie, while playing sports.

We had the same friends and the same interests, and we spent a lot of time together at practice, traveling to games, and going out with our teammates. That was the basis of our connection: proximity and similarity. We spent most of our time together doing various activities, but I had the nagging feeling that something was missing. Though I desired a deeper connection, I shared very little of my emotional world with her—or anyone else. The truth was, I wasn't actually open or available for emotional connection. Unaware of how I was contributing to our disconnection and without feeling the spark I was looking for, we broke up after a year and a half together, and I started seeing Sofia.

Sofia and I dated on and off for the rest of college, eventually both choosing to move to the same city after graduation. She was different from Katie in many ways, but our co-created dynamic would still allow me to keep myself emotionally distant in order to avoid any deep or authentic emotional connection. I knew it, too. Or rather, my subconscious mind—the part of our brain that drives all our instinctual, automatic thoughts, feelings, and reactions—knew it. This deeply embedded part of our psyche is where we store all our memories, even those we can't explicitly recall, along with our suppressed feelings, childhood pain, and core beliefs.

Sofia had been raised by an emotionally reactive mother who had frequently exploded at her when she was young, yelling and screaming or criticizing and cutting her down. Soon into my relationship with her, Sofia started treating me the same way, yelling when she didn't agree with what I said or did and calling me names or judging me when she disliked aspects of my appearance. Knowing some of what had happened during her childhood, I justified her behavior by telling myself that she didn't mean what she said or how she treated me, that she was just acting out old childhood wounds. And though that was true, I found it incredibly difficult to set boundaries or limits around what I would tolerate with her. Unable to stand my ground or communicate my hurt and upset feelings, I began to notice a growing sense of resentment toward her.

I continued to blame Sofia for my unhappiness without realizing what was really wrong—that I was deeply upset with myself for explaining away my pain and making excuses for her hurtful behavior.

After Sofia and I broke up for the final time, I met a woman named Sara, whom I dated for the next four years. Sara was a happy-go-lucky person who liked to party and have a good time, subconsciously drawing me to her: with Sara, there were always so many events and experiences to distract attention away from any negative feelings. Since she always seemed so carefree, I felt ashamed when I felt anything other than easygoing and untroubled. I started partying with her and joining her in her calendar of near-constant social outings. Attempting to soothe the growing pain and emptiness I felt in absence of a deeper emotional connection, my subconscious continued to rely on its old, ingrained habits as I stayed busy and used substances to distract myself. Though Sara never expressed displeasure with our relationship, she was frequently mean when she drank, which was often. Just as I had done with Sofia, though, I rationalized Sara's behavior by telling myself that she had just had too much to drink or didn't really mean what she was saying or doing. In those moments, I continued to suppress my emotions to try to calm or please her, putting her feelings before my own. As the months turned into years together, I began to feel the same resentment that I had felt with Sofia. Once again, I blamed Sara for not giving me enough attention and not caring about my feelings. Eventually the relationship ended.

After Sara and I broke up, I moved into a three-bedroom apartment with a roommate named Vivienne, who was older than me. Immediately, Vivienne seemed more mature than the other women I had known, and we quickly became friends and then lovers. I was attracted to her independence and emotional self-sufficiency, and we quickly bonded over similar tastes and common interests. Over time, we started sharing our worries and fears with each other deepening our connection.

Like Sofia, Vivienne had grown up in a stressful and unstable home, and she had moved out on her own when she was still a teenager. Priding herself on never needing anyone she insisted from the onset of our relationship that she wasn't the "marrying type." So, when she started talking about marrying me a few years later, I felt extremely special: *She doesn't want to marry, but she wants to marry me!* I gushed privately. We hopped a flight to Connecticut, where our same-sex partnership was legal at the time, and within a year, we moved back to my home-town as a married couple.

Shortly after we moved, my perspective on romantic relationships began to shift. Having just graduated with a doctorate in psychology from the New School for Social Research, I started to work toward my licensing hours, the hands-on training all psychologists need to complete before they can practice privately. The training was full-time and intense. For two years, I attended individual and group sessions in psychoanalysis, a branch of psychology that examines the different ways our unconscious mind drives our thoughts, feelings, behaviors, and relationship dynamics.

Suddenly I found myself immersed in a percolator of self-analysis and evaluation. During individual sessions, I began to explore my subconscious thoughts and feelings—something I had never done before—and spent group sessions evaluating how I interacted with the other students in the class. Within weeks, I realized that there was an immense emotional rift between Vivienne and me; we never talked about our deeper feelings or actual relationship dynamics, but now there I was, discussing both with total strangers. I started to think that I wasn't happy in the marriage and that the relationship didn't provide the emotional connection I so deeply craved.

In our new city, we didn't have as big a circle of friends as we'd had before, which narrowed our world to just the two of us. Without the distractions of social outings, the dynamics of our relationship became more evident, coming to the surface like air bubbles escaping from someone underwater who's held their breath far too long.

I started to regularly complain to Vivienne that I didn't feel con-nected and didn't think our relationship had the emotional depth I wanted and needed. I blamed her for being too independent and told her that she was the reason we couldn't connect on a deeper level, which sent us into cycles of heated conflict. Looking back on it all now, I cringe. Just as in my prior relationships, I failed to recognize the role I was playing in keeping our relationship on an unsatisfyingly superficial level. Because I was so largely detached from my emotions, I couldn't honor my emotions. I didn't even know what my emotions were.

As I became unhappier, Vivienne began to fight harder for our marriage. Her determination frightened me, and when I realized that I wanted a divorce, I was petrified: for the first time in my life, I felt a strong desire that directly opposed the wishes of someone I deeply cared for. I struggled for months to find a way to ask her for a divorce, trying instead to push her away with my actions. When I finally voiced my true feelings, I felt terrified and empowered at the same time: it was the first time in any relationship that I had prioritized my own desires over someone else's.

My divorce marked the first time I began to see the active role I was playing in creating the relationship dynamics that didn't serve me or those around me. On the surface, my subconscious habits of ignoring my needs, suppressing my feelings, and putting others' wants or needs before my own had led me to believe that I was a "good" and "selfless" person. But those habits weren't making me or anyone else happy. In reality, because I hardly ever expressed my true feelings, many of which I didn't even allow myself to have, I only increased my emotional distance from others. Putting others before myself wasn't selfless; it was self-abandonment. Deeply unsatisfied, I often felt agitated or upset, and I began to pick fights and cause arguments about daily issues, which had increased the feelings of resentment between Vivienne and me.

At the time, I couldn't see my own role in these repeated conflicts because my relationship habits had been ingrained in my subconscious since childhood; they were part of my instinctual way of relating to or interacting and connecting with others. I had developed and relied on those habits in my very first relationships: the ones I'd had with my family.

YOUR EARLIEST RELATIONSHIPS
SHAPE YOUR FUTURE

From the outside looking in, you might think I had grown up in a happy and close family. I would have told you the same when I was a child, as well as for most of my adult life. I always had enough to eat; I was encouraged to excel in school and sports; and I didn't experience any physical or sexual abuse. But as I've since learned, the absence of obvious abuse doesn't negate the possibility of emotional neglect and related attachment trauma.

As a child, I was surrounded by stress and illness. My older sister experienced life-threatening health crises in her childhood, and for years my mom suffered her own chronic health and pain issues, which were never openly acknowledged in my family. Similarly, we didn't talk about our feelings, whether we were happy or sad, or directly confront one another if we felt hurt or angry. We were relatively happy after all, right? Why would we ever need to discuss or confront anything?

Instead of connecting on an emotional level, I bonded with my parents and sister through stress and anxiety. Over and over again, when another health crisis or daily stress arose, our focus as a family would align in shared worry until the issue resolved. Everyone would run to care for the "urgent" needs of the stressed, sick, or otherwise upset family member, regularly neglecting their own needs in the process.

Exposed to the consistent repetition of those patterns, I learned over time that my needs and feelings weren't as important as the needs and feelings of those around me. While I *knew* my family loved and cared for me, I never truly *felt* that love or consideration in an emotional sense. When I got upset, as all children do, I needed to be listened to and emotionally soothed or comforted. Since my parents' attention was usually unavailable and consumed by the current crisis, I began to limit how much I shared with them, fearing that I would add to the family's already overwhelming stress level. Eventually, I learned not to acknowledge having needs at all—or at least, I tried not to show my vulnerability in order to avoid the possibility of feeling disappointed if no one was there to support me. To keep myself safe,

I became detached, suppressing my feelings and walling myself off from my emotional world. Those coping strategies became my defensive shield, which I instinctively used to try to protect myself from feeling hurt in relationships for years to come.

My story is, of course, my own, and yours will be different. Regardless of our unique individual journeys, our earliest attachments impact the habits we bring into our adult relationships, especially our romantic ones. Although these habits rarely serve our best interests today, they feel familiar, comfortable, and therefore safe. Because these habits are stored in our subconscious mind and repeated automatically on a daily basis, they are often difficult for us to observe, and we often struggle to consciously see the active role we play in our relationships.

We can learn, however, how to witness our conditioning and create new habits that will better meet the needs we have today. As we come to see and understand that our conditioning is a remnant of our past experiences, we can relieve ourselves of the shame we may feel as a result of our often dysfunctional relational habits. When we recognize and accept the active role we play, we can harness our ability and power to change our relationship dynamics. Because, ultimately, we will need to change the way we show up in our relationships if we want those relationships to change.

After I realized that the common thread in all my dysfunctional relationship patterns was *me*, I empowered myself to begin to shift my dynamics with others. I started to see how I only felt comfortable when I sacrificed my needs in order to avoid the discomfort I felt when disappointing others. I didn't have or set clear boundaries—or any boundaries at all. Disconnected from my authentic needs and desires and constantly overstepping my limits, I ended up feeling emotionally distant and resentful while I continued to hold others responsible, always leaving relationships in search of a more "perfect" partner. Unaware of my own subconscious habits, I blamed others for our relational issues and expected them to change without addressing my own role in creating my continued circumstances.

Only when I started to more honestly witness myself did my relationships begin to evolve. I realized that finding or maintaining healthy relationships would mean making myself emotionally healthy, too. I'd have to do something that felt very uncomfortable at first. I'd have to learn how to honor my own needs and desires by creating new boundaries with others and learning how to be patient and compassionate with myself along the way.

UNDERSTANDING HOW EARLY CHILDHOOD TRAUMA AFFECTS YOU

The truth is, when it comes to our relationships, we repeat what we experienced or learned. So if we grew up in a stressful or chaotic environment, didn't witness healthy habits, or were emotionally neglected or ignored, we repeat the same dynamic as adults in our relationships with others. Even though we may not be aware of it, our past, especially our attachments with our parent-figures, is wired into our mind and body, where it drives us to instinctively seek out and re-create the same kind of relationships as adults. These are our *trauma bonds*, our conditioned patterns of relating to others in a way that mirrors or reenacts our earliest attachments with parent-figures.

Before we dive deeper, it'll be helpful to define a few concepts that we'll explore throughout this book.

Let's start with the term *trauma*. When most people hear the word, they often immediately think of the suffering an individual might experience in the wake of a catastrophic or violent event, like a natural disaster, war, rape, incest, or abuse.

Though trauma is certainly caused by all these incidents, it also results from any stress that exceeds our ability to emotionally process the experience causing continued dysregulation to our body's nervous system. This includes the overwhelming stress that occurs when we don't have the things we need to feel safe and secure, including emotional support. When we don't consistently feel safe and secure or when we fear that those whom we rely on for our survival won't consistently be available to us, we experience a lack of certainty and control. This activates our body's stress circuit, otherwise known as the hypothalamic-pituitary-adrenal (HPA) axis (we'll talk more about that on page 73)[1], which impacts our body's ability to cope with our current circumstances.

Continual shaming of our emotions, denial of our experiences or reality, or emotional abandonment or neglect can all activate our body's stress circuit and create traumatic emotional overwhelm. This impact can occur in a single moment (which is often the case in some of the events listed above), or it can accumulate slowly over time, building up inside us, often without our conscious knowledge. When we aren't able to process our emotional responses, they become imprinted in our mind and body, staying with us and ultimately influencing our thoughts, feelings, and reactions for years to come.

In addition to the stress we experience within our homes, the environmental stress of systemic, cultural, or collective trauma affects a large majority of us keeping us disconnected from the supportive relationships we need for emotional safety and security. Collective trauma occurs when a single event or series of events—such as a natural disaster, financial insecurity, war, colonization/systemic inequities, gender/cultural oppression, or pandemics—create a lack of safety for a group of people, a community, a country, or the greater world. Collective trauma impacts the way people relate to themselves and others, affecting everyone differently, based on our conditioning and intergenerationally modeled coping skills.

Just as we all have unique emotional experiences, we all have different reactive patterns and learned coping strategies based on our specific childhood conditioning, even if we can't consciously recall what happened to us as children. If you've ever participated in traditional therapy or read about behavioral science, you're likely familiar with the concept of *conditioning*, the process by which the beliefs, behaviors, and habits that we learn through a repetition of experiences are stored in our subconscious mind, where they drive our automatic reactions, impulses, and motivations.

Though we can certainly create new habits by making new choices and having new experiences as adults, most of our conditioning occurs when we're young children and dependent on our relationships with our parent-figures. The term *parent-figures* that you'll see throughout this book refers to the people who were primarily responsible for meeting our physical and emotional needs as young children. For most of us, our parent-figures were our biological mother, father, or both, although the term can include grandparents, stepparents, foster parents, siblings, nurses, professional caregivers, or any other primary caretakers in childhood.

As children, no matter who our parent-figures were or whether we think we had a "good" or "bad" relationship with them, we instinctively looked to them for guidance, absorbing information about ourselves and our world. From them, we learned how to express (or suppress) our emotions, how to feel about and treat our body, how to fit in or be socially accepted (i.e., what behaviors were right and wrong), and how to relate to and interact with others. We learned those habits and beliefs by observing those around us, as well as by mirroring what they did.

All young children imitate their parent-figures. You've likely seen this if you've ever watched an infant smile or stick out their tongue in response to their mother or father doing the same. Similarly, young children copy most of what they see their parent-figures do. If our parent-figures shamed or stifled their own emotions, we may have learned to do the same thing. If they criticized their bodies or the physical features of others, we may have learned to criticize or shame these aspects of ourselves. If they reacted to a stressful or upsetting situation by yelling and screaming, we may do the same. If they coped with stressful or upsetting experiences by shutting down and ignoring others, we may have learned to similarly emotionally detach.

To learn how to navigate our emotional world, we first need to feel safe and secure enough to express what we're really thinking and feeling to those around us. Our ability to do this as adults is highly influenced by how we regularly felt in our earliest relationships. The concept of *attachment theory*, which was first developed by the psychoanalyst John Bowlby in 1952, explains that the safety and security of our relationship with our parent-figures influences what kind of relationship we look for and create with others for the rest of our lives.[2] If our attachment to our parent-figures was predominantly safe and secure as young children and our physical and emotional needs were consistently met, we are more likely to prioritize and meet our own needs as adults. Those with secure attachments are more likely to trust themselves and others and have emotional resilience, or are able to tolerate and quickly rebound from uncomfortable emotions. This emotional self-trust is built over time through our consistent, reliable, and predictable actions. In a relationship, trust is the feeling that you can count on someone to behave in a certain way.

Many of us didn't grow up with safe and secure attachments because our parent-figures were impacted by their own earliest relational environments in which many of their needs were not met. As a result, our physical and / or emotional needs weren't consistently identified or tended to in early childhood. Today, we may be unable to identify or tend to our needs as adults because no one helped us learn how to do so as children. We may not trust ourselves or others, often reacting impulsively because we lack the emotional resilience to deal with uncomfortable emotions, whether specific ones like stress, sadness, or anger, or all of our unpleasant feelings in general. We may continue to abandon or betray ourselves, overcommitting our time, energy, or emotional resources in an attempt to get another to care for us, or we may close ourselves off from the support of others entirely.

Whether our earliest attachments were secure or insecure, our habitual patterns of relating were wired into our subconscious mind, where they remain. It's these patterns that automatically and instinctively continue to pull us toward similar relationship dynamics well into adulthood.

YOU ARE DRIVEN BY YOUR UNMET
CHILDHOOD NEEDS

Before we can identify our attachment patterns, it's important to first understand what unmet childhood needs are. Unmet childhood needs can be physical or emotional; the former is generally easier to understand.

Physiologically, our body functions the same way. Our lungs oxygenate our blood with the air around us, our cells helps us function by converting nutrients in our food, and our muscles move us around and help us lift and carry heavy things. These structural similarities are universal to all humans, and as a result, we share the same basic physical needs: water, oxygen, nutrients, a balance of rest/restorative sleep and movement.

If your physical needs weren't met in childhood, you may not have had enough food to eat, appropriate clothing to wear, enough space for physical movement, or quiet to rest. Or you may have not felt physically safe in your environment for a number of other reasons, including financial insecurity and racial discrimination. Unmet physical needs in childhood can include more subtle inadequacies, like not being physically touched or soothed because you were often left alone or were raised by others who were uncomfortable themselves with physical contact, or not getting enough sleep because your childhood home was too loud or chaotic. Many of us continue to struggle with unmet physical needs as adults because we don't have access to the stable financial resources necessary to consistently care for our body or are unable to feel safe and secure in our own skin. Regardless of the cause, when our physical needs aren't consistently met, our body activates a nervous system response that shifts us into survival mode, pushing our emotional needs to the back burner.

What's even more common than unmet physical needs is unmet emotional needs. Nearly everyone I know, even those who had well-intentioned parent-figures, grew up with unmet emotional needs. This is to be expected, given the number of hours and jobs many of them had to work in order to provide for us financially. How can anyone who is working overtime, and not sleeping, eating, or tolerating their own stress well, emotionally care for another? They can't.

Despite these societal inequities and realities, we all have core emotional needs that need to be tended to. The deepest need we all have in all our relationships—whether as children or now as adults—is to feel safe and secure enough to *be* ourselves without losing the connection to and support of others. Feeling safe and secure enough to honestly express our perspectives and experiences helps us create emotional intimacy. When we're able to be emotionally vulnerable and honest regardless of what we're feeling, we allow more of ourselves to be witnessed and known. Look at the questions below and spend some time exploring how emotionally safe and secure you feel in your different relationships:

- Do I feel safely and securely connected to you physically and emotionally?
- Do I feel that I am / our relationship is important to you?
- Do I feel I am loved and cared for by you, even in moments of physical or emotional distance?

When we feel emotionally safe and secure, we are able to trust that another person sees, accepts, and appreciates who we are, can give us the space to change or evolve, and has our best interests at heart. If we have this safety and security in our earliest attachments, we develop the ability to trust our physical connection with our body and its ability to cope with stress and other upsetting emotions. When we feel this safely and securely connected to our emotional world, we're able to authentically share ourselves with those around us and trust our relationships knowing we can reconnect or repair after moments of conflict or disconnection.

For a parent-figure to help a child feel safe, valued (or seen, heard, and appreciated), and loved on a consistent basis, they themselves have to be able to feel these ways consistently, too. But most of our parent-figures did not feel those ways because they weren't able to regulate their emotions due to their own childhood trauma (and consequential nervous system dysregulation, which we'll explore below). As a result, most of us didn't grow up feeling the emotional safety or security we needed to be able to authentically express ourselves, causing us to feel deeply unworthy and emotionally alone.

If our parent-figures weren't able to feel emotionally safe and secure themselves, they weren't able to create the environment we needed to explore and express our authentic Self. As a result, we ended up feeling emotionally abandoned or overwhelmed by them, left alone to figure out how to navigate our own stressful or upsetting emotions and experiences. The feelings associated with childhood emotional neglect (CEN) or abandonment actually activate the same pathways in our brain as physical pain does, sending our mind and body into a continuous stress response that causes trauma.

A lack of emotional safety and security in childhood can look like being regularly ignored, criticized, or yelled at for expressing different emotions, instilling deep-rooted beliefs that you're "too much" and continued difficulty expressing yourself. Or it can look like being discouraged or prevented from pursuing a passion or interest that now causes you to feel unsure about what you like as an adult.

While there are many more than are listed, below are some other indicators that you may have had unmet emotional needs in childhood.

- Your parent-figures didn't or couldn't see you as a separate or unique individual, often treating you as an extension of themselves who needed to follow in their footsteps or adopt their beliefs, emotions, appearance, and even careers. In adulthood, you may never feel truly safe or secure to be who you are, or you may not be sure what you believe, how you feel, or what you're interested in.

- Your parent-figures didn't or couldn't pay attention to you on a consistent basis because they were distracted by their work, relationship issues, financial demands, or unresolved trauma. In adulthood, you may self-isolate or be hyperindependent, walling yourself off from any type of connection to or support from others.

- Your parent-figures often took things personally and quickly became defensive or emotionally reactive, externalizing or blaming others, including you, for various issues or conflicts. In adulthood, you may often worry about "being in trouble," look to others to make you feel better, and often find yourself placating or pleasing others to avoid conflict.
- Your parent-figures had two personas: one they displayed at home, where they were critical, shaming, or shut down, and another they displayed in public, where they were warm, affectionate, and seemingly loving toward you. In adulthood, you may often feel on edge, unsure of, or confused by the intentions or actions of those around you.
- Your parent-figures often highlighted or bragged about your accomplishments to others yet mostly ignored you unless you were achieving something or receiving accolades for your performance. In adulthood, in the absence of external validation, you may feel unworthy, unlovable, or empty.
- Your parent-figures regularly dismissed, invalidated, or ignored your perspective or feelings. In adulthood, you may find yourself stuck in polarized thinking ("right" or "wrong," "good" or "bad"), often struggling to see or validate another's perspective especially when upset or in conflict.
- Your parent-figures regularly centered their own needs or emotions, often highlighting or overemphasizing the role they played in raising you, regularly repeating or reminding you of all the things they had done or sacrifices they had made for you. In adulthood, you may feel chronically indebted to others or selfish for having any needs at all.

MY UNMET EMOTIONAL NEEDS

Although I didn't realize it until I began my own inner work, my childhood environment hadn't allowed me to feel consistently safe, valued, and loved for just being myself. When I was very young—

as well as throughout my childhood, teenage, and adult years—my mom remained emotionally distant, her attention consumed by the chronic pain she felt in her physical body. Constantly distracted and locked in survival mode, she was unable to express little emotion outside of worry about my well-being or validation around my latest accomplishment. As I was later told, she treated me and my two other siblings as if she were a "medic," feeding and caring for us without attuning to or emotionally connecting with us. My dad was an active physical presence in my life, playing with me and entertaining my restless nature, but he too remained emotionally distant, hardly ever sharing feelings outside of his daily stress or annoyances with others. My sister, who is fifteen years older than me, similarly took an active role in raising and spending time with me, especially when my mom was physically unable. But she, too, was emotionally closed off, having developed the habit in her own relationship with both of our parents.

All children have an active inner world, both mentally and emotionally—and as a young child, I was no different. But whenever I tried to share experiences with my mom, she often expressed worry, trying to quickly solve or dismiss whatever issue was causing us both to experience uncomfortable feelings. Other times, she'd try to control my behavior to relieve her own hurt, anger, sadness, or disappointment by saying things like "Oh, please don't say or do [insert undesired expression/action], or I'll get sad" or "Oh, won't you [insert desired request] for me so I don't have to worry?"

Fearful of losing my connection to my family, I regularly chose to honor their needs or desires over my own. Learning these codependent dynamics and feeling no separation between my emotions or perspective and others' feelings or perspectives, I learned to take responsibility for their emotional experiences. Caught in an internalized cycle of self-blame, I developed the habit of explaining away others' behaviors, as I later went on to do with Sofia and in many of my other relationships.

My home largely lacked emotional boundaries, adding more stress to an already overwhelmed environment. Anytime I shared intimate information with one family member, it was quickly relayed to all the others without my permission, request, or notice, in the belief that it was supportive to do so. Those violations of trust caused me to become even more self-protective, further limiting the personal details I shared. Over time, I learned that it was easier to ignore and stifle my feelings altogether. Eventually, I convinced myself that I didn't have any feelings at all because it felt safer than acknowledging those that I wasn't comfortable expressing.

This absence of boundaries in my family helped create my belief that relationships weren't emotionally safe. Because I felt distant from the people I was supposed to be closest with—my family—I feared that something was wrong with me, a fear that my mom exacerbated by continuously commenting on my "secretive" nature. I didn't feel comfortable sharing personal details of my life with my mom, though, because she wasn't able to create the emotional safety, security, or connection that I needed to authentically express myself to her. As a result, she ended up knowing little about my life, not because I was private by nature, as she told me, but because I never felt safe enough to share with her what was really going on with me.

As I got older, I instinctually began to look for and maintain the same emotional distance in my adult relationships that I had experienced as a child. Largely disconnected from my own wants and needs, I focused more on how I showed up for others, avoiding issues and conflicts, constantly fearful of disconnection or abandonment. Sometimes, I even felt ashamed of myself for having a desire or feeling that might disappoint or upset another person. I carried all these dysfunctional habits into my adulthood, continuing to rely on the same subconscious coping strategies I had adopted and used as a child to protect myself from my overwhelming and undersupported emotions.

THE NEUROPHYSIOLOGICAL IMPACT
OF YOUR CHILDHOOD

Though other early childhood relationships, including those we have with our siblings, grandparents, caregivers, friends, and teachers, can create trauma bonds, nothing has a greater impact on our current relationships than our earliest attachments with our parent-figures. Why? The answer to this question is key to understanding and unlocking the work we can do to change our relationships today—effectively and sustainably.

Our attachments to our parent-figures didn't just condition our behavior; our earliest relationships also physically programmed our nervous system, determining how we think, feel, and act. That's because our nervous system drives our thoughts, feelings, and reactions, in addition to influencing our other physiological functions.

Our nervous system is "profoundly social," according to UCLA neuroscientist Dr. Daniel Siegel, who helped pioneer the field of interpersonal neurobiology, an emerging area of science that explores the fascinating interaction that exists between our brain and our relationships. As Siegel has shown us, our brain *needs* other people to function.[3] Since the dawn of humankind, we've depended on the safety that families and groups provide. And when we're unable to feel safely connected with others, the resulting feelings of aloneness can negatively impact both our well-being and our physical safety.[4]

Today, our body and brain are still programmed to need other people. We instinctively seek out relationships, both romantic and platonic, whether we consciously think we want them or not. Though modern Western culture may promote a more rugged individualism offering an idea of the "solo self," no one is or can be an island unto themselves; having relationships throughout life is necessary for us not only to survive but to thrive. We all exist in a relationship with someone *and* something at all times, including with the environment around us and the earth on which we live (more on this in chapter 10).

Not only does our brain need relationships to physically survive and function, our relationships with others impact how our nervous system operates. As Siegel explained, "human connections create neuronal connections," meaning that our relationships with others determine how our neurons, or brain cells, connect or communicate with one another.[5] These neural connections or communications, when repeated by our brain over and over again, become the basis of our inner world, driving our daily thoughts, feelings, and reactions.

While any relationship can create new neural connections, it's our earliest attachments with our parent-figures that built our brain's basic architecture. Human infants are born with a largely underdeveloped nervous system—which is why we're so dependent on our parent-figures for the first few years of life compared to the days, weeks, or months that other mammals need before they can survive on their own. During our early years, our nervous system grows and develops rapidly, firing and forming a million new neural connections every second.[6] Although these neural pathways undergo pruning later in childhood, we create most of our neural infrastructure as infants and young children.

It's the people with whom we first connect—that is, our parent-figures—who cause our nervous system to fire and wire in certain ways. It's what they do (or don't do) when they interact with us and how we respond (child development experts call this the "serve and return") that becomes patterned in our brain. These patterns drive our brain's operating system, activating and controlling our automatic or instinctual thoughts, feelings, and reactions for life—or until we harness our brain's neuroplasticity, or its power to change.

YOUR CONDITIONED STRESS RESPONSES

Our nervous system plays a foundational role in our existence. It connects with and controls our biological organs and physiological functions. It drives our automatic thoughts, feelings, and habitual behaviors. And it determines our level of physical, mental, and emotional safety, not only with ourselves but also with others by activating a stress response when we encounter a threat, causing us to move toward or away from connection.

You likely already know something about the body's "fight-or-flight" response that's controlled by our nervous system. Fight-or-flight occurs when our nervous system initiates physiological reactions like dilated pupils and an increased heart rate and breathing rate in response to a threat, giving us energy to face danger head-on (*fight*) or run away from it (*flight*). Our nervous system can also activate a "freeze" or "shutdown" response, which slows or shuts down our body's physiological functions, usually when a threat is overwhelming or consistent. And, although it's not as well known, we've even evolved to adapt a "fawn" response to stress, with our nervous system remaining on high alert as we continuously scan our environment to identify, eliminate, or deescalate possible threats as they become apparent to us.

These nervous system responses happen automatically, most times outside our awareness. They are normal, natural, and even healthy; we need them to confront a threat (*fight*), run away from one (*flight*), play dead or conserve our physical resources (*freeze* or *shutdown*), or maintain bonds in certain communal crises (*fawn*). If our nervous system never activated stress responses, we wouldn't learn how to regulate our emotions or develop the resilience we need to deal with stress and return quickly to a state of calm and physiological and emotional wellness.

The problem for many of us though is that our nervous system doesn't return to a state of relaxed calm. Instead, our body gets stuck in a stress response, though not necessarily because we face stress all day long. Though many of us have stressful, busy lives, if our nervous system is regulated, we can toggle back and forth between a stress response and calm, everyday function. But many of us can't toggle back and forth because our body didn't develop the ability to do so when we were children.

If we grew up in a consistently stressful environment or with parent-figures who couldn't regularly meet our physical or emotional needs, our nervous system may have continued to signal that there was a fire around us long after the embers had cooled. Since our brain was still developing, those stress responses got programmed into our nervous system's standard operating mode.

Today, our nervous system is likely still wired as it was in childhood, possibly even stuck in a stress response even when there's no active threat around us. These conditioned stress responses are familiar and comfortable to our brain, as an old baby blanket is to a grown child, both biologically and emotionally. Biologically, our nervous system may struggle to physiologically downshift from a stress response, even though living in a constant state of stress isn't optimal for our body. Emotionally, we may find ourselves feeling uncomfortable, agitated, uneasy, or bored when we're not experiencing a familiar stress cycle. For some of us, if all we ever knew as children was stress, chaos, or abandonment, we may never be able to experience feelings of peace and connection unless we make the conscious choice to rewire our neurobiology.

Conditioned stress responses keep us stuck in our trauma bonds with others on a physiological level, even when we're adults. When our nervous system gets wired for stress in certain ways as children, it drives us to feel instinctually attracted to certain people only to become trapped in reactivity cycles with them (we'll talk more about these later). Our dysregulated nervous system causes us to see or re-create situations with others that fire our predictable stress states, giving us a physiological feeling of safety and control when, in reality, neither exists. Whether we gain a sense of false safety when we're picking fights (*fight*), distracting ourselves (*flight*), walling ourselves off (*freeze* or *shutdown*), or putting others' needs before our own (*fawn*), we are driven to repeat these habits, even if they're not helpful within our relationships or aren't aligned with our conscious intentions or desires. In other words, we can't help it: our brain is wired for stress when we're alone or around other people. In chapter 3, we'll talk more about how to identify when we're in a stress response and what we can do to shift out of it.

CHANGING YOUR BRAIN TO CHANGE
YOUR RELATIONSHIPS

While our relational habits are wired into our brains, we can change them. Though there are still things we don't know about the human body, science has more recently discovered that our brain is incredibly malleable. It can change over time, no matter how old we are or how much stress or trauma we experienced.

The term *neuroplasticity* refers to our brain's ability to form new neural connections throughout our lifetime. Whenever we form new neural connections, we give our nervous system the opportunity to create new instinctual or automatic thoughts, feelings, and behaviors; in short, we can change our brain's standard operating mode. Each new experience we have and every new person we meet has the potential to create new neural connections. But newness in itself isn't the answer; if we approach new experiences and new people with the same conditioned thoughts, feelings, and habits we've had since childhood, our nervous system will fire the same neural connections it always has, producing the same relational patterns and dynamics. If we truly want to change our relationships, we have to change our subconscious, which means shifting how we instinctively think, feel, and act, regardless of whether it's with new people or those we already know.

Changing our instinctual habits isn't easy; it will feel unfamiliar and uncomfortable at first. But it is possible. The first step is to learn to become conscious of or to witness the conditioned habits that live in our subconscious mind, creating and maintaining our trauma bonds with others. After we begin to witness our trauma bond patterns, we can begin to do the work to develop more adaptive and resilient ways of dealing with stress and relating to others that will better serve ourselves and relationships.

As I hope you're starting to see, you are not a passive bystander in any of your relationships. Asking others to change who they are or what they do to make us feel better doesn't often actually solve our relationship issues. By harnessing the new advances in science that we'll explore here together, it is you who has the power to change your relationships, no matter what someone else does or doesn't do. You can finally stop waiting or relying on anyone else. You can and will the change. And that change can begin now.

To change how we interact with others (and by association how they interact with us), we will need to extend our awareness beyond our brain to include our whole, embodied Self. Our embodied Self is the interconnection between our body, mind, and soul that we'll explore in detail in the next chapter.

Your Emotional Safety and Security Checklist

Take some time to consider your relationships with your parent-figures or earliest caregivers. In reviewing the following statements, check the ones that best describe your most consistent childhood experiences.

_____ I was offered comfort and support by emotionally present adults when I was upset.

_____ I was modeled boundaries and saw adults who respectfully communicated their limits without using abusive discipline or fear-inducing threats.

_____ I was given space to explore developmentally appropriate behaviors and was not parentified by adults, or made to counsel their emotions, put in care of younger siblings, or used as a pawn to manipulate or control others.

_____ I was modeled ways to safely express my feelings by adults who didn't control the emotional climate of the home with their own feelings and who regularly asked me how I felt and validated my shared emotional experiences.

_____ I was modeled how to directly express my emotional needs by adults who asked for support without using emotional manipulation techniques like giving others the silent treatment, raging, guilting, shaming, or blaming.

_____ I witnessed adults who consistently took responsibility for their actions and apologized for their role in conflicts and emotional upsets.

_____ I was given space to develop my own individuality by adults who allowed me to explore my own thoughts and ideas and didn't pressure me to conform to other's beliefs (or groupthink).

_____ I was encouraged to explore my curiosities and passions by adults who asked questions and expressed a desire to know me and my interests and had time for play and spontaneous, unstructured activities.

The more boxes you checked, the more likely it is that you had safe and secure relationships growing up. On the other hand, if you, like me, don't relate to many or any of the above childhood experiences, your earliest relationships likely didn't provide you with the safety and security needed to explore your own emotional expression. The great news is that the tools throughout this book will give you an opportunity to create safety and security for yourself, no matter what your past circumstances.

Your Relationship Experiences and Beliefs Exploration

Take some time to consider the various relationships in your life, beginning with your earliest parent-figures or caregivers. Explore the following questions and write down your reflections in the space provided or in a separate notebook or journal if helpful.

In childhood, how often (and when) were your needs (physical and/or emotional) met?

_____

_____

In childhood, how often (and when) were you left with unmet needs (physical and/or emotional)?

_____

_____

In childhood, how often (and when) were you expected to monitor or meet the needs (physical and/or emotional) of others, including your parent-figures?

_____

_____

In childhood, how often (and when) did you turn to your parents or other caregivers for safety or to protect or comfort you, learning as a result to trust others/the world around you?

_____

_____

In childhood, how often (and when) did you feel you needed to flee from your parent-figures to find safety or protect or comfort yourself, learning as a result to feel fearful of others or the world around you?

_____

_____

In childhood, how often (and when) did you experience feelings of pleasure or joy?

_____

_____

In childhood, how often (and when) did you experience feelings of playfulness or spontaneity?

_____

_____

In childhood, how often (and when) did your parents or other caregivers model negotiation and collaborative problem solving?

_____

_____

Now take some time to consider your relationships as an adult. Explore the following questions and write down your reflections in the space provided or in a separate notebook or journal if helpful.

When I think about relationships, I *think* . . .

_____

_____

When I think about love, I *think* . . .

_____

_____

When I think about relationships, I *feel* . . .

_____

_____

When I think about love, I *feel* . . .

_____

_____

2

EXPLORING YOUR EMBODIED SELF

If someone had asked me about my connection to my soul ten years ago, I would have laughed. *My soul?* At the time, I didn't know what or where my soul was or if it even existed, let alone how to connect with it. After spending eight years earning a doctorate in clinical psychology, I had developed a very academic, mechanistic outlook on the world. I believed that everything could and should be explained by the hard facts of science. And if science couldn't explain it, then it wasn't real or legitimate.

I first heard about my "soul" when I was young. Raised Catholic, I went to a parochial grade school and high school and was expected to go to Mass every Sunday, which I usually protested. At church, I learned the Christian view of the soul, which seemed supernatural or otherworldly to me—a concept I could never objectively understand. The more interested I became in science and psychology, the more the Christian concept of a soul felt illusory, even superstitious.

My perspective changed after going through the emotional crisis I now understand as my "dark night of the soul." It began, not surprisingly, at a time when I reached the end of my lifelong list of achievements, receiving my PhD, maintaining a committed relationship, and making a stable living by opening a successful private practice. Still feeling deeply unfulfilled despite everything I had already accomplished in my life, I became more consciously aware of how disconnected and unsure I felt about myself, who I was, and what I wanted—a way that I had been feeling for years or decades, even though I struggled to admit it. I imagine some of you may feel similarly now, and although it might not seem so, these feelings are often the beginning of awakening to a more deeper understanding of yourself. Though I couldn't see it at the time, my own awakening began after I hit an emotional rock bottom while vacationing with my partner, Lolly.

Those of you who read my first book, *How to Do the Work*, may remember the story: I was sitting in a rocking chair eating oatmeal and reading a book about emotionally absent mothers when I broke down and began to cry uncontrollably. Though I didn't fully understand what was happening at the time, I had finally begun to more consciously allow myself to realize that I didn't share an emotional connection with my family, especially with my mom. With the help of that book, I was starting to see all the ways I had compensated for that lack of connection, constantly dismissing or ignoring my own needs and desires in order to "connect" with her and those I loved most. For years, I'd drop everything to be available to nearly everyone in my life without pausing first to make sure I was also caring for myself. If a friend invited me out to the movies, to dinner, or for a hike, I'd immediately say yes, even if I didn't have the desire or energetic resources to go. If a loved one needed emotional support, I would do anything to try to comfort them, even if that meant jeopardizing my physical or emotional well-being. I was constantly worried others might think I was selfish or be feel disappointed if I tended to my own needs before theirs.

The irony, of course, is that prioritizing others' needs while dismissing or ignoring my own didn't help me feel safe, valued, or loved in *any* of my relationships. Instead, doing so just made me feel hollow, lonely, and unfulfilled on the inside—all the feelings that hit me like a tidal wave while I was sitting in a rocking chair reading on vacation. With chronically unmet needs, my body would never feel safe enough to shift out of survival mode and give me the opportunity to explore the deeper interests and desires of my authentic Self.

In that moment, I started to open my eyes and see all the ways that

I had put off dealing with those uncomfortable feelings, mostly by looking to others to take them away or make me feel better. When the efforts of my family, friends, or romantic partner failed to uplift me, I only felt emptier and sadder on the inside. Eventually, I only grew more frustrated and resentful that others couldn't "save" me or fill the deepening hole inside my heart.

Contrary to the messages many of us received in our families or through the media (hello, Disney and rom-com movies), the perfect partner or relationship just doesn't exist and even if they did, they couldn't take away our pain. It is not anyone's job to rescue or "complete" us because we are capable and whole exactly as we are. We are all human beings doing the best we can, and having romanticized ideas about relationships only sets us up for disappointment. At the same time, we need to learn how to tolerate disappointing others. Many of us were raised with certain idealized notions of morality or what makes us a "good person," driven by familial, cultural, religious, and societal messaging that often prioritizes the comfort of others, activating internalized guilt and self-neglecting habits.

One of my clearest memories from my childhood is my mom rehearsing a list of excuses with me after I had told her that I didn't want to go to a friend's party. In her attempt to help me decline my friend's invite, she coached me while we made up an excuse about why I couldn't go, and we practiced together. Then, with fear coursing through my ten-year-old body, I made the call to my friend and recited the excuse we'd crafted. My mom, of course, had good intentions; she didn't want me to appear rude. She had been conditioned in the same way during her own childhood. But this kind of conditioning lays the subconscious groundwork for the "good person" beliefs I know still exist inside me today, especially when I struggle to turn down an invite unless I have an "acceptable" reason, often overexplaining and overapologizing when I do. Driven to please others in order to be liked, I found myself constantly fearful of disappointing or upsetting those around me.

The reality is, the sooner we can release any illusions of perfection in ourselves or our relationships, the sooner we can begin to embrace the messy, vulnerable journey we call love. We can stop believing that others will leave us if we can't do something or if we say no because that's not true, even if our mind tells us it is. Truly healthy relationships require a commitment to learning through these moments of difference or disagreement using emotional regulation, active communication, conflict resolution or repair (something we'll talk more about in later chapters), and compromise.

These realizations may sound unnerving—and they certainly were for me at the time—but the awareness I gained during my dark night of the soul was the greatest gift I ever received. That clarity led to the start of my SelfHealing journey, when I started to take responsibility for myself, empowering myself to become an active participant in creating the change I so deeply needed. I applied this responsibility to my relationships with others: I was the only one who could realistically ensure all of my needs were known and met. And it would only be when my needs were met that I'd feel safe enough to share my natural gifts and talents authentically with those around me.

For the first time in my life, I began to see how the most important relationship I have is the relationship I have with myself. I started to realize that if I wasn't able to be honest with myself about my deepest needs and desires, I would never be able to truly or authentically connect with another person. Being honest with myself was the first step in sharing myself more authentically with others. To start breaking some of my conditioned habits, every time I noticed myself thinking about what I "should" (or "shouldn't") do or how I "should" (or "shouldn't") respond, which was often, I created a new habit of pausing (using the empowerment pause exercise you'll learn on page 120) to check in with myself. This time gave me the opportunity to explore whether there was something else I needed or wanted to do for myself instead.

For the next several years, I concentrated on exploring my own wants and needs. As I got clearer about what was true for me, I distanced and even removed myself from certain relationships that were no longer aligned. That created the space I needed to focus on accepting and caring for all of me rather than just the parts of me that were validated by others. Identifying my authentic needs wasn't easy; it meant peeling back years of childhood conditioning that had led me to think, feel, and act in ways that didn't serve my best interests. The more I stripped away the deeply embedded layers of conditioning, the more clearly I was able to connect with my authentic Self, or who I am at my core. And my authentic Self wasn't just part of me; it was *all* of me. I had a unique way of being in the world, an essence that made me *me*.

Finally, it dawned on me: this is my soul. My soul is my essence, what makes me special for being the individual I am. It is an energy that is unique to me, always swirling and shifting with the people and things around me, creating an individualized expression that no one else in the universe can possibly have.

As I continued to awaken, I started to read more about our mind-body connection, including research into the field of quantum mechanics, where I stumbled upon scientific evidence of our "soul." Quantum mechanics is the study of our world on a subatomic level—"science's most precise, powerful theory of reality," as described by John Horgan in *Scientific American*.[7] The field of quantum mechanics explains that everything in our world, including you and me, is made up of both energy and matter. Though most of us identify with the material existence of our physical body, we have an unseen energy that contributes to and animates all our physical experiences. This creates a unique vibrational energy at our core—what can be called our soul—that interacts with the world around us.

Coming to understand the concept of the soul through science was pivotal for me. At the time, I felt I needed scientific validation to recognize and accept the most vital part of my being. As soon as I had proof, though, I knew that I had to learn how to connect with this innermost part of me if I wanted to meet all my needs and heal all of me, including my connections with others.

You might not believe in the idea of a soul, as I once didn't. Or you might believe that it exists somewhere but have no idea where to find it. Regardless of what you think or feel about your soul, this book will help you connect with who you are at your core; it's the next step in your journey and the one that will ultimately enable you to *be* the love you seek.

Before you can reconnect with your soul, though, it's important to learn how to reconnect with your physical body and explore your subconscious mind. This is how we begin to integrate our embodied Self and eventually heal all our embodied relationships with others.

UNDERSTANDING YOUR EMBODIED SELF

We are what we think. Or that's what many of us believe, thanks in part to the famous French philosopher René Descartes, best known for the saying "I think, therefore I am." But we're far more complex than the thoughts that run through our mind. When we show up in our relationships, we show up as all of us: body, mind, and soul. This is why we often can't relieve our suffering or change our relationships by changing just the thoughts in our conscious mind.

To truly heal, we need to understand our embodied Self. Our embodied Self is the interwoven expression of our physical body, our mind (both our conscious and subconscious), and our soul, or authentic Self. Our soul and authentic Self are similar entities—both represent our unique essence or who we are at our core—so you'll see the terms used interchangeably throughout this book.

We can begin to embody our authentic Self when we make sure we're meeting our needs. We have three different types of needs:

- **Physical needs:** nutrient-dense foods, nourishing oxygen and water, adequate rest/restorative sleep, beneficial movement
- **Emotional needs:** to feel safe enough to authentically express ourselves and to connect with and be supported by others
- **Spiritual needs:** to connect with and express our intrinsic passions, purpose, creativity, and imagination

Making sure we're consistently getting all these needs met enables us to feel safely grounded and intentional in our responses to the world around us. We're able to feel safe and secure enough to *be* our authentic Selves within our relationships, which enables us to form authentic connections with others.

Hypothetically, we would have all learned how to meet these needs for ourselves through our interactions with our caregivers in child-hood. As many of you parents are acutely aware, infants are com-pletely dependent on their caregivers to meet all of their needs for them, all of the time. Given the reality that it's an enormous responsi-bility to care for another person, never is it more important to ensure your own needs are also being cared for. As you'll continue to learn throughout this book, it is only when our body is getting what it needs to function that we are able to navigate the multitude of stressful mo-ments we'll face while tending to another person. Many of you par-ents reading this, especially those with infants or several children, may understandably find yourselves lacking in the time, energy, or finan-cial resources required for supportive child care. Most modern-day, parents are cut off from neighbors and local communities, preventing them from accessing the practical and emotional support still available in some village-based communities. Parents these days are often over-worked and under-supported, barely meeting their own needs and, as a result, physiologically unable to meet the needs of another.

I encourage all of you parents to practice regularly extending com-passion to yourself, especially if you notice feelings of shame or other uncomfortable emotions as you continue to read about and explore the impact of unmet childhood needs. In my opinion, there is no role that has a greater impact on society than parenting, and it is necessary that we continue to come together as human beings to honor, sup-port, and prioritize parenting for being the sacred act it is.

Regularly carving out small moments for self-care practices will help you remain more calm and grounded in the face of the over-whelmingly stressful experiences of parenting. Practicing self-care can change how you show up for your children while also providing them with a healthy model of self-prioritization and self-care.

As adults, we can learn to care for our physical needs by tuning in to our physical body. We can begin to pay closer attention to our physical sensations, the real origin of our thoughts and feelings (sit tight; we'll cover this surprising fact in just a moment). We can even become conscious or aware of our subconscious mind and the conditioned thoughts, feelings, and habits that live there, driving most of our everyday actions and reactions. And finally, we can learn how to tap into our intuition and trust our instincts so that we can each embody and express the unique essence that makes us *us*.

So, what does it mean to embody something? When we embody something, we step into it as all of us: body, mind, and soul. These aren't three separate entities but one integrated self. Integration occurs when individual parts join to form a unified whole. Think of integration as a fruit salad rather than a fruit smoothie: each piece maintains its distinct qualities while all come together to form something more delicious than the individual parts.[8] (Thank you, Dr. Daniel Siegel, for this analogy.)

When we integrate our embodied Self or align our desires, intentions, and actions, we're able to show up feeling safe, secure, and whole as individuals in our relationships. When we feel safe, secure, and whole, as individuals we're able to be curious, empathetic, and receptive to others. Only then can we create the same safety and security others need to be their authentic Self, too.

When we're connected to our body and attuned to our own emotions, we can begin to safely and securely connect with others in a deeper, more authentic way. Sharing an authentic emotional connection with someone allows us to attune to them, or sense what they may be experiencing. We're open and receptive, responsive to shifts in and changes in their emotional states and are able to notice and respond to others' emotional cues, including those that are nonverbal. This doesn't mean that we need to be perfectly attuned to others all the time; that's not possible, even for the most well-meaning of us. For all caregivers reading this who have harshly judged some (or all) of your past misattunement, I hope you can begin to extend yourself grace and compassion for those moments of understandable disconnection or overwhelmed reactivity. All of us can benefit from beginning to congratulate ourselves every time we make the choice to return to our loved ones after moments of misattunement in order to rebuild the safety and security of those relationships.

When we share this kind of deeper and secure connection at least some of the time, we create a foundation of authentic or true emotional connection. When two people feel safe enough to *be* themselves, they can exist in an interdependent relationship, allowing their differences while remaining connected and working collaboratively with each other. Each individual is able to express their unique energy and gifts while allowing the other person to do the same. You can think of interdependence as the opposite of codependency, where people in a relationship are completely dependent each other to meet their needs, often at the expense of their own. This chronic self-betrayal leads individuals to adapt and modify themselves to accommodate the other. In an interdependent relationship there is a mutual meeting of needs which allows each individual to embody and celebrate true diversity by thinking, feeling, and acting differently from those around us.

When we form this dynamic, we create a bond that allows us to become more successful together than we would be on our own. We each bring our natural strengths and talents to the partnership, enabling our group to accomplish greater things (we'll talk more about that powerful phenomenon, which is known as social coherence, in chapter 10). It's like being on a sports team: each player may be a phenomenal athlete on their own, but when we come together and allow each to play their own position and contribute their own special talents, we become better than individual players can be; we become a winning team.

As we continue to explore the three-step process to embodying your authentic Self, the first step is the same for all of us: we begin by reconnecting with our body. Though each of us has lived through our own unique circumstances, I'll continue to share my own story of discovering and embodying my authentic Self in the hope that it can be of service to some of you on your individual journeys.

BEGINNING TO MEET MY BODY'S NEEDS

Before my dark night of the soul, I felt more and more disconnected from those around me and, as a result, increasingly lonely. To the outsider looking in, my loneliness might have seemed paradoxical. A serial monogamist for most of my adult life, I had spent only a handful of months in total without a romantic partner. I had a lot of friends, a busy social calendar, and a family who asked, if not expected, to see me as often as possible.

Despite having all those people in my life, I felt the embodiment of the cliché "alone in a crowded room." At my core, I didn't feel connected, supported, or even really known by anyone around me. As a result, I often thought that my relationships were never enough. I kept expecting to form a deeper emotional connection with my loved ones, and when it didn't happen, I would become disappointed, disillusioned, and, over time, resentful. I'd get excited about an opportunity to spend a weekend away with my partner, hoping that we'd finally connect on a more meaningful level, and when we didn't, I'd be disappointed and would blame her. Or I'd have high hopes for a special dinner with friends, but when the night came, the love or connection I desired remained out of reach, causing me to feel hurt or unimportant and end up emotionally shutting down or checking out entirely. My resentment would build over time until I'd move on from the friendship or, in the case of my romantic relationships, we broke up.

In my twenties, I explained away my constant unhappiness by telling myself "You're young, you live in New York City—feeling disillusioned is normal!" But after I left and moved to a new city, where I didn't have as many friends and a steady stream of social outings to distract me, I began to feel even more dissatisfied. I started to see how many of my colleagues in my clinical training program modeled a type of behavior I hadn't often seen in others: they were more in touch with their emotions and able to share them more easily and openly than I could.

As I started to explore my emotions and the ways in which I'd been suppressing them for years, I began to slowly see the role that I played in all my relationships. Showing up disconnected, I was creating the emptiness, loneliness, and unhappiness that I felt inside; those feelings weren't being created or caused by anyone else. I was out of touch with myself yet still expecting those around me to intuit and relieve my emotional suffering by helping me feel differently. I continued to expect others to "know" me but didn't know myself enough to even begin to express myself. The reality was that if I wasn't connected with all of me—body, mind, and soul—how could I possibly feel fully connected to anyone around me?

My healing journey instinctually began with my body after I had become more aware of my chronically stressed and dysregulated physical state. I wasn't consistently meeting my body's needs, even though I had enough to eat and a place to sleep. I regularly consumed whatever was readily available, including chemical-laden foods, processed sugar, gluten, and alcohol, all of which inflamed my body and brain and didn't make me feel good. My sleep was erratic: sometimes I'd go to bed early, other nights, I'd stay up late; and most mornings, I'd wake up feeling tired, even if I'd slept eight hours. My breathing reflected that chronic state of stress and was agitated and shallow, not calm, deep, and restorative. For decades, I had been experiencing persistent gut issues and brain fog so thick that I'd suddenly float into periods of mental vacancy when my mind inexplicably went completely blank.

When I started to reconnect with my body and its physical needs, I could see that I was walking around undernourished, overstressed, and continually depleted and exhausted. Over time, I could see how I regularly viewed my daily physical care as just another task or obligation that was between me and my body's need to "relax," when, ironically, caring for my body was the one thing I needed to start doing so that I could finally relax. In the absence of external motivation or validation, like someone else pushing me or visible changes to my physical appearance, I simply didn't feel motivated to take care of myself. The physical dysregulation that continued as a result of my habitual daily self-neglect wasn't just harming myself, it was also hurting how I showed up in my relationships, which were in a state reflective of my physical distress. One wrong look or word—or my misperception of either—and I'd be on edge, worrying that the other person didn't love me or was upset with me.

Do you know how you feel when you get really hungry or have a fever and don't have the capacity to deal with anything outside of your seemingly all-consuming physical needs? The same is true if we don't consistently eat nutrient-dense foods, don't sleep enough or sleep erratically, don't move enough or move too much, or routinely face more physical or emotional stress than our body can handle. These unmet physical needs may not manifest themselves as acute symptoms, but, over time, the constant trickle of unmet needs can add up to chronic dysregulation. Our body doesn't feel safe, and as a result, our nervous system can't regulate itself, causing us to show up around others as angry, distracted, checked out, or on high alert.

Today, I continue to make choices every day to regulate my nervous system by consistently committing to meet my body's needs. Though your body's daily needs may look a bit different from mine, here are some steps I took to begin to create new habits to better meet my physical needs, which we'll explore in more detail in chapter 5.

- I cut back on consuming gluten, alcohol, and processed foods/ sugars (whenever possible) to avoid the chronic systemic inflammation that all these substances can cause.
- I started prioritizing whole foods (whenever possible) to maximize the nutrients I was giving my body's cells.
- I started going to bed at the same time every night (whenever possible) to sync my sleep cycle and limit the cortisol spikes that an inconsistent bedtime can cause.
- I prioritized getting morning sunlight to help regulate my circadian clock, increasing the likelihood that I get at least eight or nine hours of restorative sleep (when possible) to allow my body to rest and repair.
- I started practicing deep, slow belly breathing on a daily basis to nourish my body with oxygen and help my nervous system regulate its stress responses.

After several months of listening to my body and meeting my physical needs, I began to feel more rested, energetic, peaceful, and ultimately more powerfully connected to and in control of my physical vessel.

WITNESSING MY SUBCONSCIOUS

When I was starting to feel confident that I was growing better able to satisfy my physical needs, I turned my attention to my emotional needs. I started to explore my subconscious mind—that deep part of our psyche that stores all of our childhood conditioning, along with all our memories, beliefs, interests, and passions.

For most of my life, I always believed that I was aware of what I thought and how I felt. I was continually mulling over my thoughts and wallowing in my feelings. I had chosen to be a psychologist, after all! Over time, though, I began to realize that the thoughts and feelings I was aware of represented only a tiny fraction of what I was really thinking and feeling. Most of my mental world was underneath my conscious awareness and driven by my subconscious mind, which steers up to 95 percent of our habitual thoughts, emotions, reactions. To identify and understand my emotional needs, I'd have to learn to become conscious of my subconscious, which, as it turns out, is not an impossible feat.

Inspired by both my psychoanalytic training and what I was learning about the power of consciousness, I peered into my subconscious mind by witnessing the automatic, conditioned habits that originated there on a daily basis. I started to realize that there was a difference between developing consciousness, or becoming aware of my thoughts and feelings, and staying caught in an endless loop of overanalyzing, overthinking, and worrying, which I had been doing for decades. Being conscious simply means noticing or witnessing, not thinking. Through a practice of conscious self-witnessing, or being a neutral observer of my mind, I began to see myself as separate from the habitual thoughts that had consumed my being for years on end, along with all of the feelings and behaviors that often accompanied them. Quite quickly, I discovered that the way I operated in the world—my very way of being—was based largely on old childhood wounds and learned coping strategies.

After paying more conscious attention to the way I cared for my physical being, I realized that I usually ate only when it was a traditional time for breakfast, lunch, or dinner or when others around me were eating. If I was starving and it wasn't a standard mealtime or no one around me was eating, I wouldn't eat, even if it meant that I'd feel off balance and agitated, at times even resentful of or upset with others for not having eaten. On other occasions, I'd rush through my meal, quickly consuming something less nutritious or nourishing. That wasn't a conscious choice, nor was it because I couldn't cook or provide myself with food. Instead, it was a conditioned habit I had developed in childhood after seeing and experiencing the eating habits of my family, learning that I "should" only eat at certain times or when and what others were.

As more time went on, I began to see that the rigid beliefs I had regarding my personal work ethics weren't serving my body's interests. When I was a child, my mom paid attention to me most consistently when I was achieving—when I got all A's in school or won a softball game as the team's star pitcher. Given the consistent validation I received for making these achievements, I learned to be an Overachiever, one of seven inner child archetypes (which we'll talk more about in chapter 4) you may be familiar with if you read *How to Do the Work*. An Overachiever learns to perform to gain attention, connection, and love, believing that they are valued or loved by others *only* when they're winning, succeeding, or otherwise meeting, or surpassing, expectations.

Being an Overachiever, I struggled to allow myself to take a break or have unstructured time to play unless those around me were also taking a break or playing. It didn't matter how long or intensely I had worked, what I had accomplished, whether I had the attentional resources to keep working, or how desperately I wanted or needed a break. When working, I rarely allowed myself to make mistakes, crossing out entries or starting new pages in my notebook or journal to avoid being reminded of my past imperfections. Now, even where I find myself today, having written three books, I continue to find myself endlessly striving for "perfection" as I catch myself critiquing and meticulously editing my work right up until my last possible deadline.

The more I witnessed my habits, the more I realized how regularly I looked outside myself and to others for answers, filtering what

I thought, felt, and did through the perception of what other peo-ple might think about or want from me. That wasn't my intent, nor was it my fault; worrying what others thought of me and putting their needs before my own were learned coping strategies that I had developed as a child to protect myself from feeling overlooked, un-considered, and hurt by those closest to me. I started to clearly see that my conditioning wasn't serving my best interests or helping my relationships. By basing most of my choices on what I imagined were others' wants and impressions of me, I was not only ignoring my own needs but also not showing up in support of others as I had long believed I was doing. In reality, I was always trying to manage others' perceptions of *me*. But if I didn't feel worthy enough to take up space in the world, how could I continue to expect others to support me or my Self-expression?

As I learned to become more aware of my subconscious, I gradu-ally changed the conditioned habits that didn't serve my best interests. While creating new habits isn't an easy process for anyone, I benefited from pausing several times throughout the day to consciously check in with myself and witness the different thoughts, feelings, and behav-iors I could become aware of in that moment. Those check-ins didn't take more than a minute, but they gave me the opportunity to decide whether I wanted to keep thinking, feeling, and acting in the same way—or whether I wanted to use that moment as an opportunity to create a new way of being. And if I noticed I was waiting for others to inspire me to move my body, I could make the conscious choice to listen to my own needs and do something active for myself instead. Or if I was relying on others to decide what we'd eat for a particular meal, I could check in with my body to see if there was any food that I felt would best nourish me.

RECONNECTING WITH MY SOUL

Staying committed to caring for my physical and emotional needs each day opened up a whole new world for me. Instead of looking outward to others for answers, I realized that I could look inward and trust myself more than I could any external source. I uncovered a place of intuition deep inside me—an internal compass that I could rely on to determine what served my best interests and the best interests of my relationships.

Accessing this inner guidance helped me identify what *I* really needed, wanted, and believed. It enabled me to reconnect with my authentic Self or soul, a part of me that didn't just live inside me but created an outward vibrational energy that interacted with the whole world around me.

Just as we all have physical and emotional needs, our soul has spiritual needs. Our spiritual needs include:

- Embracing our unique identity and significance in the world. We are able to celebrate what we're good at without feeling bad about the things that don't come naturally.
- Feeling truly connected. We are able to be vulnerable with others so that they can sense our unique authentic Self as much as we can sense theirs.
- Choosing what's in our own best interest without pressure, force, or coercion. We are able to respectfully honor our own needs and desires while giving others the space to do the same.
- Learning, seeing, and experiencing new things. We are able to cultivate unique curiosities and inherent interests and desires to help expand ourselves and those around us.
- Fully expressing ourselves and trusting in the security of our connections and relationships. We are able to feel joined or connected with others, and, ultimately, all of creation (stay tuned for more information on our powerful connection to the earth itself).

To better meet my spiritual needs, I spent more and more time looking inward, creating moments to check in and reconnect with myself. I began to set aside moments throughout the day to sign off social media and work through the discomfort of learning how to embrace free, unstructured time to relax and *be* with myself without distractions. Over time, I started to spend longer periods of time with myself, taking myself on small dates and exploring different activities I liked to do just for me, like discovering new foods, exploring new destinations, and being in nature.

A ROAD MAP TO RECONNECTING WITH YOUR AUTHENTIC SELF

Your journey back to your authentic Self will look different from mine. You experienced your own unique childhood conditioning and developed specific coping strategies as a result, which have been shaped by the events and relationships you've had since you were young. You have your own distinct vibrational energy that interacts with the world around you, creating an essence—your soul—that is unique to you.

Though your healing journey will be one of a kind, the stops you will make on your journey will be the same as mine and those of everyone else reading this book. Because we're all human, we all have the same basic universal needs. And we all have to meet these needs in the same order, addressing each sequentially.

1. We can learn to listen to our body and meet our physical needs.
2. We can learn to become consciously aware of our conditioned or habitual thoughts, emotions, and reactions so we can make new decisions that will better serve our authentic Self.
3. Finally, we can locate and learn to trust our intuition, reconnect with our soul, and manifest our unique essence or energy in the world.

FULFILLING YOUR AUTHENTIC NEEDS

Why does the sequence of your healing journey matter so much? Because we can't truly heal our relationships and evolve as individual beings until our body feels both physically and emotionally safe. If you're chronically dehydrated, sleep deprived, malnourished, or have other unmet physical needs, you won't have the energy or ability to work on yourself or your relationships. If you don't feel safe and secure enough to express your emotions, you won't be able to authentically connect with others. If you can't authentically connect with others, you won't be able to easefully be yourself, freely experience joyful play, tap into your inherent creativity, find your purpose, or feel truly fulfilled.

What I'm referring to is our *hierarchy of needs*, a concept first introduced in 1943 by the psychologist Dr. Abraham Maslow, which helps us understand human motivation. Though Maslow's hierarchy included five tiers of needs—physiological (physical), safety (personal, health, job security), love and belonging (friends, family, intimacy), esteem (self-respect, status), and what he called "self-actualization" (achieving our full potential)—I've simplified it to three foundational layers in what I call the "authentic needs pyramid," which you may remember if you read my workbook, *How to Meet Your Self.*

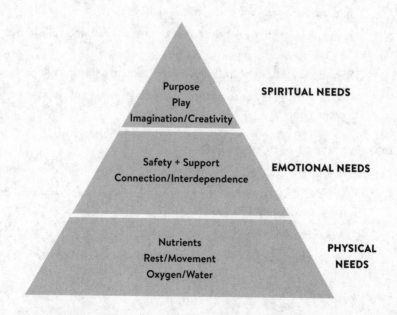

SPIRITUAL NEEDS

Purpose
Play
Imagination/Creativity

EMOTIONAL NEEDS

Safety + Support
Connection/Interdependence

PHYSICAL NEEDS

Nutrients
Rest/Movement
Oxygen/Water

Your Authentic Needs Checklist

Most of us are disconnected from our physical, emotional, and spiritual needs as a result of our childhood conditioning so it's important to first notice which needs we're currently not satisfying. Take a moment to explore the following checklist, being as honest and objective with yourself as possible as you consider the following questions and mark the response(s) that most accurately reflect your current experience:

DO I FEED MY BODY THE NUTRIENTS IT NEEDS?

_____ I listen to my body, eating when it's hungry and stopping when it's full.

_____ I choose foods that make me feel full and energized (whenever they're available).

_____ I am aware of the foods that make me feel lethargic, jumpy, or otherwise unwell and avoid them (whenever possible).

_____ I typically feel mentally alert and sharp.

DO I MOVE MY BODY?

_____ I find ways to move my body a bit each day.

_____ I know when my body needs to rest or take a break, and I allow myself that rest.

_____ I feel the sensations of my muscles contracting and expanding.

_____ I notice shifts in my body and its energy feels when I move as opposed to when I don't.

DO I GIVE MY BODY ENOUGH REST?

_____ I fall asleep quickly after getting into bed.

_____ I am able to sleep through the night without waking up (or when I do wake, I can easily fall back asleep).

_____ I wake up feeling refreshed and rejuvenated.

_____ I notice when a lack of sleep affects my moods and behavior.

CAN I DEAL WITH STRESS?

_____ I am aware of how the people in my life impact my stress level.

_____ I am aware of how the content I consume (social media, news, entertainment) impacts my stress level.

_____ I know when I'm stressed out and find moments to calm myself whenever possible.

_____ I experience moments of solitude, stillness, quiet, or nature each day.

DO I FEEL EMOTIONALLY SAFE AND SECURE?

_____ I feel safe and free to authentically express myself and my feelings in my relationships.

_____ I am aware of the things that interest me or that I'm passionate about.

_____ I am open to new experiences and set aside time to explore my creativity.

_____ I make room for spontaneous, playful, or unstructured time throughout my day.

Be gentle and compassionate with yourself if you are not yet able to mark many of the responses above. The next few chapters will explore ways you can begin to meet these foundational needs and heal your relationship with your body.

HEALING YOUR BODY

It's easy to assume that you're consistently meeting your physical needs if you're fortunate enough to have enough food to eat, a safe place to sleep, and access to clean water, adequate clothing, and health care. Even with these privileges, the reality is that most of us don't meet our fundamental physiological needs because we eat foods that inflame our body, our demanding lives stress our nervous system, or we don't get the rest our body needs to regulate our mood and emotions. Many of us—75 percent of all Americans[9]—are chronically dehydrated, and few of us, given our modern lifestyle, take the time to practice self-care, including taking the rest we all need. When unmet, these seemingly minor needs can accumulate and become major issues, sabotaging our relationships by causing us to show up tired, stressed, sluggish, or undernourished, no matter how much therapy we attend, how well we communicate our feelings, or what our partners do or don't do for us.

Because physical safety is foundational, we'll begin our journey to embody our authentic Self by prioritizing our physical needs. To do so, I've created a practice called *body consciousness* that will help you become consciously aware of your physical needs, along with your daily physical sensations like your heart rate, breathing patterns, and muscular tension. These are key indicators of whether we're meeting our physical needs or not and can help us learn and interpret our body's different cues; an ache in our stomach may mean we're hungry, tension in our muscles may mean that our energy is constricted, or fatigue may be a sign that we're overusing our body in some way. Sensations in our body, it turns out, play a surprising role in creating our thoughts and feelings. Let me explain.

Though most people assume that what we think and feel originates in our thinking brain, our physical sensations help create our thoughts and feelings. Our subconscious uses our body's sensations to interpret how we feel by recalling the emotional experiences that accompanied similar physical sensations in the past. This premise is known as the theory of constructed emotions, which was developed by a neuroscientist, Dr. Lisa Feldman Barrett, a professor of psychology at Northeastern University.[10] Though we'll talk more about this concept in chapter 5, to put it simply, we can stay locked in the experiences of our past unless we begin to practice identifying and shifting the physical sensations that cause these repetitive thoughts and feelings. By practicing *body consciousness*, we can learn to tune in to our physical sensations and manage them to some degree, helping us modify our thoughts and feelings. Becoming aware of our body's sensations enables us to change how we think and feel, ultimately changing how we show up in our relationships.

BODY CONSCIOUSNESS CHECK-IN

To practice body consciousness, you can start to take body consciousness pauses throughout your day. Taking body-consciousness pauses regularly will help move your attention away from an overactive thinking mind so you can practice attuning to or shifting your attention to your body's experience in the present moment. By checking in with your body before making any choice to engage in physical self-care (like eating, resting, or moving), you will increase your connection to your body and its different physical needs. You may find it helpful to set an alarm to alert three times during the day to remind you to pause and check in with your physical body. In this paused moment, fully shift your attention to the experience of being in your body as you explore your different physical sensations.

On the lines below, write down and take note of your experiences as you begin. You may find it helpful to repeat this list in a separate notebook or journal (or anywhere else where you can access it throughout the day) as a reminder to pause and connect with your body's physical experience.

Daily Consciousness Check-ins

Body pause: [time]
Physical sensations present:

_____

_____

_____

EMPOWERING YOUR MIND

After you've developed a consistent practice of body consciousness, you can begin to work on *mind consciousness*. Mind consciousness is the practice of becoming aware of the thoughts, feelings, and reactions that you have or do on an automatic, repetitive basis. These reflect our subconscious at work; they're our instinctual, conditioned ways of being that got programmed into our brain when we were children because we relied on them so often to feel safe, valued, and loved by our parent-figures. Now that we're adults, few of these repeated habits allow us to feel good about ourselves. They don't allow us to be our authentic Self, often sabotaging how we interact with others. These conditioned ways of being can actually even make us feel physically and emotionally unsafe or dysregulated.

As we'll continue to explore, we can learn to identify the automatic, repetitive habits that don't serve our best interests or those of our relationships. We can find and choose new ways to calm ourselves when we're upset without falling back on our old conditioned cycles. By becoming consciously aware of our *conditioned selves*, or the roles we play in our adult relationships that keep us stuck in dysfunctional patterns with others (we'll talk more about these in chapter 4), we can intentionally begin to more often honor our own needs so that we can then create the safety we need to be our authentic Self with others.

CONSCIOUSNESS CHECK-IN

As I imagine you're beginning to see, consciousness plays a powerful foundational role in our journey to embody our authentic Self. To develop my own mind consciousness, or ability to witness my subconscious habits, I developed a practice called the daily consciousness check-in. This practice will help you become conscious of the autopilot of your life. Be patient with yourself as you begin your practice; because our brain physiologically prefers to operate on autopilot in order to conserve energy, it can feel physically tiring when we start to shift our brain into a conscious state of awareness.

The steps involved in a consciousness check-in are similar to the ones you take when doing a body consciousness pause. You can start by setting an intention to pause three times throughout your day to witness or notice two things: what you're doing in the moment and where your attention is at that time.

Here are two helpful ways to create your new daily check-in habit. You can use either approach as you practice setting and keeping these daily intentions until these daily check-ins become a new habit, or until you remember on your own to pause to access moments of consciousness throughout the day.

- Set an intention to check in at three different times throughout the day, like at 11:00 a.m., 4:00 p.m., and 9:00 p.m. You may want to set an alarm or reminder on your phone to help you do this.
- Set an intention to check in during three activities you do every day, like drinking your morning coffee, preparing your after-work meal, and getting ready for bed.

To perform the check-in, ask yourself these two questions:

1. What am I doing right now (washing dishes, watching TV, talking with a loved one)?
2. What am I paying attention to? Am I fully immersed in whatever I'm doing or whoever I'm engaged with? Or am I lost in thought about other things? If so, what am I thinking about (e.g., a conversation I had earlier in the day, a recent credit card bill, an upcoming event, a stressful situation at work)?

Your goal when you practice is simply to be present in the moment, observing your thoughts as you would clouds drifting across the sky. It will be helpful to transfer the lines below to a separate notebook or journal and write down your answers to each question every time you complete a check-in. Keep it in a place where no one can see your answers, so you can practice giving yourself the freedom to write without judging or overthinking this practice. Over time, you may even begin to notice patterns in what you're paying attention to.

Daily Consciousness Check-ins

_____

_____

_____

Revisit this tool as often as needed. I continue to use it daily.

RECONNECTING WITH YOUR SOUL

From a biological perspective, your soul, or authentic Self, lives in your physical heart—and not just because the human heart is the spiritual or emotional center of the body, according to nearly every culture in the world. Known as the body's "little brain" and containing more than forty thousand neurons, the heart sends more messages to our nervous system than vice versa, impacting the health and safety of our body and mind while activating our emotional reactions to others.[11] Our heart is where our intuition and inner knowledge live, according to scientific research from the nonprofit HeartMath Institute that we'll dive into in later chapters.[12]

When we're connected with our heart, we're more likely to make decisions based on our authentic needs and desires. Being connected with our own heart actually helps us feel more open and receptive to connecting with the hearts of others. It can even help us begin to "sense" things before they happen: people who become physically and emotionally connected with their heart can actually feel changes in their chest before an incident occurs, helping them discern if something is "right" or "wrong" in their world, according to recent research on intuition.[13] We'll continue to talk more about how our heart is connected to our soul and how it impacts our relationships in chapter 7.

Heart Check-in

Many of us may know what we want or don't want but override our instinctual needs or desires because we fear losing our safe connection to others and the world around us. To begin to authentically express yourself, it'll be helpful to begin to notice the different concerns or fears that may be holding you back.

Take a moment to call to mind a recent experience with someone during which you wanted to express yourself but didn't allow yourself to speak your true thoughts, feelings, or perspectives. Now consider your responses to these questions:

What do I really think, feel, or want to do?

_____

_____

What do I think or worry would happen if I shared my true or authentic thoughts, perspectives, or feelings right now?

_____

_____

How would I feel if I shared what I'm really thinking and feeling?

_____

_____

Using the exploratory questions above, spend the next few weeks witnessing yourself throughout the day and within your different relationships, noting any patterns you may discover in the times when you tend to withhold your honest thoughts, perspectives, or feelings from others.

As you begin this practice, it's normal to find it difficult at first to connect with your heart and what it is that you really think, feel, or desire, likely because you're distracted by the thoughts in your mind. Continue to practice granting yourself grace and compassion, especially if you have never asked yourself these questions before. Continuing to practice daily body consciousness pauses and consciousness check-ins will help make it easier for you to shift your attention from your thinking mind to your physical body, where you can better hear your heart's messages. It's helpful to check in with your heart regularly throughout the day and especially before making big decisions as you continue to rebuild your connection to your authentic Self, or soul.

As you gain some clarity on what your heart may want or need, be patient with yourself as you begin to express these authentic desires to others. You can begin to practice by noticing the times when you say "yes" or agree to things that aren't true to or don't interest you. The next time you're asked to an event, and you know you don't want to go, instead of immediately agreeing, pause before you answer, giving yourself a moment to consciously choose to respond in alignment with your authentic desires. And remember as you take this time to get to know yourself, discovering what isn't true or what you don't want will eventually lead you in the direction of what is true or what you do want for yourself.

*   *   *

Understanding the concept of the embodied self and the interconnectedness among our body, mind, and soul can help us better understand our journey ahead. It's an exciting one, and although that excitement may tempt you to skip to certain chapters, it's important to continue sequentially, as true and lasting healing occurs in stages and unfolds as a living process. What awaits you along your way is a more complete, whole, and centered being. A "you" that's more *you*. By acting in alignment with your actual wants and needs as often as you can, you can embody all of you—body, mind, and soul—and begin to create the loving and fulfilling relationships that you're looking for. And to begin our journey to more authentic relationships, we will need to first understand the neurobiology of our trauma bonds.

3

UNDERSTANDING THE NEUROBIOLOGY
OF TRAUMA BONDS

I heard it often when I was in clinical practice. My clients would tell me that they were always getting into the wrong relationships or were stuck in the same conflicts over and over again. Many described cycles of shaming, blaming, criticizing, and withdrawing from or overreacting to each other. Others depicted something like a tug-of-war in their relationships, continually trying to pull their loved one closer only to feel pushed away, provoking a painful push-pull loop that never seemed to end.

At the time, I was working with couples who came to see me because they were unhappy in their relationship. My clients who were married or partnered often told me that for months or years they had felt trapped in an unloving or unsatisfying relationship that no amount of therapy or attempts at improved communication had been able to help. Those who were single frequently admitted that although they wanted a lasting partnership, they hadn't been able to find or sustain one, or if they had, the relationship had usually ended the same way, regardless of what they had done, how hard they had tried, or whom they had chosen. That sounded familiar to me, too.

What those clients had in common, was a cycle of repeating behavioral patterns or habits that they couldn't break. They were convinced instead that something was either wrong with them—that they were "unlovable," "undatable," or "broken"—or that they were a victim to uncompromising, unemotional, or unloving partners. Some of my clients even began to worry that all their romantic relationships were doomed.

If this sounds familiar to you, too, I assure you that there's nothing wrong with you or your loved ones and that loving, authentic relationships *are* possible. The relationship ruts so many of you find yourselves trapped in aren't necessarily your fault, nor are they necessarily your loved one's fault. The relationships we seek out and create as adults, especially with our romantic partners, usually aren't even the results of decisions we actively make with our conscious mind. Instead, our nervous system is wired to seek out and re-create relational patterns that mirror our earliest relationships with our parent-figures. These repeated dynamics don't serve our best interests today and often aren't authentic connections but rather trauma bonds.

In the first two chapters, you read about the work of the interpersonal neurobiologist Dr. Daniel Siegel, whose work illustrates how our earliest relationships physically shape our nervous system and dictate how we'll think, feel, and act with others for the rest of our lives. In this chapter, we'll explore the science behind why and how this occurs so that we can better understand the steps we can take—physically, emotionally, and spiritually—to break the trauma bonds habits we've developed with our friends, family, colleagues, or romantic partners.

THE TRAUMA BONDS THAT KEEP YOU STUCK: DOMINIK AND MONIQUE'S STORY

When I worked with couples, I didn't yet understand the nature of trauma bonds. Looking back, if I had been able to integrate what I know now about how our nervous system instinctually drives us to act in certain ways, I would have been better able to help my clients change their relationships. Instead, I watched helplessly as no amount of conventional therapy or other self-help tools made an impact in most people's relationship patterns: they kept repeating the same cycles, as if they were physically driven or addicted to the habits that were causing their continued suffering.

I can now see how trauma bonds played out in nearly every relationship of every client who sat opposite me in my office, including Dominik and Monique, who first came to see me when their marriage had grown disconnected and resentful.

When they had first met at a concert eight years prior, Dominik and Monique said, they had been immediately "infatuated" with each other. They shared the same taste in music, and being together, they said, had felt "easy" and "natural." A few years into their marriage, they had begun to experience significant problems. Dominik, a self-employed contractor, was landing fewer jobs and bringing in significantly less income, and Monique, a successful academic, felt that he wasn't trying hard enough to win new clients. Over time, Monique discovered that Dominik was gambling away the money he did make, which had increased the financial strains on the couple. Monique, who already kept a close eye on Dominik's activities (or, as Dominik put it, "she's constantly on my case"), began to monitor and micromanage him to a greater degree. In response, Dominik became even more secretive about his work (or lack thereof) and his gambling habits.

During couples therapy sessions, we explored Dominik and Monique's childhoods and how each might be contributing to their relationship difficulties. What we didn't discuss was how their childhoods might have impacted their physical bodies, specifically their nervous systems, and how their brains were instinctually driving them to stay locked in unhealthy relationship dynamics with each other.

Dominik was adopted at a young age into a family with a hypervigilant mother. Hypervigilant parents are similar to the "helicopter parents" you may have heard about or even experienced firsthand: They constantly monitor, micromanage, and try to control their child, driven by their internal anxiety stemming from their own nervous system dysregulation. Though well-meaning and often be-lieving that their surveillance is for their child's benefit, many hy-pervigilant parents aren't able to understand or respect their child's boundaries. They constantly oversee and overanalyze their child's thoughts, moods, and behaviors, sometimes even forcing them to pursue certain activities and interests. That was all true of Dominik's mother.

Dominik's father, on the other hand, was often distant from the family, regularly socializing with colleagues after working long hours and maintaining only minimal contact with his family. His frequent absence from home left Dominik alone to protect himself against his mother's intrusive and often shame-inducing behaviors.

When Dominik was young, he reported, he had often felt over-whelmed by his mother's hypervigilance. She was always yelling at him to be careful, even when there was no threat, and continually told him what to eat, how to feel, and what to do. She regularly in-serted herself into his early relationships with his peers, advising him how to react to the experiences he shared with her. Though her intentions may have been well-meaning, her hypervigilance caused Dominik to feel unworthy and shameful at his core, which is com-mon among children with hypervigilant parent-figures: when some-one is always trying to control or change you, it sends the underlying message that your natural way of being—your authentic Self—isn't good enough.

As his mother continued to micromanage and outright direct his be-havior at times, Dominik formed the subconscious belief that "love" felt and looked like being overseen and micromanaged for his "best interest." His earliest interactions with his mother conditioned him to believe that love and affection came with hypervigilance, even if he, like most people, didn't like how it felt to be controlled.

His mother's constant oversight didn't give Dominik any space to share his thoughts, feelings, or perspectives freely. Because his bound-aries were constantly violated, he didn't feel truly safe to be who he was, let alone allow himself to feel loved by others for being so. To cope with the persistent lack of emotional safety and security, Dominik's nervous system remained consistently stressed, on notice for the next inevitable issue or threat.

When our nervous system initiates a stress response or state of hyperactivation, our body shifts into fight-or-flight mode, giving us the focus and energy needed to face a threat or run away from it. In Dominik's instance, the perceived threat was his mother's controlling and intrusive actions, which inadvertently caused him near-constant emotional overwhelm. Though he couldn't physically run away from his mother because he was dependent on her for his survival, he fled by turning inward, as many children do, retreating to his inner world and distracting himself with his thoughts. Because he hardly ever felt safe or supported, his nervous system stayed stuck in a stress response, repeating patterns of activation in his brain's developing neural circuitry. As with all young children, those early neural pathways eventually became part of his brain architecture.

As he got older, Dominik continued to run away from any discomfort by turning inward, distracting himself with his thoughts and later with gambling. Many compulsive or addictive behaviors like gambling or using sex, work, or substances are actually a means of escaping deep-rooted pain or other overwhelming emotions. Because the neural circuitry had been wired into his brain since childhood, it felt safe and familiar to him and became the basis of the trauma bond patterns he repeated well into adulthood. His habitual flight-response most often put him into Distractor mode, one of four reactionary styles I've identified based on the body's four stress responses: fight, flight, freeze or shutdown, and fawn. All four modes are listed below, along with how to determine which type you and those around you most frequently embody.

When Dominik met Monique, everything about her felt familiar and safe. She was different from Dominik's mother in many ways, but she exhibited the same core behaviors that he instinctively understood as "love": she monitored, micromanaged, and controlled him. At first, those behaviors were subtle. Initially, she would suggest what Dominik should wear out to dinner or what to do to improve his business. But over time, her directives became more obvious, as she started to dictate her preferences for many of his daily choices. Though he didn't consciously enjoy the oversight and complained about it at times, Monique's behavior felt like the "love" he knew.

To create space and safety for himself, Dominik tried to run away from Monique, withdrawing emotionally from their relationship by distracting or distancing himself with his thoughts and actions, just as he had done in childhood. Those conditioned behaviors, though instinctual to Dominik, only increased Monique's need to control what was happening. Feeling threatened whenever he turned inward or away from her, she began to monitor him more closely, consistently asking what was wrong and trying harder to engage him or "snap" him back into the present. The less he worked and the more money he lost gambling, the more closely she monitored him, continuing the reactionary cycles between them.

Monique didn't intentionally try to micromanage Dominik. Just like him, she had her own trauma history that had resulted in conditioned coping patterns. Monique's mother suffered from depression, which frequently prevented her from emotionally attuning to her daughter and even from physically caring for her at times. Monique's father was constantly consumed by working two jobs to support the family and was rarely home. When he was able to spend time with his family and wasn't distracted by his seemingly endless to-do list and household chores, he was very attentive and loving. But his attention wasn't consistent or predictable enough to help Monique feel safe or secure.

Often feeling emotionally abandoned and alone as a child, Monique developed the subconscious belief that she wasn't worthy of having a parent consistently show up to emotionally care for and support her. Because her parents were only occasionally emotionally available to help her navigate her feelings, she had to learn to do it herself, which is overwhelming for any child. Though she always felt physically safe, she rarely felt emotionally safe with either of her parents. To try to soothe those overwhelming feelings, Monique instinctually began to try to control as many aspects of her environment as possible. She monitored her mother to try to prevent anything from happening that might upset her or send her into a depressive episode. Before her father came home, she'd compile a mental list of all the things she could do or say to prevent him from reimmersing himself in his work.

Given her lack of emotional safety and security, Monique's nervous system consistently activated a fawn response. When we're in a fawn response, we often deal with perceived threats by monitoring others, whether externally or internally. We may micromanage others or our environment in order to anticipate and avoid the next perceived threat. Locked in a fawn response, Monique often yelled at her brother if he did something to upset her mother or quietly seethed when her father got up from the dinner table to go back to work. As Monique's body repeated the same response over and over again in its best attempt to create safety, her neurobiology became wired for hypervigilance. As she got older, she could feel physically uncomfortable when she wasn't on-edge, obsessively trying to control her circumstances. Shifting consistently into Pleaser mode and acting outwardly dominating, she often ended up making those around her feel just as unsafe as she did internally.

Monique was instinctively attracted to Dominik because he was similar to her parents in a major way: he was unpredictable. She was never sure when he'd be present with her or lost in his thoughts, which was how her father had been. Sometimes he'd be happy, while other times he'd be sad, just as her mother had been. Even the nature of his work as an independent contractor was unpredictable: he'd be busy for months, then go weeks without a job. Though his unpredictability made achieving both emotional and financial security difficult, it felt familiar and safe to her; dealing with unpredictability was how she had learned to feel "love" and affection.

Monique and Dominik's unmet emotional needs from childhood and related neurobiological adaptations helped create their initial feeling of "infatuation" for each other, as well as the reactive cycles that eventually threatened their relationship. Their relationship was a trauma bond in which both unconsciously acted out the different ways each had learned to get their emotional needs met in childhood.

Like many of us, they, too, would remain locked in the same stress responses with each other until either they learned how to break these cycles by regulating their nervous systems or one or both decided to end their relationship.

DRIVEN TO RE-CREATE YOUR CHILDHOOD

Monique and Dominik didn't consciously choose to re-create conditions in their relationship that allowed them to reenact the same stress experiences and resulting coping strategies that they had grown accustomed to since childhood. A trauma bond isn't something we have active control over, at least not until we become conscious of it. Our conditioned ways of relating with others have become habitual instincts, created by the neural networks we developed as children to cope with the overwhelming emotions in our childhoods.

As we learned in chapter 1, childhood trauma includes more than abuse, neglect, incest, rape, and all the other life-altering events typically associated with the term. For many of us, childhood trauma took a subtler shape. Childhood trauma can be any perceived stress that consistently overwhelms our ability to cope with it. If our caregivers were physically or emotionally absent, we were left unable to soothe our emotional overwhelm. If we didn't consistently feel emotionally safe or were regularly undersupported whenever we faced emotionally upsetting experiences, regardless of how "good" or well-meaning our parent-figures may have been, we stored childhood trauma in our body and mind.

No matter the type of trauma we experienced as children, the overwhelming stress impacted how our nervous system developed. Because we're born with underdeveloped nervous systems, our brain grows rapidly, reaching 90 percent of its adult volume before age six and it continues to hone its functioning until our midtwenties.[14]

The human nervous system is wired to depend on other people, beginning from the moment of conception and it is our earliest relationships that create the neural connections that may last our lifetime. How our parent-figures interacted with us, handled stress, and coped with upsetting experiences influenced the pathways formed in our brains. Through a process known as *co-regulation*, the safety of their nervous system directly affected the safety of our nervous system, even when we were separated by skin and space.

This means, if we grew up with a parent-figure who was regularly dysregulated in their own stress response and unable to soothe or co-regulate with us, we felt their stress. Unable to feel soothed, our nervous system activated its own stress response, causing us to continue to feel unsafe. Repeating the same nervous system responses over and over again during that critical developmental period strengthened these neural pathways, turning some into highways that are almost instinctual for our brain to follow. We'll talk a lot more about this process of co-regulation in later chapters and explore how we can intentionally harness the constructive, restorative powers of this practice to create safety within our relationships.

NERVOUS SYSTEM 101

To understand why our earliest relationships impact us so greatly, let's dive into the science behind our body's autonomic nervous system (ANS). Our ANS is responsible for regulating involuntary physical functions like our heart rate, breathing, blood pressure, and digestion. Its main role is to store, conserve, and release energy, which helps manage how we react to perceived stress. It does this by speeding up or slowing down physiological functions that take place outside our conscious awareness, impacting our breath, shifting our energy, and even dilating the pupils of our eyes.

If most of your needs were consistently met in childhood, your nervous system likely tends toward a state of consistent regulation. This means that even when your ANS activates a stress response, it is able to quickly return to *homeostasis*. Homeostasis is our body's preferred state; it is a balance in our internal functioning where we are able to feel safe allowing us to calmly and intentionally navigate the world around us. When our nervous system is regulated, we can adapt quickly and accurately to perceived threats while being responsive to our emotions and remaining intentional in our actions, even when we experience upsetting feelings or situations. To put it simply, we are able to remain in control of how we respond to the life around us and consciously choose what we want to do next.

Most of us don't have a regulated nervous system, struggling instead with nervous system dysregulation. Our body struggles to turn off its stress response, keeping us stuck in survival mode, or a state of heightened threat, instead of homeostasis. As a result, we can't accurately determine what is a threat and what isn't, causing us to feel unsafe, easily activated, and unable to soothe our often over-whelming emotions. Overstressed and unable to return our body to peaceful balance, we can end up feeling irritable, with a limited tolerance for frustration, causing us to fly off the handle or overreact to events. Because our body will always prioritize our physical survival when dysregulated, our thoughts can easily become self-focused and we easily struggle to consider anyone's interests other than our own. When we are stuck in survival mode or are in a relationship with others who are, we end up *feeling* alone because *emotionally we are alone*. Seeing most others as a possible threat, we don't feel safe enough to open ourselves to receive connection or support from another person.

These patterns of nervous system dysregulation usually begin in early childhood, when our brain is still developing. As children, we learn how to self-regulate, or cope with stress and other un-comfortable emotions, through our experiences and moments of co-regulation with others. If our ANS didn't have the chance to develop the neural circuitry needed to toggle easily back and forth between a stressed state and homeostasis, it can get stuck in a stress response. As a result, we physiologically don't have the ability to calm down quickly or easily.

You've likely seen infants or young children stuck in a stress response. Unable to calm or wind down, some will kick, scream, or yell, all behaviors typical of children in a fight response. Others will dissociate and stare off into space, all characteristics of a freeze or shutdown response. Some become hypervigilant to their environment and display symptoms of chronic anxiety, especially when around others socially, which is common in a fawn response.

No matter which stress response(s) our bodies habituate to as young children, we'll return to the same response(s) as adults because our nervous system has become wired to do so. If we kicked and screamed as children, we'll likely kick and scream with others as adults. If we stared off into space and dissociated when we were young, we'll likely do the same today, disconnecting or detaching from others. If our safety or connection was dependent on tending to others around us, we'll likely do the same today, remaining anxious and more attuned to them than to ourselves.

Nervous system dysregulation can cause even the most conscientious people to act in ways that will sabotage the "best" relationships. When our nervous system is dysregulated, we don't have as much control over how stressful emotions impact us, so we're often easily upset or reactive around others. Our ANS becomes biologically wired to overreact to stress, and it's often only a matter of time before we find or re-create stress, even when there is nothing stressful or threatening around us.

Though chronic stress isn't physically or emotionally healthy for anyone, stress responses feel physiologically familiar to our body and, on some level, comfortable. Our subconscious mind will always prefer the familiar over the unknown, which poses the possibility of threat. Our nervous system relives the familiar because it offers a highly predictable outcome, which our brain craves in the game of survival.

When our body is in a stress response, our brain's hypothalamus-pituitary-adrenal axis (HPA) is activated. Known as the body's "stress circuit," our HPA axis floods our bloodstream with stress chemicals such as cortisol, dopamine, endorphins, and adrenaline. Though this spike of stress hormones can feel very intense, we can become "addicted" or habituated to the rush and feel physically uncomfortable, bored, or agitated when we're not experiencing our familiar cocktail of stress chemicals.

If our body grows accustomed to a stress response, it can drive our subconscious to find or re-create situations that will activate the same biochemical rush so we can go back to feeling "ourselves" again. Those of us raised in homes with a lot of chaos, unpredictability, or unsafe relationships can easily become stuck in a cycle of emotional addiction, physiologically craving the same chaos, unpredictability, and lack of safety with others as adults.

As our stressed body continues to send threat signals to our mind, it begins to race with upsetting thoughts to create the same underlying biochemistry we're used to. This addictive cycle causes many of us to feel inexplicably drawn to gossip, drama, unpredictable relationship dynamics, or situations with others that give us adrenaline rushes. Even though the drama or stress may not feel good, at least it allows us to feel *something*—which, for many of us, may be the only time we do so. If this stress causes us to act passive-aggressively, emotionally detach from others, or violate their boundaries, we may later feel regretful of the way we acted when we were dysregulated. Neurobiologically wired to prefer the familiar, we end up trapped in cycles and seeking the same kind of people or situations over and over again, only to end up feeling frequently ashamed of ourselves and our actions.

FEELING YOUR WAY TO SAFETY

Our ANS consists of two branches: our sympathetic nervous system and our parasympathetic nervous system. Our sympathetic nervous system activates our body's fight-or-flight responses by increasing our heart rate, blood pressure, breathing, and muscle tension, giving us the energy to face a perceived threat or run away from it. Once we overcome or escape the perceived threat, our body calms down again by activating our parasympathetic nervous system, otherwise known as a "rest and digest" or "safe and social" state, slowing our heart rate, deepening our breathing, and helping us feel emotionally safe again. Our parasympathetic nervous system controls our body's ability to relax.

Though spending the majority of our time in a parasympathetic state is ideal, we can become stuck in a parasympathetic response, known as a freeze or shutdown state. Freeze occurs when neither fight nor flight is an option because the perceived threat we're facing is too imminent, overwhelming, or constant. Our sympathetic nervous system is still somewhat active as our body begins to brace or guard itself against the perceived threat. When we go into a shutdown response, our parasympathetic nervous system slows our heart rate and breathing to the point where we're physically but not mentally or emotionally present, often with flaccid and weak-feeling muscles. From an evolutionary perspective, this response helped our ancient ancestors stay still or "play dead" when they couldn't realistically escape a threat. Today, many of us stay stuck in this chronic state of dissociation, disconnection, or numbing of our reality to cope with consistently perceived threats in our environment.

The body's most recently evolved fourth stress response, fawn, occurs when we attempt to avoid or deescalate a perceived threat by tending to the needs or caring for the feelings of those around us. We've learned that if we can keep someone calm, we can avoid the stress their upset would cause us. A fawn response is known as a *social state* because it's possible only when we're around others; it is often referred to as "please and appease" or, more commonly, as "people pleasing."

Learning how to shift intentionally between sympathetic and parasympathetic states can help regulate our nervous system. Over time, this flexibility will increase the amount of time we spend in a "safe and social" state when we are better able to calmly and responsively navigate both our emotions and the world around us. Accessing this state within our relationships allows us to both provide and receive emotional support and to create deep, lasting love.

YOUR FAULTY PERCEPTUAL SYSTEM

Though safety is our body's ideal state, few of us actually feel peaceful, grounded, or connected to ourselves, others, or our experiences on a regular basis, if at all. To understand why, it's important to know something about *polyvagal theory*. Polyvagal theory explains how we sense, interpret, and react to cues of safety and danger in our environment. Most importantly, it helps explain why we often unconsciously misinterpret others' behavior and end up not feeling safe enough socially to truly connect with them, even if we desperately want to.

The theory, introduced in 1994 by Dr. Stephen Porges, centers around the vagus nerve, which is one of our nervous system's main pathways of communication between our brain and body. The vagus is the primary nerve of our parasympathetic nervous system and our longest cranial nerve, connecting our brain to our heart and the rest of our body.

The vagus nerve has two branches, ventral and dorsal. The ventral branch controls our bodily functions above the diaphragm, including heart rate, breathing, vocal tone, hearing, and facial expressions. The dorsal branch controls our bodily functions below the diaphragm, including digestion.

The ventral vagal branch helps us to feel safe and social and is part of what Dr. Porges calls our *social engagement system*. When our social engagement system is activated, our heart rate is regulated, our breathing is deep and nourishing, we speak to others in soothing tones, we interpret others' verbal and nonverbal cues more accurately, and our face is relaxed and expressive. When we're in this ventral vagal state, we're able to be ourselves while extending that opportunity to others. As a result, we are able to feel engaged with and to explore the world around us, accessing feelings of curiosity, pleasure, and even playfulness and humor.

Most of us don't spend much time in a ventral vagal state. Rather, overwhelming stress activates our dorsal vagal response, causing a freeze or shutdown state. The response shuts down our digestion (we may be become constipated), slows or stops our muscle activity (we may feel weak or constantly fatigued), slows and dulls our voice, and curbs other physiological functions often making us feel immobile and detach or dissociate ourselves from reality (our mind goes blank and we feel mentally far away or somewhere else).

While we're in a dorsal vagal state, our ventral vagal branch can stay somewhat "online," allowing us to remain active and engaged enough to attune to others' perceived needs. At the same time, our dorsal vagal response keeps us "offline," or disconnected from our own needs. This happens when we're in a fawn state, trying to keep ourselves safe by prioritizing the needs or wants of others. We may feel hyperaroused and hypervigilant, always alert to the needs of those around us, or hypersensitive, always thinking or worrying about another person (which may lead us to think that we're being "empathetic" with others). By being attentive and receptive to changes in the emotional states of others, we try to anticipate

THE POLYVAGAL THEORY: THE AUTONOMIC LADDER
Understanding the Nervous System

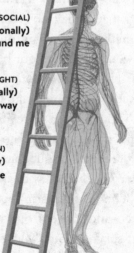

CONNECTOR MODE (SAFE AND SOCIAL)
I feel safe (physically and emotionally)
I'm connected to others/the world around me

ERUPTOR OR DISTRACTOR MODE(S) (FIGHT-OR-FLIGHT)
I feel unsafe (physically or emotionally)
I need to fight back or run away

PLEASER MODE (FAWN)
I feel unsafe (physically or emotionally)
I'm hypervigilant to others/the world around me

DETACHER MODE (FREEZE)
I feel unsafe (physically or emotionally)
I can't cope and am immobilized or shut down

*Adapted from Deb Dana

and avoid stressful, upsetting, or otherwise threatening experiences. Take a look at the image on the previous page for a visual perspective of these nervous system states.

The overall state of our nervous system depends on various cues that we constantly perceive and receive in the environment around us. Our subconscious is always scanning our surroundings for signs that we're safe or in danger; this is known as *neuroception*. Given our evolutionary success as humans in social groups, our subconscious is primed to look for cues from other people, including their facial expressions, gestures, and vocal tones. If their behavior appears to indicate they feel safe, we'll feel safe, too. But if no one else is around or the cues we receive appear threatening, we won't feel safe and our nervous system will shift into a fight, flight, freeze or shutdown, or fawn response.

If you've ever experienced turbulence on an airplane, you can understand how neuroception works. When the plane starts to bump and shake, the first thing most of us do is look at other passengers to see if they look scared. If the people around us appear calm—their posture is open and relaxed, their facial expression is soft or kind, their breathing is regular—we'll likely feel calm, too. But if they give off cues that they feel nervous and are visibly reacting to the same threat, we may not feel safe, and we'll shift into fight-or-flight. If something is really wrong—the turbulence persists or worsens—our ANS may activate our body's freeze or shutdown response, slowing our physical functions and causing us to detach or dissociate from what's happening around us.

Though from an evolutionary standpoint the process of neuroception was designed to keep us safe from active threats in our environment, our subconscious doesn't always accurately perceive or interpret the behavior of others. Instead, our past conditioning and childhood trauma influence how our subconscious receives cues of safety and danger from those around us. We often see and sense what our subconscious "wants" us to see and sense, not necessarily what's actually happening in our environment.

In the instance of turbulence on a plane if we're afraid of flying, have heard stories of plane crashes, or have experienced traumatic turbulence in the past, our subconscious is more likely to interpret signals of danger from those around us, even if no danger exists. When this occurs, we won't feel safe, and our body will activate a stress response. If, on the other hand, we fly often enough to feel more comfortable or are familiar with turbulence, we may find ourselves able to remain calm in the cabin and even possibly help calm the fears of scared passengers around us.

Perhaps not surprisingly, our earliest relationships and environments have the biggest impact on how accurately our subconscious interprets social behavior. If we were bullied or shamed in childhood for the way we looked or dressed by our parent-figures or peers, we may filter glances our way as indicating the same disdain, or we may assume that others are always talking about our appearance behind our back. If our parent-figures continually demanded high achievement or perfection from us as children, we may filter our actions or the actions of others through our own imaginary, often unattainable expectations or feel as though we never really measure up.

If you, like me, were abandoned (emotionally or physically) as a young child, you may interpret any moment of distance or disconnection with a partner or close friend as an indication of similar abandonment. In those of us with this core abandonment wound, we easily perceive moments of distance as a sign of conflict or upset within our relationships. I used to panic when a partner didn't respond to my text in what I thought was a timely manner, offered a clipped or shortened answer in response to one of my questions, or remained quiet when we were spending time together. In those moments, I would often obsessively ask if anything was wrong, convinced that they were upset with me. That all stemmed from my own childhood, when my mom would give me the silent treatment and stop speaking to me or ignore my existence altogether, sometimes for weeks at a time, when she was deeply hurt by or disapproving of my actions or choices. Fearful of upsetting my mom, my dad enabled that treatment, sometimes even playing messenger between us, ultimately leaving me feeling abandoned by the two people I needed most.

Early in my relationship with Lolly, I regularly found myself upset with her consistent desire and requests for time alone, which hurt my feelings and activated my deeper wounds. Lolly, though, was not abandoning me. Instead, she had been raised by parents who modeled hyperindependence, and she had learned to be self-reliant. While her distance wasn't an actual threat to our relationship, I inaccurately perceived it to be, even though there was no actual threat present.

Research actually shows that all childhood trauma, even bullying by our peers, can cause structural change in our amygdala,[15] the part of our brain that detects threats in our environment, as well as in our prefrontal cortex,[16] the region responsible for our "executive functions," like our ability to plan, make decisions, and manage our social behavior. These structural changes as a result of childhood trauma create a state of hypervigilance whenever our nervous system is on alert. When this state becomes chronic or consistent over time it can manifest itself as social anxiety or complex post-traumatic stress disorder (C-PTSD), with related difficulties managing emotions, exercising inhibition, and, ultimately, having relationships.[17] When our nervous system remains on high alert, we constantly scan our environment, engage in worst-case scenario thinking, and often become overwhelmed with racing thoughts while we anxiously wait for the other shoe to drop. Within our relationships, structural changes in our brain can cause us to mistakenly perceive aggression in both neutral facial expressions and calm tones of voice.[18] When our amygdala is on high alert, we are more likely to see indicators of aggressive behaviors when none are present. The reality is when we experience overwhelming stress or have suffered past trauma, it continues to impact what we think and believe as well as how we perceive ourselves, our relationships, and the world around us.

If our neuroception is primed to misinterpret signs and perceive everything as possible danger, we can easily stay locked in a vicious cycle of conflict with others, that is mostly self-created. Our faulty neuroception won't allow us to feel safe enough to open ourselves up to connecting with others on a deeper, more vulnerable level. Feeling constantly at risk of rejection, we'll feel too exposed being vulnerable and allowing ourselves to be seen as we are. Though we may look to others and even expect them to help us feel "better" or more connected, we won't be open to receiving their comfort or connection because we don't feel safe enough to do so. Instead of being comforted by the physical presence, closeness, or touch of someone who is calm and grounded, some of us may even retract in fear.

Neuroception is an unconscious process that we don't have conscious control over, though we can learn to shift how we instinctively interpret and respond to social cues from others. The first step is to become aware of those situations when we subconsciously assign old meanings to what we believe is happening around us. If someone we love sends us signals or tells us they want to be alone, we can break our habit of immediately assuming that we're being abandoned, reconfirming our deepest fear that we're unworthy of love. Instead, we can accept and respect their need for space or solitude as something we all need from time to time.

Similarly, we can become conscious of our tendency to be consumed by worries or concerns about how we look so we can begin to accept different versions of beauty. Or we can notice our endless quest for perfection and our tendency to be consumed by critical or diminishing self-thoughts, and choose instead to honor our individual strengths and quirks, regardless of how they "measure up" to others. I continue to practice these habits to help myself feel safe enough to just be *me* while remaining open and receptive to others and the world around me.

The more conscious we can all become of our subconscious perceptions and beliefs, the better able we'll be to remove the conditioned filters that prevent us from accurately interpreting the behaviors of others around us. In chapter 6, we'll talk more about how to expand our practice of mind consciousness and develop a new habit of conscious self-witnessing to become aware of our conditioned beliefs, feelings, and reactions that don't serve our authentic Self.

YOUR DYSREGULATED NERVOUS SYSTEM

Each of the four stress responses is associated with behaviors, no matter who we are or where or how we grew up. Becoming familiar with these common indicators can help you identify when you or a loved one is in a stressed state, enabling you to better determine when you or they may need time or support to regulate or calm down.

Eruptor Mode (Fight Response)

Those who are in Eruptor mode feel most comfortable when they're in a fight, seeking out or creating conflict any chance they get. Their nervous system is wired to be hyperactive, keeping them always looking for something—anything!—that could be an affront. When they find something offensive or the proverbial shoe hits the ground, they kick, scream, throw a tantrum, or explode on others. They're often defensive, can't see their own part in current circumstances, and don't calm down easily, often holding a grudge or considering revenge. They often transition from nitpicking to throwing a tantrum to waiting and watching for the next issue. Their neuroception has been conditioned to perceive most social behavior as an insult, slight, hurt, or provocation.

Sofia, my ex-girlfriend from chapter 1, was often in Eruptor mode. She always felt that she was being taken advantage of or that others were out to get her. She was regularly in conflicts, whether it was with a cashier at the grocery store who didn't notice she was next in line or a friend who took too long to respond to her text. She frequently erupted at others, either by muttering under her breath, giving them dirty looks, or outright yelling or arguing when something didn't go her way.

Sofia isn't a bad person, and she's not to blame for her Eruptor tendencies. She grew up in an emotionally explosive home, where yelling and screaming were daily occurrences. From a young age, her nervous system dealt with her stress and other overwhelming emotions by shifting into fight mode. That dysregulation caused her to instinctually scan for and perceive or find threats, even when none existed, which kept her body in the felt "safety" of her familiar nervous system response. As illogical as it may sound, when she wasn't in a fight, she felt physically and emotionally unsafe and uncomfortable, likely because it signaled being in a more vulnerable state of openness.

Distractor Mode (Flight Response)

When those in Distractor mode feel threatened or unsafe, they run away from their perceived problems, whether they do so emotionally by pushing people away or physically by allowing themselves to be consumed by their work or other obligations. They may keep themselves busy or throw themselves so intently into their work, family obligations, to-do list, hobbies, or other pursuits that they don't have the time or space to sit with themselves and feel their feelings. Some people in Distractor mode numb themselves with drugs, sex, alcohol, food, or other substances or activities. In general, they'll do anything to avoid confrontation, ghosting others or changing the subject if a stressful or uncomfortable conversation arises that could possibly lead to a conflict or issue. I've often found myself in Distractor mode, avoiding or distracting myself from my uncomfortable emotions or difficult tasks by procrastinating with unnecessary projects like scrolling a topic on social media, rearranging my bookshelf, or tidying the house.

Aisha spends a lot of her time in Distractor mode. A successful doctor with two kids and a prominent attorney husband, she wakes up at five every morning to jog, volunteers after work by seeing low-income patients for free, and offers to organize every family party, holiday or community event and work celebration that she can. By continually playing Super Doctor, Super Mom, Super Daughter, and Super Host, Aisha never has time to sit with herself; she's constantly in flight, running away from possible conflicts, confrontations, and other uncomfortable emotions. Remaining continually busy allows her to avoid potentially stressful feelings or moments when she might have to look inward, even if regularly pushes her body past its physical limits.

Aisha isn't to blame for being in Distractor mode. Though her mother was a loving person, she couldn't properly attune to her daughter because she was distracted by soothing Aisha's father, a well-known artist who was often in Eruptor mode. Under the shadow of her well-known father, Aisha grew up in a family that overemphasized achievement and productivity, instilling in her the subconscious belief that she must always do and achieve to be valued and loved. Though her achievements in her job, volunteer work, and fitness feel validating to Aisha on some level, as they do to many of us, her constant striving prevents her from meeting her body's need to rest and recharge. Wired for flight, her nervous system is comfortable only when she's fleeing the stressful experience, whether it's by jogging, staying constantly busy, or otherwise distracting her attention away from her deeper emotional discomfort.

Detacher Mode (Freeze or Shutdown Response)

Those in Detacher mode cope with perceived threats by freezing or shutting down completely. They deal with their feelings by dissociating or separating, climbing into what I call their "spaceship"; their body may be in the moment, but their mind is zooming far away from the present and their current problems or perceived pain. Detachers are different from Distractors; those in Distractor mode often experience racing, hyper-focused or self-analyzing thoughts, while people in Detacher mode usually experience a kind of mental "blankness." Generally speaking, they stop engaging in any significant way with the thoughts in their mind, the emotions or sensations in their body, or the environment around them. As I experienced, Detacher mode can often progress into or alternate with Distractor mode when stressful events occur for too long or our attempts to self-regulate by numbing or distracting ourselves no longer work.

My mom was often in Detacher mode. She was always physically present, going through the motions of making meals and running our household, but emotionally, she was checked out, unaware herself that she was shut down. She would tune into and out of conversations and frequently orbit around us in her own "spaceship."

My mom's habit of living in Detacher mode began, I imagine, during her own childhood. Her mother (my grandmother) was a cold, distant person who, due to her own generational trauma, was unable to express love or other emotions. Keeping herself emotionally walled off from everyone, even her own children, was her only way of keeping herself emotionally safe. Due to similar intergenerational trauma, my mother's father (my grandfather) believed in the old, harmful adage that children are to be seen, not heard, and would come home many nights after work only to completely ignore his family in favor of reading the daily newspaper. Because my mom grew up with little to no emotional support, she learned to dissociate herself from reality as a way to cope with her stressful and upsetting life experiences. Like her own mother, she disconnected from her emotions to keep herself safe, ultimately disconnecting herself from her own children and passing down the same intergenerational abandonment wound to my siblings and me.

The depth of my abandonment wound became clear to me when I found myself inexplicably becoming incensed with my ex-wife Vivienne's humming. One day, as I felt my body clench in response to her joyful tune, I recalled memories of Mom always humming and singing to herself, lost in her own world, far away from the rest of us. When Vivienne did it, my neuroception interpreted the cue not as the joyful play it was but as detachment, since that had always been the case in my childhood. It was not Vivienne's humming that caused my reaction but my own nervous system, which associated the sound with the inherent threat of my mom's absence.

Pleaser Mode (Fawn Response)

When those in Pleaser mode perceive a possible threat, they anticipate or neutralize it by saying yes, keeping the peace, or doing whatever else they can to defuse or avoid the conflict altogether, usually sacrificing their own needs in the process. Like that of people in Eruptor mode, the nervous system of those in Pleaser mode is hypervigilant, causing them to misread signals of safety as cues of danger. But those in Pleaser mode react by fawning or giving in instead of fighting when they perceive a problem.

My sister, who is fifteen years older than I am, has spent a lot of time in Pleaser mode. Throughout her childhood and teenage years, she constantly monitored her environment and relationships, especially with our mom. She often played the role of caretaker to me and my mom, hovering around us both and always assessing our mom's health status and overall physical condition. She continually asked us if everything was okay or if we needed care or help in some way. Until she became aware of that pattern, she continued to do so with her son and most others in her life, always available to anyone who needed her, regardless of whether she was physically or emotionally able to meet their needs or not. Unable to create separation or boundaries between her own emotions and those of others, she regularly took responsibility for how others felt and shifted into Pleaser mode in an attempt to soothe the associated discomfort.

My sister likely began to shift into Pleaser mode when she was regularly hospitalized as a child. Worried that her illness was the cause of extreme stress and fear in the home and without any emotional support from our parents during that frightening time, she developed deep-rooted fears of abandonment and became consumed by constant worry. Finding herself dependent on my parents but lacking an emotionally safe and secure relationship with them, she was left with no choice but to manage her internal overwhelm by controlling or monitoring the environment around her, adopting a pattern of hypervigilance that would last into adulthood. For many years, until she began to regulate her nervous system, she continued to unconsciously scan our home for the next possible threat, dropping everything to neutralize it before it caused any more stress.

Like my sister, I often shift into Pleaser mode, worrying about what others think of me or need from me to try to prevent imaginary conflicts or issues. During times of high stress, I've said things I didn't want to say or withheld things I had wanted to say in order to avoid or prevent a possible conflict. I've often said yes to plans with friends that I knew I wasn't interested in or didn't have the time, energy, or financial resources to commit to. To support my school peers or work colleagues, I used to regularly take on extra work when I was already overcommitted to my own projects. For decades, I hardly ever spoke up or shared my perspective on family decisions, deferring instead to what the majority wanted or felt was needed at the time. When dating, I regularly struggled to be honest about my feelings and even ghosted others instead of directly expressing my lack of interest in a relationship with them.

Connector Mode (Safe and Social)

Those in Connector mode have a well-regulated nervous system and their body can respond when a threat is present, then return easily and quickly to a state of grounded relaxation and calm. Their neuroception is largely accurate, enabling them to realistically perceive threats and the social behavior of others without misreading either to be signs of misinterpreted danger. Those in Connector mode can open themselves up and are receptive to others and what's happening around them, allowing them to handle conflicts, stressful situations, and upsetting emotions more calmly and efficiently. They are curious about and able to hold space for differences in perspectives and are able to negotiate and collaboratively solve problems. They can set boundaries, give and accept social support, build authentic relationships, and make responsive choices considering their own needs as well as the needs of the greater collective.

This state of openness to connecting with others is possible only when our body feels safe. Felt safety can occur only when we have access to the physical and emotional resources necessary to consistently meet our physical and emotional needs. Throughout this book, we'll continue to explore ways to support ourselves and replenish our resources so that we can build a foundation for this safety.

HOW TO CREATE NERVOUS SYSTEM AWARENESS

Nervous system stress states are automatic and involuntary and we can't really control them. Though when they do occur, we can notice and use the practice of body consciousness that we'll discuss in more detail in chapter 5 to calm the emotional dysregulation they cause. The more we're aware of the physical cues that our body sends our brain when our nervous system is activated, the more we can sense when we're in a stressed state.

Though everyone is unique, the following chart can help you begin to understand what the various stress responses may look and feel like in your daily life. Read through the indicators on the facing page and see which ones you notice in yourself right now. Then spend the next few weeks starting to notice any shifts that occur in your body's physical sensations and mental outlook that might indicate when you're in a stress response. To notice when your nervous system is activated, set an intention to begin to practice body consciousness check-ins (see page 54) more frequently throughout the day.

Nervous System Checklist

ERUPTOR MODE (*FIGHT RESPONSE*)

I notice myself taking things personally, becoming overly defensive, dominating the conversation, arguing with others, feeling angry or enraged, harboring resentment, holding grudges, or nursing vendettas. I may bully, shame, belittle, or become highly critical or judgmental of myself or others.

BODY:

_____ I feel unable to relax and may feel uncomfortable, unsettled, agitated, or anxious.

_____ My heart is racing.

_____ My body is sweating or shaking, and my shoulders may be squared or my chest puffed out.

_____ I'm breathing quickly and shallow, from my chest (instead of from deep in my belly).

_____ My muscles (in my jaw, neck, upper back, psoas) are tense, and my hands and fists may be clenched.

_____ I'm talking loudly, maybe even screaming or yelling.

_____ My eyes are hyperfocused or fixated on something or someone in my immediate environment ("tunnel vision").

MIND:

_____ My thoughts (about myself or others) are highly critical.

_____ My thoughts are highly emotional and may even be stuck in all-or-nothing loops (like repeatedly thinking "I am a total failure" or "They are completely wrong" in response to a stressful or upsetting event).

DISTRACTOR MODE (FLIGHT RESPONSE)

I notice myself retreating into my thoughts or attempting to escape through my work or to-do list or by eating, drinking, or using other substances. I change the subject or leave uncomfortable conversations or hide from, avoid, or "ghost" others when I perceive for fear an upset or conflict.

BODY:

_____ I feel unable to relax and may even feel uncomfortable, unsettled, agitated, or anxious.

_____ My heart is racing.

_____ My body is sweating or shaking, and my posture may be hunched (so that I look smaller), or I feel as though I want to retreat into the background.

_____ I'm breathing quickly and shallow, and from my chest (instead of from deep in my belly).

_____ My muscles (in my jaw, neck, upper back, psoas) are generally tense and may be trembling or shaking.

_____ I may not be talking much, may be talking at a low volume, or may be rambling or trying to change the subject of the conversation.

_____ My eyes are distracted or I'm avoiding eye contact with my immediate environment altogether and they're fixated elsewhere (i.e., like on my phone or TV screen).

MIND:

_____ My thoughts are racing, and I may have difficulty concentrating on tasks or thinking clearly and critically.

_____ My thoughts are hyper-fixated a certain subject, topic, or issue.

DETACHER MODE (FREEZE or SHUTDOWN RESPONSE)

I notice myself shutting down, checking out, or disconnecting entirely. I feel numb or empty. My mind often feels blank, and I struggle to connect with my thoughts or feelings or verbalize them to others.

BODY:

_____ I feel generally detached or apathetic and may even feel depressed, hopeless, despairing, or unmotivated.

_____ My heartbeat is slowed or imperceptible.

_____ My body may be cold or numb and is generally shrunken, and my head may hang low.

_____ I'm breathing from a constricted chest and may even be holding my breath or feel an overall stiffness in my midsection.

_____ My muscles are generally weak and feel fatigued or heavy.

_____ I feel physically exhausted, energetically depleted, or mostly numb and unable to feel any emotions or physical sensations at all.

_____ I may be silent or my speech is flat, monotone, or forced (I'm nodding or giving one-word responses).

_____ My eyes have a blank or far-off stare.

MIND:

_____ I feel spaced out and may feel unsure of what is real versus imagined.

_____ My mind feels blank, and I may have difficulty concentrating on tasks or thinking clearly and critically.

PLEASER MODE (FAWN RESPONSE)

I'm fixated on the physical or emotional states of others and may even take full responsibility for anticipating their needs, feelings, or actions. I regularly notice myself overexplaining or defending my thoughts, feelings, or choices to others.

BODY:

_____ I'm disconnected from my body and often have difficulty noticing how I feel.

_____ My attention is hyperfocused on others or the environment around me.

_____ My breathing may mirror that of people with whom I'm spending time.

_____ My energy may reflect the energy of others around me or my environment.

_____ My eyes are constantly scanning someone or something in my external environment.

MIND:

_____ My attention is always on the lookout for the next possible issue ("waiting for the other shoe to drop").

_____ I'm distracted by thoughts or worries about others being mad or upset with me or concerns about external circumstances in general.

Your Regulated Nervous System Checklist

CONNECTOR MODE (SAFE AND SOCIAL RESPONSE)

I notice myself feeling calm, safe, and open to engaging or connecting with someone or something around me. I'm curious and able to see things from a different perspective, hold space for complexity and contradiction, and remain grounded and responsive to whatever arises.

BODY:

_____ I feel physically awake, relaxed, and alert.

_____ My body posture is open, relaxed, and at ease, with my arms hanging loosely alongside my body.

_____ I'm breathing slowly and deeply from my belly.

_____ My heart is beating calmly.

_____ I feel peaceful and relaxed in my body.

_____ I am able to make eye contact with those around me.

MIND:

_____ I can think clearly and plan for the future.

_____ I am open to and curious about others and the world around me.

_____ I am in a flow with my interests or passions and able to access my unique creativity.

When our nervous system is activated, we often act like a trapped animal. Because we feel threatened, we'll do anything to preserve our survival without concern for others. Recognizing this tendency and accepting it as innate human behavior can help us release the shame we may feel about our actions or words when we're in a stress response. By becoming aware of the signs of nervous system dysregulation so that we can identify when we're dysregulated, we can begin to understand why we may do or say things in our relationships that create or exacerbate interpersonal stress.

When we learn to recognize when we're reacting in a stressed state, we can make a conscious choice to act or respond differently. We can decide to take a step away or a timeout, excusing ourselves from a situation or not interacting until we feel both calm and are both able and willing to be open to connect socially again. Ming, the parent of a toddler, recently commented in our private membership portal that she noticed how much calmer she felt when navigating her dysregulated child's temper tantrum *after* she paused to take a few seconds to ground herself first. Whereas she used to "feel like a bad mom" for focusing on herself before she did her child, she was relieved to hear that her instinct was backed by science.

Like Ming, we can all begin to use some of the mind-body practices we'll continue to discuss throughout this book to bring our body back to safety. These practices will be particularly useful if we can't remove ourselves from an interaction or are otherwise unable to leave a stressful environment.

Nearly all of us have trauma bond patterns we repeat within our relationships, whether with our friends, family, colleagues, or romantic partners. We re-create the same dynamics with others because we're neurobiologically driven to do so: our nervous system and subconscious mind are wired to reenact within our relationships today the ways in which we learned to feel safe, valued, or loved as children. Until we regulate our nervous system, we'll continue to create or reinforce our trauma bonds with others, no matter how much insight or awareness we have. Thankfully, we can all regulate our nervous system, a process that we'll continue to talk more about in the following chapters.

4

WITNESSING YOUR CONDITIONED SELVES

Mona couldn't stop staring at her phone. *Why isn't he texting me back?* she wondered. *It's been two hours! I must have done something wrong. Maybe he's with another woman.* And the thought behind all the others: *I'm just not good enough for him.*

Mona had been dating Juan for more than two years, and even the security of what was a relatively long-term relationship didn't prevent her from panicking every time he didn't respond quickly (or quickly enough, in her opinion) to her texts or calls or seemed distant, distracted, or disinterested in any way. When he stayed late at work, she suspected that he was having an affair. When he wanted to spend time alone or out with friends, she assumed that he must be unhappy with her. If he was quiet, grumpy, or low energy, she figured that he had finally grown tired of their relationship. Mona was always, it seemed, looking for evidence to indicate whether her relationship was going to work out.

When two hours dragged into three, Mona started to panic. *It's finally happening*, she thought. *He's breaking up with me!* She sent another text: "What's going on? Is everything OK?" The more time passed, the more nervous she became. She had a ton of projects to finish that day—she worked from home as a graphic designer—but she couldn't concentrate. She'd already skipped her afternoon online yoga class, even though she'd paid for it, and rescheduled several work calls because she was too anxious to do anything other than stare at her phone. She wasn't even listening to her favorite playlist, which she usually found comforting, since she was too concerned about missing the ding of a possible text.

When another hour had passed since her last message, Mona texted Juan again: "Can you please text me back? Or just call me? I'm getting worried." Her anxiety was now all-consuming. Should she drive to his work and look for his car? She decided to try calling his phone . . . straight to voice mail! *He's blocked me!* she thought. She started crying as she dug around in her purse for her car keys. Even though Juan usually left the office by that time, she would drive over anyway, and if she saw his car outside, she'd walk in and confront him about what was going on.

As Mona was getting ready to pull out of the driveway, her cell phone rang. It was Juan; he'd forgotten his phone charger that morning, and his battery had died shortly after her first text. He'd just plugged in his phone and seen all her other messages. "Is everything OK?" he asked.

Mona wanted to squeal with relief, "He's not leaving me!" At the same time, she wanted to scream in anger, "Why didn't you charge your phone at work? You could have asked a colleague to borrow a charger! Is it because you didn't want to text me back?" But she didn't scream anything and broke down crying instead as Juan tried to make sense of how he'd upset his girlfriend yet again.

FROM CORE WOUNDS TO CONDITIONED SELVES

Mona wasn't inherently an insecure or paranoid person. Instead, she suffered from what so many of us do: a core abandonment wound. We develop this wound if we were physically left by a parent-figure who died, was incarcerated, gave us up for adoption, or simply stopped coming home one day, separating from the other parent or suffering a health crises or accident. We also develop this wound if we were consistently left without the emotional support while going through emotionally overwhelming experiences as children.

In Mona's case, though both her parents cared for her deeply and were physically present in her life, they had married at a young age when they didn't yet know how to emotionally support themselves or each other, let alone attune to their developing daughter. They fought constantly, and when Mona was three, her father abruptly moved out after one particularly explosive argument, eventually filing for divorce. Several years later, he married another woman and started a new family. Although she saw him and her half siblings regularly, she never felt part of their family or as though she was even her father's daughter anymore.

Though Mona doesn't explicitly remember much about her parents fighting or the details of the night when her father left, her body and brain do. That's because all the experiences we have in childhood, even when we're too young to consciously recall them, are recorded as our implicit memories, those that exist inside us as instinctual thoughts and feelings. Because our hippocampus, an area of our brain responsible for conscious recollection, doesn't fully develop until age three, most of us can't directly recall what happened to us before then even though our developing nervous system stores those experiences. Before our brain has language abilities, the overwhelming events we experience are imprinted on implicit or preverbal regions of our mind, according to the groundbreaking work of Dr. Bessel van der Kolk, the author of *The Body Keeps the Score: Brain, Mind, and Body in the Healing of Trauma*. Simply put, even if we can't actively call to mind the experiences that impacted us as children, the impact on our conditioning is still there, driving our thoughts, feelings, and reactions today.

To complicate things, if we faced chronically stressful environments outside and inside our childhood home, our body produced more cortisol, which further impacted the functioning of our hippocampus, helping to explain the life-long difficulties recalling the past that many of us have noticed, including myself.

When we experience trauma at a young age, we lack the emotional maturity to contextually understand the subjective nuance of our individual circumstances. This causes us to have immature and self-centered (or egocentric) thoughts as we try to make sense of what is happening or has happened to us. We often think, *I'm what causes Mom to always come home in a bad mood; Dad drinks because I'm bad;* or *If I were more lovable, Mom wouldn't be depressed.* Whatever thoughts we had as children, if we thought them often enough, they eventually became part of our neural patterning and deep-rooted beliefs.

When a parent leaves the family, as Mona's father did, especially when the child is young, the child can't understand that the conflict or separation has nothing to do with them. Instead, they may feel as though Dad or Mom left *because* of them, that they weren't worthy or lovable enough or were too intrinsically flawed for their parent to want to stay. This causes deep-rooted shame that the child internalizes and carries with them into adulthood.

Because my mom was constantly dissociated, distracted, and lost in her own world, she wasn't able to emotionally connect to or attune to me. Without the developmental maturity to know the real cause of her distance, I assumed that it was because of me and my overwhelming emotional world. Feeling shameful about myself for causing our disconnection—or so I believed—I stopped sharing my feelings with everyone, believing it was the safest way to maintain my relationships.

Either form of abandonment, physical or emotional, results in adults who still believe that they're not worthy or good enough to be loved and supported within a relationship. Because Dad or Mom left us, we subconsciously assume that others will leave us, too, as soon as they find out that we're as flawed, unworthy, or broken as we've come to believe we are. Though we're particularly prone to feeling this way in our romantic relationships, where we are the most vulnerable both physically and emotionally, we can have similar worries about being left out within our friendships or find ourselves feeling like an imposter in our professional relationships.

Believing we're unworthy, some of us become "chasers" as adults, constantly pursuing or pushing others to try to verify, validate, or prove that they still love us and want to be with us. As a chaser, we may seek out new romantic interests or even casual sexual encounters in the hope of feeling good enough. We may find ourselves constantly stressed about our job security when our boss or colleagues don't praise our latest project. If we're in a committed romantic relationship, we may struggle to give our loved one the space they need and interpret moments of distance or disinterest as confirmation of our overall unworthiness. Whenever we perceive the slightest possibility that we're being abandoned by another person, we easily become reactive as Mona did, texting, calling, or pursuing our loved one, sometimes in unreasonable or irrational ways. We may break down emotionally, becoming inconsolable, all-consumed by overwhelming feelings, or shut down and nonfunctional. Because, as children we subconsciously believe that *who* we are caused Mom or Dad to leave, we modify *how* we are in the world. As a result, we never truly allow ourselves to *be who we are* or our full and authentic Self, continuing instead to embody only the parts of us that were accepted as children.

While some of us weren't abandoned in childhood, we were wounded in other ways when we were shamed, criticized, ignored, or otherwise overwhelmed by our parent-figures. Every time we heard "Stop being so dramatic" or were teased when we cried, we felt hurt by those we needed the most at that time. Every time our boundaries were ignored or disrespected when we were told what we should or shouldn't think, feel, or believe, our emotional intuition was invalidated. Every time a part of our external self-expression like our appearance or performance was highly praised, valued, or acknowledged more than our deeper interests or pleasures, our authentic Self was diminished. Every time we were seen as an extension of our parents, pressured to bring pride to the family, or told to pursue an interest, career, or path others had been unable to follow, our natural inclinations and talents were dismissed.

Regardless of what our individual childhood wounds were, those early hurts caused us to modify ourselves in order to feel safe and remain connected within our earliest relationships and environments.

Those adaptations became our childhood coping strategies or ways of fitting in. Of course, these coping strategies don't go away when we grow up; our past conditioning is stored in our nervous system where it continues to drive our instinctive reactions as adults. Because of our learned habits, most of us continue to play the same roles in our adult relationships, even though the conditioned parts of us are immature, reactive, and based in trauma.

These adaptations are what I call our *conditioned selves*, the consistent roles we've learned to play in our relationships based on the ways we learned to feel safest and most loved in childhood. Rooted in years of research and related ideologies, the concept of conditioned selves stem from an evidence-based method of therapy known as Internal Family Systems (IFS). Developed in the 1980s by the psychologist Dr. Richard Schwartz, IFS maintains that our minds are made up of different "parts," which developed in response to our earliest unmet needs and that continue to live as mental constructs inside us, directing how we act and react with others.

Our conditioned selves are the neurobiologically wired parts of our subconscious minds. Because the thoughts, feelings, and reactions we had as children were patterned into our nervous system, where they continue to exist today, our conditioned selves are a physically and emotionally embodied part of us. Unless we take the time to become aware of or witness the ways in which they drive us to think, feel, and behave with others, they will keep us locked in the same reactive neurophysiological patterns and habitual ruts.

In this chapter, we'll meet our conditioned selves. To help you start exploring, below are seven archetypes and the common thoughts, feelings, and habits that accompany each. Most people I've met or have worked with relate to one or several of these seven conditioned selves witnessing their presence in most if not all their relationships. You may likely recognize yourself in at least one of the seven descriptions you'll read below.

Before we can more deeply explore our conditioning, though, we need to meet our inner child—more specifically, our hurt inner child. Our hurt inner child is the little being inside us all who was aban-

doned, shamed, criticized, ignored, overwhelmed, or hurt when our
needs weren't consistently met by our parent-figures. When we reconnect with our hurt inner child, we're better able to see our core
wounds and the childhood coping strategies we developed as a result.
Understanding and witnessing this painful and reactive part of us gives
us the opportunity to cultivate compassion for ourselves and others as
we continue to repeat the same dysfunctional habits, despite wanting
or needing change. Reconnecting with our hurt inner child will help
us identify which conditioned selves we most commonly embody in
our adult relationships, giving us the opportunity to begin to break
away from playing these trauma-based roles.

THE (HURT) INNER CHILD INSIDE US ALL

We all have an inner child; it's the part of us that's born free, whole,
and connected to our inner essence, or authentic Self. Our inner child
loves to play, freely speak their mind, and is expressive, spontaneous,
creative, trusting, and innocent. Imagine what you might be like if
you felt truly free *to be fully you*. That would be your true Self before
you were exposed to all of the life experiences that changed your natural way of being—that is, before all the imprinting, teaching, scolding,
chiding, shaming, criticizing, rule making, and other forms of conditioning that we were all subjected to, whether it was functional or
dysfunctional.

Our inner child usually doesn't stay free, whole, and joyful for long.
As children, we all experienced moments or situations that caused us to
feel insecure, scared, or hurt. If those moments or situations occurred
often enough or were overwhelming enough, we eventually learned to
suppress our natural instincts and our playful, expressive, spontaneous
side to keep ourselves safe. The more consistently we suppressed our
natural instincts, the more wounded our inner child became.

Though emotions were a normal part of our childhood and life
experiences, few of us were modeled healthy emotional expression
by our parent-figures. If we grew up in a household where certain

emotions weren't tolerated—we were told to stop crying or were ignored whenever we were sad—we may have learned that only certain feelings are okay to express. If we regularly witnessed emotional explosions or overwhelming outbursts, we may have come to believe that those were appropriate ways to express ourselves when we're upset. Or if our parent-figures suppressed or hid their own feelings, emotionally dissociating or disconnecting themselves from us, we may have developed similar habits.

Here are a few common ways many of us were modeled dysfunctional emotional expression and communication in childhood.

COMMON DYSFUNCTIONAL COMMUNICATION STYLES

Emotional invalidation. An attempt to get someone to believe their emotions are the issue instead of the actual problem or conflict at hand. This can involve saying "You're too dramatic," "You're too sensitive," or "You just need to get over it or move on" whenever feelings are expressed.

Projection. A defense mechanism of attributing undesired traits or behaviors in oneself onto others. This can involve making accusations such as "You're probably the one lying" in response to a stated concern.

Scorekeeping. A control dynamic in which two people avoid addressing conflict or underlying emotions by bringing up past wrongdoing to one-up the other. This can involve bringing up a past issue in response to a current concern.

Name calling/shaming. The use of insults as a way to control or modify others' behavior. This can involve using derogatory language, character attacks, or mean-spirited comments or "jokes."

Icing. The act of shutting down, withdrawing, or pretending a person isn't present as a way of avoiding issues or displaying disapproval. This can involve completely ignoring others by not speaking to them or not responding when spoken to ("the silent treatment").

Avoidance. The act of denying, ignoring, or sweeping issues under the rug. This can involve refusing to take ownership of one's behaviors, often by refusing to admit to or lying about one's actions, leaving out certain details, refusing to talk about problems or issues, or ignoring the reality of the problems or issues entirely.

Deflection. The habit of consistently changing the subject to redirect blame toward another (externalization) and avoid personal accountability. This can involve blaming others for being the cause of their verbal, emotional, or physical abuse by saying things like "If you hadn't X, I wouldn't have Y."

Many of these communication styles occurred in my own family. No one in my family showed many feelings other than worry about our daily life and health-related issues. Consumed by anxiety, there was little opportunity for anyone in the family to feel at ease, joyful, or playful, at least not for long. That constant stress created an underlying, fear-based tension, which often manifested itself in outwardly controlling behaviors. My dad, locked in survival mode from his childhood, was regularly stressed by being the sole provider of our family's financial security. He manifested that stress by micromanaging our home, obsessively organizing and monitoring the cabinets and pantry, and always saving old food and items, including those that were used, like wrapping paper and ribbons from holidays. If anything was moved or misplaced and was no longer where he had put it, my dad shifted into Eruptor mode, yelling, screaming, and releasing the pent-up rage caused by years of dysregulation and unmet needs while also hurting those around him, even the ones he loved most.

From my family, I received a consistent message that talking about or expressing emotions would either be ignored or only add more stress to an already-overwhelmed environment. Because no one in any of my earliest relationships modeled healthy emotional expression, I didn't know what feelings really looked like. Emotionally under-supported, I started suppressing my inner world and true way of be-ing, appearing outwardly cold or aloof, not in any way even needing the support of others. Though this characteristic wasn't an inherent part of my personality, it was one of the ways I learned to keep myself emotionally safe in my childhood relationships.

I didn't even tell anyone after I saw my best friend get beaten up by a group of older peers when I was in my early teens—something I can't imagine keeping to myself now. Although I was scared and even got hurt myself while trying to run away to escape her attack-ers, I kept the whole experience secret, more fearful of how my mom and family would react if they found out. I lay alone in bed that night, shaking and crying myself to sleep without any emo-tional safety or support when I needed it most. That experience only continued to strengthen my growing belief that there must be something about me that prevented me from receiving emotional support.

Just as I avoided showing unpleasant or difficult feelings, I also sup-pressed pleasant emotions when growing up. It wasn't until I was in my early twenties and my mom was about to undergo a high-risk heart surgery that I verbally told her I loved her. Because that senti-ment was rarely expressed directly in my home, I can still remember how vulnerable I felt when I first began to say it aloud.

If you did happen to grow up in an emotionally expressive family, your inner child may have been wounded if you were criticized for having certain interests or hobbies, shamed for how you looked or acted, physically or emotionally abandoned as Mona and I were, in-consistently supported as Monique was, micromanaged or controlled as Dominik was, or expected to put the needs of your parent-figures or family before your own, as was the case for Diego.

Diego was raised by a single, nonnative, non-English-speaking mother. Because she struggled to communicate, she relied on her son to help navigate the family's new life in an unfamiliar land. Regularly told how mature he was for his age for acting as the man of the house, Diego was often left to take care of his two younger siblings while his mom was at work. From a young age, he was depended on to care for the family and provide emotional support to his understandably stressed mother—her obvious need for support only made him feel guilty whenever he even thought about pursuing relationships outside his family.

Though Diego's mother was doing the best she could navigating the family's stressful circumstances, her behavior parentified him, reversing the traditional parent-child role. Relied on to care for his mother and younger brothers, Diego was never able to be a kid and play when he wanted to, get upset when he felt angry or sad, pursue the things that interested him, or given the attention and space to learn how to prioritize and meet his own needs. Instead, he regularly learned that his family benefited when he ignored his needs. As he grew up, he continued to be subconsciously attracted to individuals who appeared in need of some sort of help or support, even though he increasingly felt resentful of their neediness.

Today, Diego continues to play the role of the Yes Person, one of the seven conditioned selves that we'll explore later in this chapter. Priding himself on his identity as a "nice, responsible, and family-oriented person," he regularly bends over backward trying to keep others happy, ignoring his own needs in the process.

Witnessing his hurt inner child helped Diego become more aware of the different ways he still plays this role in his relationships as well as the growing feelings of discontent and dissatisfaction inside him. These feelings naturally arise whenever we are suppressing our true needs or desires. And by continuing to suppress parts of ourselves, we never give ourselves the opportunity to be accepted and loved fully and authentically.

Because Diego didn't have the safety or security to pursue what he really needed, wanted, or was interested in as a child, he remained deeply disconnected from those aspects of himself as an adult. After spending years directing all his energy toward supporting, helping, and loving others, he understandably felt burnt out. Yet at the same time, he didn't know how to stop playing that role and often felt too proud to ask for help or support from others. Most of the time, he was too distanced from himself and his own emotions to even know that he could benefit from some.

No matter how we were hurt as children, many of us learned that we needed to suppress our needs, overlook our true interests and curiosities, and modify our authentic Self-expression in order to fit in with those around us. And as adults, our hurt inner child still lives inside our subconscious mind, where it drives us to think, feel, and react in the same ways we did as children. When we encounter anyone or anything that appears similar to something that overwhelmed us in the past, we instinctively return to the well-worn neural pathways of our familiar stress responses and learned childhood coping strategies. Because we subconsciously prefer our familiar neurobiology, our brain's reticular activating system (RAS), a network of brain cells that helps moderate our behavior, begins to filter out any evidence that the experience is dissimilar in any way, locking us into a self-confirming safety cycle that keeps us trapped in old, dysfunctional patterns.

Our wounded inner child lives inside our body as much as in our subconscious mind. When our core wounds are activated and we feel insecure, scared, or hurt in the same way we were as children, our heart rate rises, our breathing quickens, and our muscles tense up. This is our nervous system's fight-or-flight response, trying to help us to cope with our perceived stress in familiar ways.

This issue is, these survival-driven reactions prevent us from thinking calmly or rationally. Believing that our safety is at risk, our brain will do anything and everything to protect us, including driving us to act in selfish, irrational, or hurtful ways and ultimately preventing us from *being* the love we seek.

After Diego learned about his hurt inner child and witnessed his habitual tendency to play the role of the Yes Person, he began his journey toward reconnecting with his authentic Self. Today he is on his way to rediscovering his true passions and purpose as well as connecting with others in ways that allow him to open himself up to the possibility of authentic love.

MEETING YOUR (WOUNDED) INNER CHILD

Even if you can't consciously recall your specific childhood wounds, you can still witness and heal your hurt inner child and, as a result, your relationships, too.

Though I know it can feel silly or uncomfortable for many of us at first, we need to be able to acknowledge and accept that we all have a hurt inner child that drives our daily reactions. Doing so creates the space to develop a more compassionate understanding of our dysfunctional habits or other shame-inducing aspects of our conditioning. There isn't actually anything wrong with us; we're not flawed, broken, or unlovable, as many of us perceive ourselves to be. Instead, we've adapted in the ways we needed to do in order to keep ourselves as safe as possible in our lived experiences. Our hurt inner child isn't trying to sabotage our life but exists to protect us from our painful past circumstances.

Though the dysfunctional relationship habits we developed as a result of our childhood trauma aren't our fault, they are our responsibility as adults. We can empower ourselves to become conscious of the deep inner pain that drives us to hurt ourselves and others by beginning to make new choices about how we want to act in the current moment.

We can all begin to reconnect with our inner child when we allow pause and space to explore or notice, without judgment, all the different ways we attempt to get our emotional needs met in our adult relationships. On a universal level, we all yearn to feel safe and secure enough to *be* ourselves, freely sharing our thoughts and perspectives, pursuing our true passions and interests, and tapping into our ideas and creativity. It is only when we are able to fully express ourselves that we are able to share a "felt" presence with others, allowing us as individuals to feel supported and capable of dealing with life's emotional ups and downs. Experiencing our emotions in the presence of another person allows us to communicate with all of us—body, mind, and soul—and to create the "embodied" emotional connection necessary for deep, authentic relationships.

Going through my dark night of the soul, I came to realize that I had never really shared my emotional world within my relationships, despite complaining I wasn't emotionally connected with anyone. As in my childhood home, I created patterns of stress- or complaint-based communications and dynamics in my relationships, where I expressed only feelings of anxiety and worry about my latest crisis to my friends and partners. In a repetition of my earliest relationships, I didn't allow for the creation of a deep and authentic connection with another person—although as an adult, I continued to hold the other person solely responsible. I continued to embody my Overachiever self at the expense of my authentic needs and desires, not because others didn't let me be me but because *I* struggled to let *me* be *me*. I was too shut down and fearful to be fully vulnerable with others or admit that I even had feelings in the first place.

As I reconnected with my inner child, I started to see inside me pain that I had struggled my entire life to put into words. As I began to come to terms with my mom's lifelong emotional absence, I also gave myself the time and space to begin to grieve for the relationship I hadn't had with her, which helped me be more honest about the one I did have. I recognized the little emotional connection we'd had and gave myself permission to no longer hold myself responsible for that which had never been. Taking actual space away from my mom and the rest of my family allowed me to see that, as an adult, I am now safe enough to exist in the emotional distance that was always there, a distance that was once a threat to my survival. Letting myself finally become vulnerable to my own pain allowed me to develop a true capacity for empathy, to be truly present to the pain carried by others.

I continued to extend grace and compassion to myself as I began to see all the ways my suffering had grown out of a desperate desire and expectation to be seen and loved for a Self that I refused to let others see. It was a deep pain—and a growing resentment that at times erupted outward as I was subconsciously driven to perceive myself to be neglected, unconsidered, or uncared for.

As I developed more empathy for my own experience, I became better able to show my wounded inner child the compassion, care, and consideration she had always deserved. At first, the practice of extending myself empathy felt surprisingly vulnerable and uncomfortable, and it may be the same for you if, like me, you didn't experience moments of true understanding or attunement as a child. Over time and with practice, my inner child was able to relax into a deeper sense of worthiness for being exactly who she is. Though I know no one can take away the pain that comes when you don't bond with your Mom, I am now learning how to provide myself the mothering I always needed.

As you reconnect with your own inner child, you may encounter similar deep-rooted feelings of grief or loss that underlie your unmet needs and relationships that never were. To recognize and tend to our emotional needs within our relationships, we have to accept that we have emotions in the first place. This may sound obvious, but many of us are so disconnected from our body that we don't realize that we experience the emotions that we do. Our emotions contain evolutionary messages (we'll explore this idea more in the next chapter) and reconnecting with these sensory signals is foundationally important to both our survival and well-being as humans. We're constantly gathering sensation-based information to signal to our brain and nervous system whether we're safe or unsafe. And when we're safe, we can relax and be authentically express ourselves, however it is we are feeling.

Take a moment now to think about your last week and the various emotional experiences you may have had. Were there moments when you felt sad, angry, scared, surprised, or joyful? When you felt those ways around another person, did you feel safe and secure enough to directly communicate to them how you were feeling? Or did you feel safe and secure enough to express your emotions in another way while in their presence (by non-aggressively yelling, crying, or laughing)?

Exploring the different ways in which you express your feelings with others can help you better understand your emotional habits in your current relationships. Ask yourself:

- Are you able to remain calm and express your feelings in a way that's safe for you and others are around?
- Do you become activated and erupt, chase, detach from, dissociate from, or act out toward others?
- Do you harm yourself in some way, by using substances, ignoring your personal work or hobbies, or sacrificing your sleep, nutrition, or other self-care needs?
- Do you harm others in some way, by acting physically or emotionally explosive, abusive, or violent with your words or behaviors?

When we deal with our emotions in immature, unreasonable, or irrational ways, it's a sign that a hurt part of us is lashing out. Start to pay attention to these moments: If you can more objectively witness the times when you're reactive, it will help you reconnect with your deeper emotional wounds. In these moments, take some time to consider why you may be feeling insecure, scared, or hurt by asking yourself:

- Do you feel worried that you might be hurt, abandoned, or left by another?
- Do you feel ignored, overlooked, or unseen by another?
- Do you feel undervalued or criticized for your contributions to the relationship?
- Do you feel overvalued or singled out for only certain aspects of you?
- Do you feel pressured or controlled by another?

Exploring why you feel activated can help you reconnect with your hurt inner child and witness how your old childhood wounds may be impacting your relationships today.

Some of us are already aware of the ways in which we act immaturely, unreasonably, or irrationally in our relationships. If Mona was honest with herself, she knew that her instinctual thoughts, feelings, and reactions with Juan were irrational, even though she felt that she couldn't help having them. Similarly, you may know that you react disproportionately to distance or separation or take certain remarks or actions personally, even when others are well-meaning. You may know that you have a tendency to fly off the handle or become reactive when you're dysregulated, feeling hurt or upset by others. You may instead act passive-aggressively, ice others out, or give them the cold shoulder or silent treatment when you feel that you've been slighted. Or you may be hypervigilant, trying to micromanage or control others as a bossy child would do on a playground.

Let's revisit Mona's journey to reconnect with her hurt inner child. She started to acknowledge and accept what she already knew on an instinctual level: that she was reactive and irrational when she perceived moments of distance in her relationships. Without judgment, she began to develop more compassion for herself when she heard her hurt inner child's voice whispering "He doesn't love you anymore, he will leave you, you're unworthy." She realized that this voice was a subconscious by-product of old wounding rather than an accurate indicator of what was happening in the present moment.

Now when Mona heard her hurt inner child's voice, she began to pay attention to her body. She noticed that her heart rate usually shot up, her breathing became shallow, and her muscles tensed—all signs that her nervous system was in a fight response. As she became more aware of these different physical sensations (we'll talk about how to do this in chapter 5), she was able to identify when she felt threatened, which made her more likely to misinterpret others' behavior and act out. In those moments, she started to practice mind-body techniques to regulate her nervous system and soothe her hurt inner child, defusing the intensity of her emotional reactivity. That allowed her to strengthen the wise voice in her head by reminding herself "You just feel threatened right now and may be misinterpreting Juan's behavior.

He's probably busy, his phone died, he needs space, or he's feeling uncommunicative, all of which has nothing to do with you. You can help yourself feel safe right now without becoming reactive or acting in ways you won't feel proud of later."

WITNESSING YOUR HURT INNER CHILD

Our inner child is the subconscious part of our mind in which we carry our unmet needs, repressed childhood emotions, and habitual coping strategies. When these deep subconscious wounds are activated, we often unconsciously shift into the ways we navigated our emotions as children in the hope of protecting, preventing, or soothing our pain.

Take a look at the list below and spend the next few weeks witnessing your own hurt inner child. Remember that these wounded, reactive states are often signs of emotional suffering, so try to be nonjudgmental and compassionate as you reconnect with your deep-rooted pain.

_____ I'm emotionally explosive and raise my voice, say things I don't mean, slam doors, or throw things.

_____ I'm highly defensive or am unable to listen to another's thoughts or feelings without taking them personally, feeling attacked, or becoming emotionally reactive.

_____ I'm dismissive of another's feelings or invalidate, deny, or try to change how they feel in order to relieve my own discomfort.

_____ I fall into polarized thinking, viewing things as all good or all bad or having a difficult time seeing contextual nuances or another's perspective.

_____ I center conversations or experiences around my feelings or have a difficult time expressing curiosity or empathy about another's internal world.

_____ I try to control or dominate conversations by changing the subject to ones I'm interested in or insist on sharing only my own perspectives or experiences.

_____ I actively find ways to distract myself from or avoid uncomfortable conversations, topics, or experiences by scrolling on social media, turning on the TV, or leaving the room entirely.

_____ I remove, withdraw, or emotionally distance myself, shutting down or giving another the silent treatment.

_____ I close myself off from receiving connection or support from another or intentionally suppress my needs and emotions, choosing instead to remain "tough" or emotionally distant.

_____ I use alcohol, food, or other substances to numb myself or engage in other self-harming behaviors when stressed, upset, or otherwise uncomfortable.

The more you frequently notice these reactions, the more likely your inner child is wounded. As you become more consciously aware of these reactive parts of yourself that want to be seen and valued for their once-protective presence, you can begin to practice extending them compassion and love.

Identify Your Hurt Inner Child Habits

Spend a few weeks continuing to witness your hurt inner child in your daily life. The more consistently you notice your wounded reactions, the better you'll be able to recognize themes. You can use the following prompts to explore any common patterns you discover.

When my inner child wound is activated, I tend to think _____.

I tend to feel _____ [identify your physical sensations].

In my relationships, I tend to act _____.

Afterward, I tend to think _____ and/or feel _____.

YOUR CONDITIONED SELVES

As we now know our conditioned selves are part of our nervous system. When we fire the same neural circuits over and over again, they wire together, increasing the likelihood that our brain will continue to repeat the same response to similar events in the future. Like a well-traveled trail through a dense forest, the most consistently used circuits become the easiest and most instinctual pathways for our brain to follow. Neurobiologically, our conditioned selves feel familiar, safe, and even natural to us as adults.

No matter how familiar they may be, though, our conditioned roles can keep us trapped in our dysfunctional cycles or trauma bonds with others. Thankfully, we can create real transformation by identifying the various conditioned parts we play with others. Once we recognize our habitual roles, we can start to make conscious choices to more authentically express ourselves.

The Seven Conditioned Selves

We all have unique childhood wounds and have developed unique coping strategies to manage them. That said, there are commonalities in the strategies children often use to meet their emotional needs. After spending time with my clients, in my global community, and in my personal relationships, I've identified seven conditioned selves that we often play in our adult relationships. These are Caretaker, Overachiever, Underachiever, Rescuer/Protector, Life of the Party, Yes Person, and Hero Worshiper.

Those of you who read *How to Do the Work* may remember these as our *inner child archetypes*. Inner child archetypes are simply common patterns in how we relate to our childhood relationships and environments. Over time, these archetypes become part of our brain's neural circuitry, eventually solidifying into the conditioned selves that we're neurobiologically driven to embody or inhabit daily.

As you read through the following descriptions, keep in mind that you may identify with only one conditioned self or with several at the same time. We can shift into different conditioned selves, depending on whom we're with or the period of our lives. We can consistently embody one conditioned self in our romantic relationships and a different one with family, friends, or colleagues or supervisors at work.

Our goal in this section is to witness the conditioned self or selves we embody most often in our various relationships. Doing so helps us identify the habits that don't serve us or help us sustain the relationships we want. Once we become aware of our conditioning, we can begin to make conscious choices that will create new habits that better serve us and our relationships. This process is called *integration*. Integration doesn't mean that we're no longer compelled to act in habitual ways but that we're more aware of the times we feel inclined to play these roles in our relationships. When we become conscious of our unconscious habits, we give ourselves the opportunity to begin to make choices outside our neurobiologically programmed patterns and create lasting change. The "Conditioned Selves Assessment" exercise on page 119 will help you begin this process of integration.

Here are the seven different conditioned selves defined.

Caretaker. Gains a sense of identity and self-worth through meeting others' needs in relationships. Believes that the only way to receive love is to be needed by others or to care for them physically or emotionally, often while neglecting their own personal needs or desires. May seek out relationships, experiences, or careers where care is required or may play this role at the first sign of need. The Caretaker's nervous system is often hypervigilant and in Pleaser mode, scanning the environment to assess the needs of others.

Overachiever. Attempts to be the "perfect" friend, child, partner, or spouse. Requires constant external validation and is often focused on or consumed by how they measure up to others. Regularly attempts to carry most of the responsibility in a relationship, often struggling to ask for or receive support. The Overachiever's nervous system is often stuck in Distractor mode as they seek distraction in self-assessing, self-analyzing, or self-criticizing thoughts, especially when external validation isn't present.

Underachiever. Attempts to keep safe from evaluation and judgment by hiding any and all undesirable parts from others, believing that the only way to be loved is to stay small and unnoticeable in relationships. Has low self-worth, fears criticism, and often can be emotionally distant, avoidant, or disengaged to protect against possible rejection. May occasionally act out to receive negative attention that validates deep-rooted feelings of unworthiness. The Underachiever's nervous system often shifts between Distractor mode, as they distract themselves with self-deprecating or self-shaming thoughts, and Detacher mode, slowing down their motivation and energy systems, which can result in delayed decisions or actions.

Rescuer/Protector. Regularly finds themselves in relationships that allow them to rescue, protect, or otherwise be of service to others whom they perceive as helpless, incapable, or dependent. May gain a sense of felt superiority for not needing personal help and find it difficult to ask for or receive support, even when necessary. The Rescuer/Protector's role is similar to that of the Caretaker, but whereas the latter strives to care for others' physical needs, the Rescuer/Protector is more concerned about tending to and defending those whom they perceive to be emotionally vulnerable. The Rescuer/Protector's nervous system is often hypervigilant and in Pleaser mode, unconsciously scanning for those who need their rescue or protection.

Life of the Party. Fears uncomfortable emotions or experiences and avoids conflict at all costs. Often avoids voicing issues or opinions that might cause upsetting feelings or disappointment.

Typically appears to be happy but is usually disconnected or detached from reality. The Life of the Party's nervous system is often stuck in Deatcher mode, numbing, dissociating, or distancing from most or all stressful or uncomfortable thoughts, feelings, and experiences.

Yes Person. Tends to be agreeable with no expressed preferences in relationships, and is often referred to as a people-pleaser or "pushover." Regularly engages in codependent dynamics, neglecting their own needs to drop everything for others. Prides themselves on acting "selflessly" (or being a "martyr") by showing up for others no matter what and often ends up over-giving and under-receiving support and care within their relationships. Regularly adopts the beliefs, habits, and even hobbies of their partners, friends, or family and can feel lost or helpless without others to direct them. The Yes Person's nervous system is often hypervigilant and in Pleaser mode, constantly putting others before themselves.

Hero Worshiper. Tends to look up to those they're in a relationship with or put others on a pedestal. Believes that others know what's best for them, is easily influenced, and can be dismissive of themselves, often viewing others as a model for how to live. In idealizing others, they often blame or shame themselves for thinking or feeling differently or having separate needs. The Hero Worshiper's nervous system is often hypervigilant and in Pleaser mode, giving more attention and weight to the thoughts, opinions, beliefs, and feelings of others as opposed to one's own instincts.

Not all the habits associated with our conditioned selves are dysfunctional or should be avoided. Many of the behaviors listed in recent pages, like caring for others and being motivated to achieve goals, aren't dysfunctional in themselves. They become dysfunctional when our childhood wounds drive us to continually take the same actions, even when it's not in our best interest or the best interests of our relationships to do so. Becoming more aware of our conditioned selves gives us the opportunity to consciously and intentionally choose our actions instead of allowing the remnants of past pain and other learned behaviors to direct our current actions.

Like many of you, I felt for years that I had no choice about many of my Overachieving habits, even if I wasn't aware of the idea of a conditioned self. Today, I sometimes still allow my childhood fear of rejection to direct my reactions and choices, as I continue to find it difficult to express vulnerability or personal needs with others. When my mom was dying, I struggled to ask for support from my partners. Instead, I pushed them away to cry alone in my bedroom, and when they didn't come to comfort me, I felt angry and resentful, believing that they should just "know" that I needed or wanted them to. Not only was that one of my immature, conditioned beliefs, I was not, in reality, acting like someone who wanted or needed comfort. Just as my mom had done to me so many years before, I was unfamiliar with how to connect with others when I was emotionally upset, so I continued the same pattern of disconnecting from both my discomfort and my opportunity for much needed love and support.

I'm continuing to become more consciously aware of how often and when I play the Overachiever with others. I'm growing better able to recognize when I'm putting unrealistic expectations on myself. And in those moments, I practice consciously reminding myself that no one expects me to be perfect and that trying to be inhibits me from connecting with others on a deeper, more authentic level. This conscious awareness then gives me the opportunity to begin making intentional choices that better serve my authentic needs and help me connect more deeply with others and the world around me.

The next year, before the one-year anniversary of my mom's death, I decided to take a weekend trip alone so that I could be more fully present with my emotions, regulate my nervous system, and create much needed feelings of safety, regardless of how I was feeling in each moment. This time and space allowed me to find my way back to a more regulated state in which I could feel safe enough to open myself up to connect with the love available around me. When I returned, I was able to vulnerably ask for the support I needed. And, in that moment, I was truly okay with however others were available to support me, as I no longer expected or needed another person to take away all my sadness and grief. Not only can no other person do that or even be emotionally available for me at all times, I have learned that the support I really want is for someone to be present and connected with me regardless of what I'm feeling. More simply, I, like each and every one of you, want to feel less alone in our pain and suffering.

Explore Your Conditioned Selves

Most of us shift back and forth between our conditioned selves and our authentic Self throughout the day, sometimes even on a moment-to-moment basis. While many of us aren't connected with our deeper needs or sure of who we really are, one of the ways we can reconnect with our authentic Self is to identify the conditioned selves we most often embody.

To explore your conditioned selves, spend some time witnessing or journaling about the typical patterns you see in your relationships with friends, family, colleagues, or romantic partners, using the following exploratory prompts. Remember that it's possible to see more than one conditioned self in different relationships. The goal of this exercise is to identify your conditioned selves so that, going forward, you can begin to recognize when you're tempted to play these habitual roles in your current relationships.

Your Conditioned Selves Assessment

Take a look at the following checklist and spend some time nonjudgmentally witnessing yourself in your various relationships. Check the habits that you notice most commonly, and remember you may even notice that you embody different selves in different relationships or over time.

THE CARETAKER:

_____ When I am in a relationship, I feel a strong pull to be needed or depended on.

_____ I am often hyperaware of others' physical needs or even try to predict what they'll be.

_____ I feel that I am most loved when someone is reliant on me for care in some way.

THE OVERACHIEVER:

_____ I am always focused on whether others think I'm good enough.

_____ I pride myself on being "the best" lover/friend/daughter/son, etc.

_____ I'm usually the first to engage with, reach out to, or show up for the other person, even if it's not reciprocated.

THE UNDERACHIEVER:

_____ I tend to avoid relationships or have commitment issues.

_____ I struggle to be vulnerable or feel emotionally connected to others.

_____ I avoid criticism and any situation in which I might feel rejected or abandoned.

THE RESCUER/PROTECTOR:

_____ I'm attracted to people and relationships in which the focus is solely on the other person.

_____ I feel loved or important when a person is emotionally vulnerable and needs me to be there for them.

_____ I tend to be fiercely protective of the people I'm in relationships with and take their sides or viewpoints, regardless of what they are or if I agree with them.

THE LIFE OF THE PARTY:

_____ I regularly avoid conflict in my relationships.

_____ I usually don't address my feelings or like talking about things that might make me or others feel uncomfortable.

_____ I think the best way to deal with a stressful or upsetting situation is to pretend that everything is okay.

THE YES PERSON:

_____ I tend to "go with the flow" or defer to my loved ones' needs or desires the majority of the time.

_____ When I am in a relationship, I tend to adopt the preferences of my friends or loved ones, like dressing similarly, sharing the same beliefs, pursuing the same hobbies, or changing my schedule to accommodate theirs.

_____ I agree to do things that others want me to do even if they interfere with my work, rest, or self-care.

THE HERO WORSHIPER:

_____ When I first meet someone, I tend to be enamored of them and view them as perfect.

_____ I often hide or change "shameful" parts of myself to try to be more like those I idealize.

_____ I overlook any flaws or issues in my loved ones and tend to focus solely on their positive aspects.

Empowerment Pause Exercise

As we've been learning, our experience of life is shaped by and filtered through our conditioned brain. Gaining awareness of our habitual reactions and patterns empowers us to start shaping and creating the experiences we want to have instead of feeling stuck, unfulfilled, or powerless in our circumstances. This empowerment comes from an area of our brain known as the _prefrontal cortex_, which controls our intentional responses, along with our ability to plan, focus our attention, curb our impulses, delay gratification, predict consequences, and manage our emotional reactions.

You can begin to practice activating your prefrontal cortex by taking a moment to pause before reacting to the thoughts, feelings, and impulses that come and go throughout your day. This practice can enable you to gain awareness of your reactivity and create a space in which to choose new, more intentional responses.

The following exploratory questions and exercises can help you explore your own experiences with reactivity and responsiveness. Spend time thinking about and writing down your thoughts and feelings in a separate notebook or journal if helpful.

Take a moment to call to mind a time when you found yourself instantly or explosively reacting to an experience without giving your behavior much thought and explore the following questions:

How do you physically feel during and after this moment of reactivity?

_____

_____

How do you emotionally feel about yourself and any others who may be involved in this moment of reactivity?

_____

_____

Take a moment to call to mind a time when you experienced another's instant and explosive reaction to an experience and explore the following questions:

How do you physically feel during and after experiencing another's reactivity?

_____

_____

How do you emotionally feel about yourself and the individual who was reactive?

_____

_____

Take a moment to call to mind a time when you found yourself able to remain grounded in your responses or choices and explore the following questions:

How do you physically feel during and after this moment of responsiveness?

_____

_____

How do you emotionally feel about yourself and about any others who may be involved in this moment of responsiveness?

_____

_____

Remember, there are no "right" or "wrong" answers; the work to consciously change our conditioned patterns and habits begins with this self-exploration, which can be empowering in and of itself. When we're able to gain conscious awareness of our conditioned habits, we can begin to make intentional choices within our relationships instead of constantly reacting to and re-creating our old childhood wounds. We can then curiously explore the different ways the roles we've played since childhood may not be serving our authentic Selves or our relationships. This work to integrate our conditioned selves helps restore our sense of safety and security, regardless of what's happening with others in our lives. Creating safety and security for ourselves through our daily choices creates new neural pathways in our brain. Over time and with consistent repetition, these new neural pathways can become permanent and the habits associated with them instinctual.

This doesn't mean that you won't ever repeat conditioned thoughts, feelings, or reactions again or won't feel instinctively pulled back to your familiar habits. Becoming conscious of your conditioned self or selves means that you will gain access to new choices that will better align you with who you are, who you want to be, and the people and relationship dynamics that will truly fulfill you. And as I imagine you may not be surprised to hear, it is a regulated nervous system that gives you access to these new choices. We'll begin our journey to regulate your nervous system in the next chapter where we'll continue to explore the life-changing practice of body consciousness.

5

HARNESSING THE WISDOM OF YOUR BODY

Before we dive deeper into body consciousness, let's take a few moments for a brief exercise to help you reconnect with your body exactly as it feels right now.

Starting with the top of your head, begin to notice any tension you may be holding in your muscles (jaw, neck, shoulders, lower back, legs, and so on). Breathe slowly and deeply into any areas of tightness or constriction, releasing your jaw and flattening your tongue if it is touching the roof of your mouth, lowering your shoulders and rolling them down your back if they are raised or hunched forward, and releasing any tension in any other muscles. Take another moment or two to notice any shifts or changes in your mental or emotional state after relaxing your body in this way.

Many of you may have probably discovered stress or tension you hadn't previously noticed. Some of you may have even found it difficult to feel your body at all in this moment. Though this exercise may not seem to have anything to do with solving issues in your relationships, it's actually a critical piece of the puzzle. As you'll discover throughout this chapter, true physical and emotional safety and security begins in our body, and until we can feel this safety and security within ourselves, we can't feel safe and secure with others.

When I was young, I adapted to my stressful environment by disconnecting from my physical body as a survival strategy and ignored the signals it was constantly sending me. I was unaware of when my muscles were tense or my breathing was quick and shallow—a state that continued well into adulthood, preventing me from recognizing what my body needed as well as what I was actually feeling. You see, our physical sensations play an important role in our emotional life, communicating our body's ongoing assessment of our environment to our brain. But I was too disembodied to feel anything, living most of my life in my head, cut off from my physical self.

Being in my body felt unsafe mainly because it was unfamiliar and therefore uncomfortable. When I was a child, no one modeled for me what it was like to feel safe and secure living in a physical body. Instead, I was exposed to body shaming and insecurity in my home. My mom and sister were always on a diet or adopting other food-restrictive behaviors. They were critical of their own bodies and those of others around them, and my mom often commented on any weight gain or changes in body size of anyone in the family, including herself.

As I got older, uncomfortable in my own skin and growing more intolerant of feeling the sensations in my stressed body, I closed myself off from the physical aspects of my existence. Even though I desperately wanted to feel emotionally connected with others, I wasn't connected to my physical self to access my emotions in a way that would allow me to bond with another person. The reality was, I had difficulty feeling *anything* at all.

It took me years to develop a state of body consciousness, or to become aware of my body's physical sensations so that I could start to regulate my nervous system consciously and intentionally. Because most of us didn't grow up in safe homes or have safe and secure relationships with others, we continue to live with nervous system dysregulation that keeps us disconnected from both our inner and outer worlds.

WHAT IS BODY CONSCIOUSNESS?

We are all aware that we have a physical body. We use it for almost everything we do and generally know how it feels when we walk, sit, sleep, work out, have sex, hold hands, eat food, drink wine, run in the rain, dance in the snow, or nap in the sun. Many of us are conscious of our body's basic needs on a fundamental level: we're usually aware when we're hungry, thirsty, tired, sick, or injured. Some of us may even be focused on our body's well-being and try to eat healthfully, exercise, get enough sleep, or adopt other habits that we think can improve how our body looks or feels.

Even those of us who are health minded, though, are rarely body conscious or aware of how safe or unsafe we feel in our physical self. The term *body consciousness*, as I use it in this book, does not mean a state of self-consciousness about or hyperawareness of how our body looks, whether to ourselves or to others. Instead, it describes our ability to sense what's happening *within* our body.

We develop body consciousness when we enhance our ability to witness our physical sensations, then use this sensory input to help regulate our nervous system and our behavioral responses. Learning to identify when our nervous system is stressed creates the opportunity for us to shift ourselves out of a reactive, avoidant, or dissociated state into a more open and receptive one. As we become more attuned to our physical sensations, we can begin to discern not only obvious signs of physical stress, like the rate of our heartbeat or breathing, but more subtle signals, like if our energy is light, heavy, calm, or agitated; if our shoulders are hunched or straight; if we are speaking softly or loudly, quickly or slowly; and if we can maintain eye contact or smile easily.

These sensations may seem unremarkable, but they reflect the state of our nervous system while also communicating information to our brain that helps determine our emotions. When we're able to consciously perceive these sensory shifts, we can begin to understand the emotional messages they send our brain. With this awareness, we can give ourselves the space to calm down when we know we're activated and the opportunity to create safety by using the intentional mind-body techniques we'll talk about later in this chapter.

Maintaining a consistent state of body consciousness isn't easy. The stress and trauma stored in our body affects our ability to pay attention to our current experiences. Most of the time, our mind is reacting to the stress and tension stored in our body, causing our mind to wander and us to struggle to focus on the present moment and be fully aware of what's happening in and around us. Because of these stress-induced thought spirals, few of us are truly present in our body during our daily life; instead, we're in our mind, racing through thoughts about the past or trying to predict the future. While it can be helpful to reflect on the past or imagine the future at times, we need to be immersed in the present moment and connected with our body in order to be truly *in our own presence*. And if we're constantly focusing on what someone else is thinking or feeling about or around us, we may never know how we really feel being *in their presence*.

In addition to the impact of this stored stress in our bodies, some of us have learned body-shaming habits from the cultural and societal messages we have been exposed to. The lack of diversity in skin color, ethnicity, body size, and physical ability in television, media, and movies has deeply impacted our body-based beliefs, sending the subconscious message that there is an ideal version of who is acceptable, attractive, or desirable. If our body's skin tone, shape, or functioning is different, we may struggle to feel safe and accepted because of our natural physical appearance and our stress response may remain chronically activated.

Physical touch is universally important to all human beings, helping to comfort and soothe our emotional experiences. However, it is our individual experiences with touch (or the lack thereof) that can cause us to have conflicting feelings about physical contact that can lead to confusion, anxiety, and ultimately unmet needs. In order to feel comfortable being physically close with another, we first have to feel comfortable with our own body. To do so, we need to learn how to trust in our ability to stay connected with our own body and safe within our own boundaries as we move physically closer to one another. Knowing that we can stop or slow down whenever we want allows us to expand our ability to be physically soothed, comforted, and even stimulated by another.

If we have a dysregulated nervous system, as most of us do, spending any amount of time noticing our body won't immediately feel safe to us. Feeling unsafe is why so many of us disconnect from our body in the first place, living inside our head instead. And many of us may notice that we continue to avoid those sensations that are connected to emotional memories that are too deeply uncomfortable to endure.

YOUR EMOTIONS BEGIN IN YOUR BODY

Emotions are part of our shared humanity. They color and give meaning to our life, guide us, and make us feel alive. From an evolutionary perspective, emotions help us interpret our environment so that we can identify threats and stay safe. The more quickly we're able to register fear or signal the presence of a threat to others, the safer we'll remain as individuals and groups.

Though the words *emotions* and *feelings* are often used interchangeably, they describe two different phenomena. Emotions are our subconscious reactions to our physical sensations, and feelings are our conscious experience of our body's sensations.

Most people assume that our thoughts create our emotions and our emotions define who we are at any given moment: I think this emotion, and this emotion makes me *me*. If I tend to think sad or depressing thoughts, I might assume that this makes me a sad or depressed person. Or if I think angry, anxious, or worrying thoughts, it makes me an angry, anxious, or worried person.

Many of us also assume that what's happening around us or in our immediate external environment causes our emotions: *This situation now is causing me to feel X, Y, or Z*. We often think that someone else made us feel a certain way: *What you're doing now is making me to feel this way*. It's empowering to realize that these assumptions aren't true. Emotions aren't facts or even accurate representations of what's happening to us. In fact, most of the time, our emotions aren't even reactions to what's going on in the present moment.[19]

If you're wondering *How can it be that my emotions aren't a product of the present moment?*, you're not alone. For decades, psychologists believed that our emotions were immediate responses to what we saw, heard, or experienced. In recent years, neuroscientists have overturned that idea, thanks in part to research by Dr. Lisa Feldman Barrett, a psychology professor at Northeastern University who introduced what's known as the *theory of constructed emotion*. According to this ground-breaking theory, emotions begin in the body as physical sensations, which our subconscious then uses to predict how we should feel based on how we've felt in the past when we've experienced the same sensory state of being.

If our heart is racing, our breath is quick, and our blood is pulsing through our veins, our brain may interpret these sensations as fear or excitement, depending on what we've experienced in the past when we felt similarly. So, for instance, if we're preparing for a big speech and have had unpleasant experiences with public speaking, our subconscious may interpret our sensory state as fear. But if our past experiences with public speaking have been positive, our subconscious may interpret the same sensations as excitement. Our emotions are really just mental concepts created by our body and driven by our past. Or, as Dr. Barrett put it, our emotions are "constructions of the world, not reactions to it."[20]

The fact that our emotions are body-brain constructs, not hardwired reactions to our reality or relationships, means that we don't have to be prisoners to what we feel. The theory of constructed emotion gives us the opportunity to perceive our emotions as self-creations, not reality, and empowers us to change how we feel by shifting certain physical sensations.

In psychology, our ability to sense our inner sensations is known as *interoception*. Interoception, sometimes called inner sensing, constantly occurs on an unconscious level as our subconscious scans our body's sensory input to interpret the safety or threat of our environment. We can intentionally enhance our ability to practice interoception by practicing body consciousness to help identify our emotional state by consciously witnessing our body's sensations.

Accessing this active state of body awareness allows us to intentionally change how we feel in the moment by actively shifting our body's sensations, soothing ourselves if we're stressed. Body consciousness is a life-changing practice we can use to help make conscious choices about how we want to feel and show up in our relationships.

MY JOURNEY TO BODY CONSCIOUSNESS

It took me years before I felt safe enough to spend consistent time in my physical body to begin to identify its needs and the emotions stored there. I preferred to live in the safety of the spaceship in my mind, obsessing over my thoughts without ever dropping into my physical experience. I was unaware of and unable to listen to the messages my body was sending me every day, which prevented me from being able to identify or meet my physical needs. As a result, I was often reactive and incapable of regulating my emotions, on many occasions finding myself trapped in cycles of inexplicable and inescapable agitation and discomfort.

For most of us, the process of disconnection begins in early childhood. For me, I believe it started in utero, when I was immersed in the stressed physiology of my mom's dysregulated nervous system. If your mom didn't feel safe inside her body, you probably didn't feel safe inside her body when you were developing, either.

My mom discovered she was pregnant with me at age forty-two, fifteen years after giving birth to my sister. She was at a different stage of her life, not trying or expecting to have another child, and given her chronic anxiety about her health, when she began to experience morning sickness, she assumed that she had stomach cancer. When her doctor told her that she was pregnant, I imagine she was fearful of the diagnosis and could understand if she was feeling overwhelmed by the thought of having a third child whom she'd worry about.

While I was developing inside my mom, I absorbed her stress and apprehension—a normal state for her that was only amplified by her advanced maternal age. Because she was anxious and disconnected from herself, she remained unable to regulate her own emotions or her body's cortisol levels, and as a result, when I was inside her, I couldn't, either. My body was so stressed in utero that I was born with a sucking mark on my thumb. Looking back now, I have compassion for myself, who was, I believe, desperately trying to self-soothe before being born. Unable to calm my overwhelmed nervous system, I likely entered the world already dysregulated and feeling unsafe in my body. Research corroborates my experience, showing that elevated levels of the stress hormone cortisol in a pregnant woman can cause larger amygdala volume in a developing child, leading to a dysregulated stress response and anxious behaviors.[21]

Growing up, I continued to absorb the unspoken messages from my family that there was little or no space for me to express my separate or different needs, and so I gradually stopped doing so. Like many who grew up with parents from an older generation, there was a Depression-era mentality in my home that as long as there was food on the table and a roof over my head, there was nothing else, including emotional support, that I could possibly need.

As part of an Italian American family, I was modeled highly ritualized eating habits in which my mom used food as a gesture of her love and care. Every night we ate together as a family at "dinnertime," which in my family happened to be at 5:30 p.m., right after my dad came home from work. My attendance at those nightly mealtimes was a felt obligation or unspoken expectation, regardless of whatever else I had going on. That was especially true on Sundays, when my brother's family and my two uncles usually came over for a big pot of Italian pasta and sauce (or gravy, as I grew up calling it). Because my mom was deeply insecure in her connections to us all, she used food as a primary way to show her love. She regularly looked to us for validation during those meals, hoping we'd proclaim that her food was delicious or clean our plates as an indication of our approval and reciprocated love. Seeking to please, I would often finish my whole plate and take seconds when my mom urged me to do so, usually after advising me to "eat more now" so I "don't end up being hungry later."

Food was one of the main means of consistent connection within my family. During our shared meals I consistently learned that it was important to tend to the expectations and feelings of others, even when my body told me otherwise. I would eat when or what was convenient for those around me even if I wasn't hungry or disliked the taste to avoid offending anyone. I'd take an extra helping when my mom suggested I do to avoid disappointing or denying her request. I continued those habits as an adult by scheduling my mealtimes and making food choices based on the schedules, needs, or suggestions of those around me.

As a child, I learned to overlook other physical needs, too, like having a consistent sleep schedule and regular physical activity, because neither was prioritized or modeled in my home. I didn't have a set bedtime and would regularly stay up late watching TV with my family, who also stayed up late. Outside of playing sports (which was motivated by my desire to be seen by my family as successful), I wasn't encouraged to exercise, and although my dad was active, my mom frequently remained on the couch or in bed in pain.

Other than regular commentary on or criticism of the size and health of their bodies, no one in my family directly spoke about or showed their physical body. I never saw anyone in my household naked, so I assumed it was to be avoided—one reason why I never really felt comfortable showing much skin. My mom and I never discussed anything about puberty or a woman's menstrual cycle, so I didn't tell her when I got my period. By that age, I already felt so ashamed about most aspects of my developing body that I couldn't imagine sharing those kinds of vulnerable experiences with anyone anyway. That deep-rooted shame resulted in a critical, noncompassionate relationship with my body, and I regularly overlooked my basic needs, often rushing through my self-care or treating my body roughly when I did tend to it at all.

My disconnection from my body created my disconnection from my emotions. I didn't sleep enough or move in healthy ways and ate foods that inflamed and stressed my body. These habits only made it more difficult for me to regulate my overwhelming emotions, which continued to color my perceptions of the world.

Over time, I adopted a cool, apathetic exterior—my family began to call me "Nothing Bothers Me Nicole"—to hide the painful reality of my inner world, which was full of deep-rooted feelings of abandonment, loneliness, and shame. Without the safety and security to be myself, I used my outward attitude to protect against increasing feelings of unworthiness; if I never showed my vulnerabilities, I would never be at risk of having them or myself feel rejected.

To keep myself protected, I became hyperfocused and perfectionistic about my appearance, obsessively looking at and trying to hide the various scars I had been accumulating on my body over time. I ritualistically spot cleaned dirt and other stains off my clothes and shoes in the hope of removing any evidence of wear-and-tear or other imperfections. That obsessive behavior carried over to my physical environment, where I fanatically arranged items in my childhood bedroom in attempts to soothe the increasing feelings of stress and tension I was storing in my body. All of those behaviors seemed to my family just to be part of who I was or my "quirky personality," as they put it, when, in reality, they were coping strategies to try to regulate my nervous system and manage my overwhelming emotions.

Eventually, I became aware of how disconnected I was from my body and the stress I carried in my physical self. Though I didn't realize it for a few decades, my body was locked in a stressed state, with my muscles tightening and constricting more with time, especially in my back, neck, and jaw. With increasing physical tension, my body never felt like a truly safe place for me to rest or relax. As I shared in my first book, *How to Do the Work*, I fainted twice over the course of several months, once at the home of a childhood friend and again after spending a significant amount of time with my family over the holidays.

My body was overwhelmed by nervous system dysregulation, overwhelming emotions, and childhood trauma, and it was starting to shut down. Though I thought I was taking care of my health when I decided to become a vegan in my midtwenties after I learned about industrial animal farming, I still wasn't listening to my body and its host of unmet physical needs. Like most of us, I operated on autopilot, eating whatever was around me or whatever and whenever others ate, barely exercising, while not prioritizing my sleep or ever really allowing my body to truly rest—all habits I had learned in childhood.

Getting things done without paying active attention can, of course, help us deal with many of the complex experiences we have to navigate daily, like acquiring what we'll eat, coordinating our daily commute, and remaining aware of the changing social etiquette. But the habitual tendency to mindlessly engage with daily life can also lead us to eat without tasting our food, overexert our muscles when they need rest, and interact with others without actually connecting with them.

Because my body was overwhelmed by decades of unmet physical needs and accumulated emotions, I didn't feel comfortable spending much time in it to feel or understand to my physical sensations. I had no idea how fast my heart beat, how deeply or calmly I could take in the air around me, whether my energy was constricted or light, or how my muscles felt. Those sensations created my emotional land-scape every minute of every day, but I wasn't paying attention to them. And I didn't know why I should or how I could.

During my dark night of the soul, I learned a lot about our physi-cal body, which was when I discovered that our emotions live inside us—in the physical cells of our muscles, fascia, and organs. Your issues are literally in your tissues, or so the saying goes. Our emotions get activated when our body has a biological response (hormonal, neu-ral, and cellular) to trauma. Shocked and inspired, I began spending more time consciously aware of my body every day, using my Fu-ture Self Journal (FSJ) to help me keep that daily intention. (You can download your own free copy with a how-to guide on my website, www.theholisticpsychologist.com.)

At first, it was difficult to feel what was happening inside my body since I'd been disconnected from it for so long. Most of my sensations felt uncomfortable. My heart rate was often erratic, my breathing was shallow and constricted, and my jaw always seemed to be clenched.

At the same time, I knew those sensations were telling me something, that I was existing in a state of fear and stress. My nervous system dysregulation was causing me to shut down, which explained my fainting episodes (a progression of the freeze response) and why I couldn't remember so many moments in my past that others could easily recall. I was basically living in a state of numbed overwhelm.

Learning about the evolutionary function of our emotions and our nervous system responses helped me understand why I never felt able to truly relax or find peace in my body. It explained why a "perfect" appearance or environment calmed me only temporarily. It explained why the alcohol and other substances I had relied on from such an early age had never really taken away the deep-rooted pain inside.

Though that realization was alarming, it was also incredibly empowering, setting me on a path to create body consciousness. Using my FSJ, I recorded my daily intention to check in with my body every day, several times throughout the day. Then, every few hours, I would set an alarm on my phone to remind me to do a body consciousness check-in (see page 57).

That practice helped me recognize how often I looked to others to meet my physical needs and how I still relied on my mom for health advice, even when I knew how to take care of myself. It helped me more clearly see how sharing my health-related stress or worry was my attempt to connect with my mom and others emotionally. I saw how regularly I continued to prioritize my "obligations" or "achievements," diving right into my to-do list instead of taking a moment in the morning to connect with and care for my body. I noticed how consistently I felt as though I had to "earn" moments of rest or relaxation by first completing a task, like sending a work email, always pushing myself to be "done" with my never-ending list of projects.

I was starting to see all of the ways I was carrying the dysregulation that had lived inside me since I was a child wherever I went as an adult. It was like the famously titled Jon Kabat-Zinn book *Wherever You Go, There You Are*.

I also saw that the more I turned inward and spent time with my body rather than cycling through the loop of my conscious thoughts, the more capable I became at sensing my physical sensations and recognizing when my nervous system was activated. And during the times when I knew something deeper was happening inside me, I started to become curious about what was prompting my reactions.

Over time, I became better able to discern when I was actually hungry or needed to move or rest my body, which helped me feel more grounded and less irritable in general. I started to stretch the tense muscles in my body that had been frozen or constricted from years of stress-related tension and began to eat more nourishing foods. I maintained a regular sleep schedule for the first time in my life, going to bed and waking up earlier to sync my natural circadian rhythm with the sun. I started moving my body and stretching my muscles almost daily while taking rest when my body needed it.

Becoming more connected to my body, I started creating safety for myself whenever I felt my nervous system becoming activated. When this occurred and I sensed I was shutting down or going into a freeze response, I practiced the Wim Hof Method, a breathing method that helps activate our sympathetic nervous system and pull us out of a shut-down parasympathetic state. When I noticed that I was over-stimulated or going into fight-or-flight mode, I took some slow, deep belly breaths to help calm myself down. We'll explore these different breathing techniques on page 140.

Today, I still use intentional breathing and other mind-body practices to regulate my nervous system and help me navigate my emotions. Since I'm often activated within relationships, like most of us are, I try to practice body consciousness when I'm around others or before I react impulsively to help me make sense of and manage my emotions. If I don't hear from my partner as quickly as I'd like and begin to worry about the security of our connection, I can drop into my body to practice the body consciousness pause. If I feel that my heart rate is elevated, my face is flushed, and my energy is agitated, I know that my nervous system is in a stress response. Although these feelings are real, I can now acknowledge the possibility that I'm reacting to old wounds rather than new slights. With this understanding, I may be able to reinterpret my situation. It's likely that my partner still loves me and just needs space or is going through something stressful and needs time alone. In such moments, I can calm my body so that I don't send a snarky text or do something else I might regret. I can go for a walk, practice deep belly breathing, or stand outside with my feet firmly planted in the grass, all of which can help bring my body back to safety. When my heart rate slows and my energy lightens, I can reassess the situation more calmly and objectively.

To tell the truth, I still struggle to consistently maintain body consciousness. Instead of living with and feeling my physical sensations, I sometimes ignore my body, running away from it by looping through my distracting thoughts, keeping myself busy with my endless to-do list, or numbing myself by watching mindless TV for hours on end. In such moments, I extend myself grace and compassion, understanding that these actions were my best (and only) way to regulate my big and overwhelming emotions as a child. I sometimes do still allow myself to check out for a few hours with my favorite TV programs, knowing that those moments can give my nervous system the rest it needs to rebalance and replenish itself especially when I'm feeling particularly stressed or overwhelmed.

Thankfully, I've paid attention to my body long enough to know that whenever I'm connected and listening to my body, I'm better able to meet my needs and calm my nervous system, no matter what's happening around me or within my relationships. When I'm calm, grounded, and connected within myself, I'm better able to feel calm, grounded, and connected when I'm with others. And it's only in those moments that I feel safe enough to be *me*, that will give me the opportunity to truly connect to *you*.

PRACTICING BODY CONSCIOUSNESS

The first step in our journey to connect authentically with another person is learning how to be present in our own body by practicing body consciousness. When we consistently begin to pay more attention to *being* in our body, we can begin to make intentional choices to help regulate its different emotional states. This is how we cultivate emotional resilience, giving us the opportunity to have a feeling without reacting or behaving in ways that don't serve ourselves or our relationships. When we are emotionally resilient, we are able to deal with stress and other upsetting emotions and are flexible in our responses to our changing circumstances rather than staying stuck in our habitual or conditioned reactions.

Since many of us have been disconnected from our body for so long, spending time with our full range of physical sensations can be both difficult and uncomfortable at first. We may not be able to tell if our heart is beating quickly or slowly or if our energy is open and light or constricted and heavy. Practicing the daily body consciousness pauses you learned about in chapter 2 will help you reconnect with your body's sensations.

Using Body Consciousness to Witness Your Emotions

As we explored in chapter 3, we can all learn to identify when we're in a stress response, as well as which particular response we're experiencing. If we're able to notice and identify when we're in a freeze or shutdown response, feeling detached from what's happening around us, we can move or shake vigorously to reawaken our body to help us reconnect to the present moment. And if we notice we're overstimulated in a fight-or-flight response, we can move and breathe more slowly to calm ourselves down. Once our body returns to safety, we can then open ourselves back up to connecting with others.

We can even learn to witness how different emotional states feel in our body so that we can use our actual physical sensations to shift our emotional experiences. Remember, we all experience emotions a little differently, so the physical sensations that signal fear in one person may indicate excitement in another. At the same time, all humans experience the six core emotions—anger, sadness, fear, joy/happiness, disgust, and surprise—in similar ways. The chart below can help you identify your emotions based on your physical sensations, along with the messages that these sensations may be sending you.

EMOTION	SENSATIONS	MESSAGE
Anger	Muscle tension Flushed face Clenched jaw/throbbing temples Clenched fists Elevated or loud tone of voice or speech	Boundary violation or unmet need
Sadness	Heaviness or low energy Drooped shoulders Difficulty smiling Lump in the throat Ache in the chest or stomach Flat or whiny tone or speech	Loss
Fear	Increased heart rate Shakiness "Butterflies" or a "pit" feeling in the stomach Quickened/shortened breath Sweating (hands, armpits) Quickened speech and dry mouth	Threat to safety
Joy/Happiness	Light and expansive energy Warmth throughout the body Smiling or laughing Upbeat tone/speech	Interest, pleasure, or well-being
Disgust	Clenched or sickened stomach (possible gagging) Wrinkled nose or covered nose Averted eyes/body language	Aversion to something offensive (physically, emotionally, or morally)
Surprise	Increased heart rate and overall energy Hyper-alert attention/visual scanning Widened eye and jaw (mouth opened slightly as in a gasp)	Unexpected event or violation of expectation

This practice helps us develop emotional awareness so that we can learn how to witness an emotion when it's present. Using body consciousness to identify our physical sensations gives us an opportunity to consciously try to change those sensations so that we can change our emotional experience of the world around us.

As you become conscious of different physical sensations, many of which may have been present for some time, it is helpful to also begin to witness the way you think and talk about your emotional experiences. If you notice the urge to overidentify with certain emotions or your emotional state in general by thinking or saying things like "I'm scared, stressed, or angry," practice saying "*A part of me* feels scared, stressed, or angry." Over time, this practice can help you hold space for the many different emotions we can and often do experience at once, which more accurately reflects the multidimensionality of our shared human emotional experience.

Create Safety by Regulating Your Nervous System

Even if we've been living in a stressed state for years, as many of us have, our nervous system is still capable of regulating at any time. When we create safety for ourselves regardless of what's happening around us, we increase our tolerance for uncomfortable emotions, perceive our environment and other people more accurately, and respond calmly, kindly, and in ways that better allow us to connect us with the people we love.

The following pages contain, in my opinion, the most effective practices to create the internal safety needed to help regulate our nervous system. Some of them, like intentional breathing and grounding in nature, are best used in the moment to create immediate safety. Others, like nutrition, sleep, energy work, and boundary setting are lifestyle shifts that can help us more consistently meet our physical needs over time. Though some of you may find that eating a nourishing meal just one day, getting one good night's sleep, or doing a single session of energy work helps you feel calmer, most of us have ignored our physical needs for so long that we'll need to adopt these habits consistently over time before we notice the impact.

It's helpful to notice where your attention is as you practice the different exercises below. If your attention is lost in worrying or upsetting thoughts, including replaying whatever experience may have activated your nervous system, your body will remain stressed and will not be able to fully calm down. Continue to be patient with yourself and your body as you commit to the following practices; you didn't become dysregulated overnight, and it'll likely take longer than a single day of practice to regulate your nervous system. You also don't have to commit to all the practices listed here at the same time. Pick one that stands out to you, and begin there. Using your FSJ, you can set a daily intention to practice this one technique for a few days, weeks, or months.

Intentional Breathing Practices

One of the most effective ways to regulate our nervous system is with our breath. Some breathing techniques, like the Wim Hof Method, are better suited to thaw or energize a freeze or shutdown response, while others work best for calming a fight-or-flight state. Because we're all unique, I suggest trying different techniques to see what is most helpful to you.

Deep belly breathing. This type of breathing can calm a fight-or-flight response by relaxing our nervous system when our sympathetic branch is in control. Try to practice deep belly breathing anytime you feel stressed and/or incorporate it into your regular routine by practicing it every morning just after you wake up or every night before bed.

1. Find a comfortable position or safe space where you can relax for several minutes. If you can sit or lie down, that's ideal, but you can also practice this exercise standing up.
2. Place one hand over your chest and the other right below your rib cage.
3. Take a deep breath through your nose and feel your stomach rising with the inhaled air.

4. Exhale slowly through pursed lips, feeling the air leave your body and your stomach sink.
5. Repeat for one or two minutes.
6. Reassess your physical sensations and notice whether your heart rate drops, your muscles relax, and you feel your energy calm.

Wim Hof Method. This type of breathing can energize our nervous system when we're stuck in a freeze or shutdown response and our parasympathetic nervous system is dominant. It's helpful to practice Wim Hof breathing anytime you feel frozen, dissociated, or numb, and also begin to incorporate it into your regular routine if you often find yourself in this state.

1. Find a comfortable position or safe space where you can remain for several minutes.
2. Take thirty quick, deep breaths, inhaling through your nose and exhaling through your mouth.
3. Then take one deep breath and exhale, holding the exhale until you need to breathe in.
4. Inhale again, as deeply as possible, and hold for ten seconds.
5. Repeat until you feel your body begin to energize or your awareness return to the present moment.

Grounding Yourself in Nature

Having direct physical contact with nature, known as earthing or grounding, has been shown to stabilize our body at the deepest levels, balancing and improving nearly every aspect of our physical function.[22] Grounding allows us to coregulate with Mother Earth, or simply use her natural energy to bring our own body back to safety. This isn't woo-woo thinking but science, as the earth's natural electrical charge has been shown to activate our parasympathetic system, improve heart rate variability, or HRV (we'll talk more about HRV in chapter 8), reduce inflammation, improve sleep, increase energy, ease pain, lower stress, boost overall well-being, and normalize the body's biological rhythms, including our HRV.[23] Even moving ours eyes back and forth like we're viewing or gazing at the earth's horizon line can help activate our parasympathetic nervous system, sending calming signals to our body and mind. Whenever possible, it's beneficial to spend at least thirty minutes outside each day, physically connected to the natural world.

Here are a few ideas to help you co-regulate with Mother Earth.

- Stand barefoot or sit on a patch of grass.
- Swim in an ocean, river, or lake.
- Take a barefoot walk on the beach.
- Hug or sit up against a tree.
- Garden or work in the soil.
- Build a snowman or make snow angels.

NUTRITION

If you're consuming a diet that inflames your nervous system, as many of us do, you'll have a difficult time feeling safe and regulating your emotions. The health of our microbiome, the multitude of microorganisms that inhabit our intestinal tract, directly affects the health of our central nervous system, thanks to a pathway known as the gut-brain axis. Most of us have more unhealthy gut flora than we should, which can cause a condition known as dysbiosis, increasing our risk of disease and nervous system dysregulation.

When the bad bacteria in our gut outnumber the good bacteria, we can suffer from leaky gut syndrome. This condition occurs when the cells lining our intestines weaken, allowing toxins and food particles to enter our bloodstream, causing inflammation and nervous system dysregulation. Many factors can cause leaky gut, including too much stress, gluten, processed sugar, or alcohol; a nutritionally imbalanced diet; and the overuse of some prescription and over-the-counter drugs.[24]

Prioritizing nutrient-dense, organic, whole foods that nourish the body rather than inflame it can help heal dysbiosis, leaky gut, and nervous system dysregulation. When I started eating more whole foods and less processed ones, I noticed that I felt calmer and more regulated after a few months. Since changing our nutritional lifestyle habits is not a quick fix, it's important to make dietary shifts that you can sustain not just for days or weeks but for a longer period of time. Instead of adopting a an all-or-nothing mentality of what you can and cannot eat, think about prioritizing certain foods and minimizing your intake of others.

FOODS TO PRIORITIZE FOR NERVOUS SYSTEM REGULATION

- **Whole foods.** When you consume unprocessed or minimally processed whole foods, you minimize your intake of many items that inflame your nervous system. That said, these foods can often be expensive or less accessible than processed foods are. Affordable whole foods can sometimes be found through community gardens, food-sharing programs, co-ops, or food pantries.
- **Foods high in B vitamins.** B vitamins, especially B_{12} and folate, play a critical role in supporting our nervous system and preventing mood disorders such as anxiety and depression.[25] Most of us don't consume enough B's, especially B_{12}, which is found only in animal products like meat, dairy, and eggs. I noticed a significant shift in my mood after I started eating more organic and grass-fed animal products after years of avoiding those foods. You can try supplementing with something called methylated B_{12} and folate. Methylated B's can be absorbed by people who have genetic variants of the MTHFR gene, a common condition that prevents some people from properly digesting B_{12} and/or folate. Just be sure to speak with your medical practitioner before taking any new dietary supplement.
- **Foods high in marine omega-3 fats.** Eicosatetraenoic acid (EPA) and docosahexaenoic acid (DHA) are two marine omega-3s found primarily in fatty seafood that are necessary for a host of physiological functions, including nervous system health, cognitive health, and the prevention of many mood disorders. Though omega-3

fats are found in plants like flaxseeds, walnuts, and chia seeds, the marine omega-3s (EPA and DHA) are by far the most beneficial for nervous system health and regulation. You can find these fats in salmon, sardines, mackerel, cod liver oil, trout, mussels, oysters, and tuna.

- **Foods high in vitamin D.** Vitamin D is critical to regulating our nervous system, boosting our mood, and helping set our circadian clock so that we have more energy during the day and can sleep better at night. Most of us don't get enough vitamin D, even if we spend plenty of time in the sun, which helps our body manufacture the nutrient. But our skin can't make enough D if we live at latitudes above the 37th parallel, which includes most of the contiguous United States, even in summer.[26] This is why we need to consume foods high in D, including fatty fish, egg yolks, cheese, mushrooms, and low-sugar foods fortified with D. You can also take a vitamin D supplement; ask your medical practitioner for dosage recommendations.

- **Antioxidant-rich plants.** Fruits, vegetables, legumes, nuts, and other plant-based foods high in antioxidants provide us energy and protect our nervous system, according to research.[27]

FOODS TO MINIMIZE

Note: Limiting or restricting food of any kind may not be appropriate for anyone with current or past disordered eating issues. If this is you, you may want to skip this section.

- **Sugar.** Sugar is one of the most inflammatory substances we can consume, if not *the* most inflammatory ingredient in our food supply today. Having too much glucose in the body stresses our cells, dysregulates our nervous system, and disrupts our microbiome. Over time, the more you limit your intake of sugar, the less you'll crave it. Added sugars are common in processed and convenience foods, so consuming mostly whole foods in their simplest form will help you minimize your sugar intake without having to read labels closely.

- **Gluten.** Though clinical studies have not conclusively linked gluten to inflammation for those who don't have celiac disease (an immune reaction to gluten that affects only 1 percent of the population), a diet high in the protein, which is found in wheat and other grains, can cause unhealthy microbes to flourish in the gut and can even contribute to intestinal permeability, harming the health of our gut-brain axis.[28]

- **Processed foods.** Processed foods cause inflammation and prioritizing whole foods over processed items, whenever accessible, is the simplest way to eat to help your nervous system regulate, increasing you stress resilience.

- **Alcohol.** Even if you don't consume alcohol in excess, a steady drip of booze into your bloodstream, whether it's via a glass of wine every night or a big evening out once or twice a week, can depress your nervous system, impairing your ability to think about the long-term consequences of your actions and loosening your inhibitions. Because of its effect on the functioning of our prefrontal cortex, alcohol use can lead to emotional instability and volatility, negatively impacting our relationships.

In addition to prioritizing the foods you eat, changing *how* or *where* you eat can also benefit your nervous system. Far too many of us eat on the go or while rushing through work, watching or reading stressful or upsetting news, talking to a partner or child, or cruising social media. In these moments, our choices may be activating our body's stress response, taking us out of the "rest and digest" state we need for proper nourishment. By changing how we eat and creating as calm an environment as possible, we can increase the likelihood that our body will absorb the nutrients it needs.

SLEEP WELLNESS

We need at least seven hours of nightly sleep on a consistent basis to be able to maintain a healthy parasympathetic state and connect with others. Prioritizing our sleep can significantly benefit our relationships, especially if we're chronically sleep deprived, which many of us are. If we don't have enough energetic resources, we're more likely to be agitated, irritated, impatient, and easily reactive around others. And yet, most of us don't prioritize sleep, instead putting our work, social outings, digital habits, and favorite TV shows before our bedtime. For those who experienced abuse or other trauma especially during nighttime, sleep itself may feel unsafe, resulting in difficulty falling asleep or staying asleep due to nightmares. As I did, its helpful to establish a regular nightly routine to help calm your body and activate your parasympathetic "rest and digest" system before bed. Here are some helpful tips to create a soothing bedtime ritual:

- Go outside first thing in the morning, even if it's cloudy, to expose yourself to natural light. Natural light in the morning can help regulate our circadian clock, our body's twenty-four-hour internal cycle, to help us fall asleep at night and wake up more rested in the morning.
- Avoid activating social media and stressful or upsetting news at least an hour before bed, as both can excite and stress our brain. You could even try leaving your phone in another room to avoid being stimulated before you sleep (and looking at it if you wake up during the night).
- Practice deep belly breathing for several minutes while lying or sitting in bed.
- Practice gentle yoga before getting into bed. Yin yoga, which is slower paced than regular yoga, can be especially helpful.
- Turn off your phone and all other Wifi or bluetooth devices. Most of our new technology gives off electric and magnetic fields, or EMFs, emitting a low level of radiation. Over time, consistent exposure to this invisible energy can begin to impact the functioning of nervous system and our nightly sleep.

- Meditate for several minutes before bed or in bed especially if you find yourself worrying about what happened today or what will happen tomorrow.

As you see, many of the things that will benefit our sleep are actions we can take throughout our day to set our body up for rest at night.

PHYSICAL MOVEMENT

Physical activity allows us to harness our energy and move it through our body, reducing our feelings of anxiety, stress, and even depression while regulating our nervous system. Regular movement can help release painful emotions and stored trauma, rebuild muscles, and rewire neural circuits in new ways.

Gentle exercise like yin yoga, stretching, and walking can help calm our nervous system when we're in fight-or-flight mode. Vigorous exercise, on the other hand, can stimulate our sympathetic nervous system when we're in a freeze or shutdown state. As anyone who's experienced a good, sweaty workout may already know, physical activity releases endorphins, chemicals that help our nervous system cope with pain and stress.

The way you move your body doesn't have to resemble any type of traditional "exercise." Even the gentlest forms of movement and stretching provide benefits. And doing something you enjoy, whether it's dancing in your living room, playing a fitness-based video game, or running around the yard with your dog or children, will make you more likely to move.

Personally, I like to stretch for fifteen to thirty minutes daily, sometimes by taking a YouTube yoga class (*Yoga with Adriene* and Travis Eliot's yin practices are my go-tos). I try to get in a long walk and a more vigorous workout every few days and make a point to carve out small moments for more playful activity like dancing to a favorite song or hitting a tennis ball against my garage door.

You can even start to use exercise in an intentional way to calm your nervous system, specifically choosing your movement based on the stress response you're experiencing.

- **For fight, flight, or fawn**, you want to activate your parasympathetic nervous system. The best way to do so is with gentle movement like stretching, walking, yin yoga, tai chi, or qigong. You don't need to practice for hours; start with ten minutes of any movement that you can do at home, at work, or anywhere else you feel safe. Find a private, quiet room or go outside if you can't find a safe space indoors. If you're new to yin yoga, tai chi, or qigong, you can practice with videos provided by amazing teachers who share their gifts on YouTube for free. Learning a few moves of the one you like best will enable you to practice in the future without having to look at a screen.

- **For freeze** or whenever you feel dissociated or shut down, you want to activate your sympathetic nervous system. The best way to do so is with vigorous or intense movements like sprinting, jumping rope, walking briskly uphill, lifting heavy weights, cycling at high RPMs, or playing tennis or basketball for ten minutes. You can try vigorously shaking your body for five minutes by waving your arms, swinging your legs, and rotating your core at the same time. If vigorous movement isn't an option or you're looking for more ideas, try cold therapy, submerging your hands or washing your face in ice-cold water for one to two minutes.

ENERGY WORK AND OTHER TECHNIQUES

All the cells in our body produce energy. When we're stuck in a stress response, our cellular energy can become frenetic, frazzled, or deficient. Energy practices such as acupuncture, acupressure, and Emotional Freedom Technique (EFT) tapping can help rebalance unhealthy energy by realigning our body's meridians, or energy pathways.

- **Acupuncture** practitioners insert thin needles into specific points of the body to redirect stuck energy and stimulate nervous system function. Studies show that acupuncture balances sympathetic and parasympathetic function and reduces chronic stress and anxiety.[29]

- **Acupressure** uses the same bodily points as acupuncture to align energy and boost nervous system function. But instead of inserting needles, practitioners use their hands, elbows, and even feet to apply pressure that can release you from a stress response.
- **EFT tapping** uses acupuncture points, but you don't need to see a practitioner to benefit. Instead, you learn how to tap areas of your body to relieve stress.

Other techniques shown to relieve stress responses and regulate the nervous system include:

- **EMDR therapy**, short for eye movement desensitization and reprocessing therapy, is a form of therapy in which a trained practitioner leads you through a series of eye movements while you recall memories of traumatic past experiences. The therapy has been shown to help the body and brain heal from trauma while activating the parasympathetic nervous system.[30]
- **Bilateral stimulation** is a form of therapy that rhythmically stimulates the right and left hemispheres of the brain to help calm the nervous system. EMDR is a type of bilateral stimulation administered by a practitioner, and there are also ways to use touch and sound to achieve similar effects. For more detailed exercises, you can reference my workbook, *How to Meet Your Self: The Workbook for Self-Discovery*, or look online for resources to guide you.
- **Tension, Stress and Trauma Release (TRE)** is a somatic (body-based) practice that can help release deep-rooted muscular stress, trauma, and other emotions by completing shaking or vibrating exercises. You can find a workshop or TRE practitioner online.

SELF-REGULATION TOOL KIT

Following are some additional self-soothing and self-regulating options to help activate your parasympathetic nervous system and calm your body's emotional reactions.

- Teach your body to surrender or relax into your emotions and physical sensations by breathing deeply into areas of discomfort.
- Comfort your body with a soothing touch or a self-hug, which helps release oxytocin, a hormone that increases our sense of connection and helps moderate anxiety.
- Use a weighted blanket or gently rock your body to relax your body's energy.
- Smile to increase your production of feel-good serotonin and dopamine.
- Soothe your brain and body by listening to the sounds of nature (raindrops, gusts of wind, bird's chirping, etc.) or to music specifically created to calm the nervous system, like binaural beats or solfeggio frequencies.
- Listen to music to shift your mood by choosing tunes that match your current emotional state or energy. If you feel upset, sad, or angry, picking music that allows your brain to access these emotions can help support their flow through your body. Over time, once these emotions begin to release, you can gradually shift into listening to more upbeat or happy music to help increase your dopamine level and decrease your cortisol level.
- Calm your nervous system by co-regulating with a pet: pet or cuddle your own, offer to walk a friend's dog, or volunteer at a local animal shelter.

BOUNDARY SETTING

Boundaries are protective limits that we set with others to help us meet our body's physical and emotional needs, which helps create safety for our nervous system. We can set physical boundaries by eating what and when we want, going to bed when we choose, and prioritizing how and when we exercise. We can set emotional boundaries by saying no to people, events, situations, or tasks when we don't have the energetic, attentional, or emotional resources for them, even if the people we love are asking for our support. We can set these boundaries when we begin to feel on edge, are irritable with others, feel overwhelmed or on the verge of tears without explicit reason or cause, or are unable to think or express ourselves clearly.

Boundaries are choices we make for ourselves, not ultimatums we give to others. When we ask ourselves what *we* can change to help feel physically or emotionally different, we empower ourselves to ensure our own safety and security, regardless of what's happening (or not happening) around us. Setting limits in these instances can also help us replenish our energy so that we can be there for our loved ones in the future. Recognize, too, that our boundaries can change depending on our emotional state, how connected we feel to the person we're interacting with, and our body's energetic resources, including the amount of stored stress or tension we face.

As I hope this chapter has illustrated, a consistent practice of body consciousness can help us become aware of the patterns of nervous system reactivity that may be keeping us stuck in cycles of conflict, disconnection, or dissatisfaction within our relationships. Consistently meeting the needs of our physical body by eating nutrient-dense foods, spending time both moving and resting, and breathing deeply and calmly is foundational to creating a safe environment for our nervous system to regulate itself in.

As we continue to practice the empowerment pause (see page 120), we can start to notice the sensations inside us that drive us to say hurtful things we don't mean, keep ourselves endlessly "busy" or always on the go, say yes when we really mean no, or check out from difficult conversations or our relationships altogether. When we are able to consciously witness the sensations associated with our different nervous system responses, we can make conscious choices to bring our body back to safety. Only when we are in this grounded state can we intentionally choose our responses to our relationships and the world around us, ultimately allowing us all to *be* the love we seek.

As you learned in chapter 2, our body isn't the only participant in these reactive cycles. Next we'll talk more about the conditioning that lives in our subconscious mind and can drive these seemingly instinctual cycles with ourselves and others.

6

CREATING CHANGE THROUGH MIND CONSCIOUSNESS

Trevor couldn't understand why his last relationship had gone up in flames—yet again. He was smart, successful, attractive, and fit, all characteristics he thought made him the ultimate catch. *Women should be flocking to me!* he thought.

Though Trevor had no difficulty attracting dates or engaging in sexual experiences, sustaining a romantic relationship was another thing altogether. It didn't have anything to do with what he looked like or how much money he made, as he had once thought. What was sabotaging his relationships was his ego story continually running through his mind about who he was and who he had to be to feel worthy of love.

We all have an ego, and every ego has its stories. These narratives are created by our subconscious mind to make sense of the world around us. Our ego may create the story that "we're not worth their time" if someone we're interested in doesn't text us. Or our ego may interpret being passed over for a work project or business opportunity to mean that we're an unqualified imposter or fraud. Though we can't ever be sure of all the factors involved in a potential lover's preferences or a boss's decision, our mind creates stories and assumptions, assigning meanings to our experiences to try to help us deal with the discomfort of not knowing. The more frequently we assign the same meanings to similar experiences, the more these interpretations form a cohesive narrative or storyline that accompanies us through life. Even though it's impossible to know all of the objective "facts" surrounding our circumstances, we continue to assume that our interpretations are factual representations of reality.

Most of us have several different ego stories, some that change over time. But our biggest ego story—the one that we've been listening to the longest and is most influential to our sense of self—is the story that our subconscious made up during our childhood to help us better manage the stress of having needs neglected by our parent-figures. No matter your personal ego story, it usually boils down to deep-rooted shame about being not lovable enough, good enough, or worthy enough for someone to want to meet your needs.

As children, we lacked the emotional maturity and perspective to know that it wasn't our fault if our parent-figures weren't always able to help us feel safe, valued, and loved in the ways we needed. In a childhood state of egocentricism, we couldn't evaluate situations maturely or from another person's perspective and, as a result, personalized all interactions and experiences. When our developing brains couldn't understand the many factors that contributed to a person's abilities or choices in any given moment, we reasoned that anything we or others did indicated something about *us* and *who we were*. Because our wounded inner child believed that *we* were the problem, we began adapting or modifying ourselves in order to fit into our environment and relationships. We tried to keep ourself safe and connected through the habitual patterns of our trauma bonds, trying to feel "loved" in whatever ways were available.

Today, we probably still subconsciously believe that we're not worthy, continuing to suppress or hide those parts of ourselves that we believe make us instinctively unworthy. Sometimes we even hide those undesirable parts of ourselves from ourselves, keeping them repressed in our subconscious, unable to admit that they're even a part of us at all. You may have even heard these repressed parts referred to as "shadow" parts.

You may be asking yourself why, if most ego stories include difficult, uncomfortable, or limiting aspects, do we repeat them over and
over again? Because the human mind craves certainty, our ego works
tirelessly to confirm, reconfirm, and reinforce the stories we've repeated and grown comfortable with since we were young.

Anytime we think thoughts about ourselves—*I'm undesirable; I'm
too sensitive; I'm not good at anything*—that's our ego at work, helping
to create, define, and maintain our identity. Our ego's primary job is
to protect our hurt inner child, and to do so, it spins stories about who
we are to help us understand, justify, and compensate for the ways in
which we didn't feel safe or secure in the past.

Examples of common ego stories include:

- I'm too much or too sensitive to be loved by others.
- I'm needy or helpless.
- I'm worthless and deserve to be alone.
- I'm cursed, and nothing good ever happens to me.
- I'm loved only when I'm doing something for others.
- I'm an imposter and worthy of love only when I appear to be
  perfect.
- I'm always going to be left, abandoned, or cheated on.
- I'm more important than others, and my needs or opinions are
  the only ones that matter.
- I'm weak, and I'd feel too vulnerable to share how I really feel.
- I'm always being violated or taken advantage of.

Most of us are unaware of our ego story. Instead, we think our ego
story is our truth because it's become such a familiar pathway of our
subconscious mind. Since we were children, our brain has fired the
same ego-driven thoughts and intrepetations again and again, creating and reinforcing the associated neural networks. As these networks
grew stronger, our ego began to filter our daily experiences to confirm
these forming beliefs. Whenever our subconscious is presented with
information that contradicts or conflicts with our ego, it will quickly

and adamantly reject it as a threat to our perceived identity. We easily get stuck repeating the thoughts and reactive patterns of our ego, our experiences continuing to confirm the identity-based narratives from our childhood. Over time, we become more and more limited in both our thinking and perception and end up feeling more threatened, reactive, and often out of control as a result.

Thankfully, though, we can choose to develop *mind consciousness* or to become aware of these powerful subconscious beliefs by learning how to witness our ego story and the ways in which it drives us to think, feel, and react with others that don't serve our best interests or align with who we want to be. As we gain a greater awareness of our subconscious conditioning, we can begin to challenge our ego's underlying beliefs of unworthiness and make new choices that aren't colored by the hurt of our inner child.

TREVOR'S EGO STORY

Before we get into the process of developing mind consciousness, I want to go back to Trevor, since his ego story helps illustrate how our subconscious narratives can impact our relationships. Some of you may identify with Trevor's story because you've experienced something similar or have been in a relationship with someone like him.

Trevor had many ego stories, but the one he'd been listening to the longest was the one that was largely responsible for short-circuiting his romantic relationships. His ego story was: *I'm a man, and emotions make me (and all men) weak.* Here's how his hurt inner child came up with that belief.

Trevor had grown up in an upper-middle-class family in a safe, financially privileged neighborhood. His father, once a high-ranking officer in the military, was the CEO of a bank, which gave his mother the financial ability to stay home and raise their son. Trevor attended a good school, was encouraged to be physically active, ate healthy, home-cooked meals most nights of the week, and was allowed to pursue the hobbies that interested him, including costly ones like skiing, horseback riding, and guitar playing.

Though he had very few unmet physical needs, Trevor grew up with near-constant emotional abuse. His father was a physically and verbally domineering man who ruled the family with an iron fist. When Trevor expressed a normal emotion like sadness, loneliness, or fear, his father would respond by telling his son "Stop crying," "Man up," "Shape up or ship out," or "Toughen up, or you'll never make anything of yourself." His father, who frequently shifted into Eruptor mode, often exploded in fits of rage, sometimes for no apparent reason. To cope, Trevor began to adopt a cool, distanced facade, often using humor or deflection to deal with uncomfortable emotions, whether his own or those of others. He learned from his father to be consumed with status, wealth, and physical appearance, since that was how Trevor's dad felt he and other men were valued in the world.

Trevor's mother didn't protect her son from the near-constant emotional or verbal abuse in their home, helping him feel emotionally safe or secure. Though she loved Trevor deeply, she was frightened of her husband and fawned around him, enabling his temper and his harsh treatment of their son. This dynamic left Trevor with little to no emotional support since both his primary caregivers were unavailable: his father scared him, and his mother was too sacred to do anything about it. Trevor began to feel immense pressure to step in and mediate tense or volatile situations between his father and mother, using the same tactics he saw his mother use to try to please or calm his father.

Trevor was too scared to express his emotions or needs, so his nervous system remained on high alert, always ready to protect him against future attacks. Like his father, Trevor developed a two-faced exterior, remaining stoic or silently seething most of the time, then in reactive moments exhibiting rageful and abusive behaviors toward those closest to him. Though he mostly hid his dark feelings from the outside world, they created a highly complicated experience later in life for his romantic partners, who felt invalidated and silently enraged by his Jekyll-and-Hyde personality.

Wired for fight, Trevor learned from his father that anger was an effective way to control his environment. As an adult, Trevor used anger to intimidate others so that he felt more powerful, subconsciously compensating for all the times he'd felt helpless in childhood, as well as helpless against the emotions he feared made him weak. His hairtrigger temper was especially evident in his road rage, which frightened any partner who had to sit next to him in the passenger seat, and when he erupted at restaurants, parties, stores, or the office when he felt overlooked or slighted in some way. Trevor's nervous system was constantly scanning his environment, looking for evidence that he wasn't valued, which he usually found, even if none existed. Everything looked like a threat because everything in his childhood had been a threat: his authoritarian father, his passive mother, and the impossibility of expressing any emotions that might make him appear weak.

In his romantic relationships, Trevor suppressed all emotions other than anger, caught up in his ego story that real men don't show their feelings. He was regularly the Life of the Party, always acting as though everything was fine. Because he was unable to authentically express his wants, needs, and desires with others, he couldn't truly connect with his partners, who often saw him as angry, unfeeling, and harsh—not the nuanced, complex, kind, compassionate, generous, and loving man he was capable of being when able to authentically *be himself.*

Trevor's ego story prevented him from attuning to his partners since most emotions, even those expressed by others, scared him. During his childhood, no one had modeled healthy emotional expression for him or helped him learn how to adaptively cope with his or others' feelings. Growing up in an avoidant and explosive environment, he had never learned how to attune to his own upsetting emotions, which made him uncomfortable whenever others expressed their feelings around him as an adult. He often used logic to shut his partners down, unintentionally explaining away or invalidating their feelings when they shared their concerns with him. If his partner had

had a tough day at work, Trevor suggested that her boss was a jerk
or that she needed to get a promotion or apply for the job he had
recommended months before. Or if she told him that she felt lonely,
he questioned the validity of her feelings, reminding her that she had
just been out with friends the other night. As a result, his partners
never felt safe enough to honestly express themselves around him, and
many stopped sharing their emotions altogether, causing them to feel
isolated and often frightened within the relationship.

YOUR JOURNEY TO MIND CONSCIOUSNESS

Your ego story is likely different from Trevor's. Some of us have no
problem expressing our emotions within our relationships, but our
ego story keeps us trapped in patterns of emotional dumping, abandonment anxiety, or other dysfunctional behaviors that are driven by
our inner child wounds. No matter what our individual ego story may
be, it's likely creating cycles of shame-driven reactive behaviors as we
continue to hide parts of ourselves and as we desperately strive to feel
good enough.

When we develop mind consciousness, though, we can witness our
ego story and begin to appreciate ourselves for who we really are, not
who we had to be to feel safely connected in childhood. This will give
us the opportunity to begin to take away the power of our ego story
and its impact on our relationships. And it's how we start to create
new narratives about who we are and want to be. By doing ego work,
we can finally begin to believe that we're worthy enough for just *being
who we are*, without needing another's actions or validations to make
us feel whole and lovable.

Before we explore how to use mind consciousness to witness our
ego, I want to emphasize the importance of continuing the foundational body-based practices to help regulate your nervous system before beginning this process. If your nervous system is dysregulated
because of consistently unmet physical needs, developing mind con-

sciousness will be very difficult. If you're undernourished, exhausted from too little sleep, or fatigued from too little or too much movement, your body will continue to feel unsafe and you will likely continue to experience stress or fear-driven reactions, no matter how much ego work you do. If you've been taking steps to consistently meet your body's needs so you can better regulate your nervous system, you're ready for the next step in your journey back to your authentic Self.

YOUR SUBCONSCIOUS CREATES YOUR REALITY

Most of us spend the majority of our time in our head, obsessing over or analyzing what we think and feel. We believe that the narratives running through our mind are accurate accounts of ourselves and our experiences. Many of us even believe that we can will or think our way into believing or behaving the ways we want to.

None of this is true. Our thoughts and feelings do not make up our identity or who we are. Who we are is guided by our intuition, as we learn to trust the instinctual feelings in our heart, residing more in our body than in our mind. And, until we become aware of our heart's messages or desires, our daily habits and cycles of reactivity will be driven by our subconscious mind and dysregulated nervous system. When we become conscious of these inner powerful forces by witnessing both the habitual thoughts in our mind and the physical sensations in our body, we give ourselves the opportunity intentionally direct our creation of and reaction to our life.

Though most of us believe that we perceive the world around us accurately, we, in reality, see only what our subconscious wants us to see, based on our past experiences. And, to speed up processing time so we can move toward the safety of predictability, our brain often makes snap judgments, distorting or misrepresenting the available information. When our subconscious does this within our relationships and makes predictions based on our past, it can cause us to do or say unreasonable things or continue to hide the parts of ourselves we've come to believe make us unlovable or unworthy. This is especially true in our romantic relationships, where our subconscious habitually relies on our earliest relational experiences to predict our future. Because my mom was unable to consistently be emotionally present and attuned to my needs, my subconscious, desiring the safety of certainty, drives me to filter all of my relationship experiences through the age-old script that neither I nor my needs will be considered.

Using what happened in my past to predict that my partners aren't willing or interested in supporting my emotional needs limits the possibility of a different future outcome or experience. Because my subconscious has convinced me that I shouldn't even try to share my feelings with my partner, I end up shutting myself up in my room when I need or want support or making passive-aggressive or snarky comments that indirectly express my need or desire, snapping that "I wish I had someone to help me" instead of directly asking for the type of help or support I need or want. And, when I do decide to share my feelings with my partner, my subconscious often causes me to perceive any slight reaction—the look on their face or the tone of their voice—as an indication that I'm burdening them, just as I predicted and expected.

As I imagine you're beginning to see, most relationship conflicts aren't actually about what's happening between two people in the present but are instead reenactments of what happened between us and others in our past. When our subconscious makes predictions within our relationships, we can easily apply past trauma to our present interactions and make decisions based on old inner child wounds. Here are some examples of what that can look like, based on early childhood trauma.

- If you were repeatedly criticized by your parent-figures—told what to think, how to feel, when to act—your subconscious may interpret everything your loved one does or says about you or to you as critical, regardless of whether it is or not, causing you to be continually defensive. Your subconscious filters another's communications as a threatening indication of how negatively they *really* think or feel about you.

- If your parent-figures frequently yelled, slammed doors, or barged into your bedroom, your subconscious may perceive any loud noise or sudden gesture—a slammed door, a shut cabinet in the kitchen, someone walking behind you without your conscious awareness—as a reason to startle or scare. Your subconscious perceives loud noises or sudden gestures as threats because believing that someone is coming to yell at or scold you.

- If you grew up in a home with scarce or unavailable resources— your family lived from paycheck to paycheck and struggled to make ends meet, your parent-figures didn't have enough time for you because of financial insecurity, or you were shamed for wasting food or other resources—you may have grown up with a constant fear of not having enough or running out of what you need. Your subconscious may perceive what others say or do as indicative that they don't have enough resources for you, including enough time, support, attention, or love. You may act protectively in your relationships, always making sure you get your half or worrying that there's not enough even when there's plenty to go around, sometimes even quickly consuming whatever is available in order to "conserve" for possible future scarcity.

YOUR SUBCONSCIOUS'S FAVORITE STORY

If our physical or emotional needs weren't consistently met in child-hood, our subconscious can end up believing that we're inherently flawed. This belief creates an implicit threat of abandonment— that others will reject or leave us once they see we're unworthy or unlovable—causing our nervous system to repetitively activate a stress response. Over time, this nervous system dysregulation causes more reactivity within our relationships, as we feel consistently over-whelmed by the emotional and physical discomfort inside us.

Our subconscious will continue to overlook or filter out any evi-dence that we're worthy so that we can keep operating in our familiar neurobiological confines. Believing that unworthiness is part of who we are, intrinsically and undeniably, we interpret anything others say or do as reinforcement of this belief. As you can imagine, this can have detrimental effects on all our relationships.

Jada's story illustrates how our earliest childhood beliefs of unworthiness can impact our adult relationships. You may also know someone like Jada, who constantly perceives what happens to her and others as an injustice or maltreatment. Jada grew up in an economically underresourced home with three older siblings and one younger brother. Her parents worked long hours in order to feed the family of seven, and although they were "good" and "loving" people, they were physically unavailable most of the time—and too exhausted when they were home to attune to their children. Their physical and emotional absence caused Jada and her siblings to grow up feeling deeply unworthy of having someone meet her needs. Often behind on rent, the family was forced to move frequently, and the children were transferred from school to school. Struggling to fit in, Jada's siblings coped with their feelings of unworthiness by bullying her both physically and emotionally. Lacking any type of foundational safety, Jada started to feel that the world was filled with unsafe people—after all, not even her own family was kind to her. Her ego story soon became "I'm not worthy of being treated with respect."

The older Jada got, the more her ego story caused her to see the possibility of injustice in most daily circumstances. Feeling deeply outraged and, at the same time, powerless and alone, she was constantly on guard for possible threats, often adopting a combative attitude in an attempt to keep herself safe, especially from those who held positions of power. That misguided and hypervigilant self-protection often activated a disproportionate reaction whenever she thought someone slighted her, becoming indignant or even rageful if she was passed over for a project at work, she scrolled by a social media post that offended her, or someone mistakenly cut in front of her in line at the coffee shop. Her subconscious perceived moments of possible conflict everywhere and hastily relied on polarized ("us" or "with me" versus "them" or "against me") thinking to automatically group others into categories based on perceived power dynamics. Usually, she'd take the side of the underdog, even if they were harming others.

In both her romantic and professional relationships, Jada's ego story attracted her to partners whom she believed she could easily defend or who needed her protection. That was her trauma bond pattern, her childhood wounds causing her to play the role of the Rescuer/ Protector with others. Her subconscious was always on the alert for signs that those she cared about were being taken advantage of, and when her mind inevitably found evidence of that, she would become reactive and defensive, yelling at whoever was causing the perceived injustice. She continued to project her internal experience of powerlessness onto others, seeing people as vulnerable and in need of rescuing. In her ego's reality, she was just trying to stand up for others the way she wished her parents had stood up for her. Though in her interactions with others she wasn't able to hold space for any differences in perspectives and often came across as self-righteous and often abrasive even though she meant well.

Meet Your Ego Exercise

You can witness your own ego by beginning to pay attention to the thoughts or stories you frequently tell yourself about yourself, others, and the world in general. During the next couple of days or weeks, nonjudgmentally take note of these types of thoughts as they occur throughout your day, writing them down on the lines below or in a separate journal or notebook if helpful. By recognizing these stories for what they are—tales made up by your subconscious mind—you can stop reacting to them as your truth and start responding to them in new ways. Continue to extend yourself compassion during this exercise, acknowledging that these narratives once helped protect you and your inner child from your deepest pain.

Examples:

"I'm not good enough."

"Others aren't trustworthy."

"The world is unsafe."

"I am _____."

"Others are _____."

"The world is _____."

MEET YOUR EGO-GUIDED MEDITATION

Meditation practices can help you enhance your ability to witness and more objectively explore the thoughts you have as just thoughts, with no judgment, meaning, or value. Removing the

strength and meaning from your thoughts can, over time, help you begin to see that your ego story doesn't define you and will give you the opportunity to create new beliefs that better align with your intrinsic worthiness.

If you're new to meditation, you may be wondering where to start. Though the idea can be intimidating, there is no right or wrong way to meditate. Remember, your goal is simply to be present in your body in the moment, observing the thoughts you're having without judgment, as though you are watching clouds drift across the sky.

Though meditating with your eyes closed in a quiet space can limit distractions from your external world, helping you better see your internal one, you can also learn to be consciously present while around others. As you grow your meditation practice, it's helpful to begin to notice your ego-based thoughts in real time. Learning how to shift into this state of witnessing in the moments when you're in a reactive ego state can help create the space needed for you to pause, rethink, and make more authentic, heart-based choices.

EGO CONSCIOUSNESS AND YOUR
CONDITIONED SELVES

If our ego story feels so much like our identity and truth, how can we convince it otherwise? The answer is that we can't. Though you may have heard otherwise, our goal is not to "kill" or overpower our ego. Our ego is actually a critical part of our experience as a human, one that has kept us safe in overwhelming environments or situations since we were children. Now that we're adults, our ego's presence lets us know when something from our emotional past may be coloring our current experience. Over time, we can use our ego's presence to cue our conscious mind to bring ourselves back to safety and the present moment.

Though our ego is an important and protective part of each of us, it's not *all* of us. When we let our ego story color how we think about ourselves and interact with others, we operate in a space that I call *ego consciousness*: we automatically assign meanings and value to who we are, who others are, and what they think of us based on our unmet emotional needs. We can't help but hide parts of ourselves as our ego story tricks us into believing that those parts aren't worthy.

When I'm in a state of ego consciousness, I believe that my Over-achiever self is what makes me *me*. I'm compelled to act as though my self-worth is dependent on whether I'm succeeding in my relationships by impressing others, appearing without imperfection or vulnerability, or fulfilling what I assume are their expectations of me. My subconscious is always analyzing what others say and do for evidence that they like or value me. Because at my core I don't believe I'm worthy, I look to others for validation to help make me feel better about myself. The irony, of course, is that no amount of praise ever takes away my deep-rooted feelings of of unworthiness: that belief comes from me, not from others.

Ego consciousness often drives me to agonize over whether others are truly happy with and want to be with me. If I plan a special event for a loved one, I can spend the whole night obsessing over whether they really like what I've done for them—instinctively believing that their satisfaction with the event is a reflection of whether they're satisfied with me. Because my subconscious is primed to find clues that I'm never good enough or doing an adequate enough job, I can misinterpret their response as a sign that they dislike the experience and, by extension, think less of me. Feeling hurt for these imagined reasons, I'll usually end up sulking in a corner or accusing my loved one of being ungrateful.

Of course, not everyone identifies with the habits of an Overachiever. If you relate more as a Caretaker, your subconscious believes that you're valued only when you are caring for others. When you feel threatened and are in a state of ego consciousness, your subconscious will continue to scan your interactions to assess whether you're adequately tending to those around you, believing that your self-worth is dependent on doing so. You might constantly ask if others are okay, look for anything you can do for them, or overanalyze their reactions to the services you provide, needing to know if they *really* liked what you cooked for them or *truly* appreciated you for organizing their medical or financial care. Your ego story makes it impossible for you to stop showing up to care for others and putting their needs before your own, since your subconscious will tell you that you're unworthy if you don't. Though showing up to care for others is part of an emotionally supportive relationship, when you continually put others first, it can prevent you from tending to your own needs.

Devin is a self-professed Hero Worshiper who constantly looks to others to show and tell her how to think, feel, and act because she's so unsure of her own inner voice. She grew up in a strict religious home with a mother who always prided herself on being a "good" and moral devotee. Her father drank almost daily, consuming several beers after work and many more on the weekends. Usually mildly intoxicated, he would often make mean or sexually inappropriate jokes in public—otherwise, he played the role of the happy-go-lucky family guy, showing no upsetting feelings. Because he never became angry or out of control while drinking, Devin's mother tolerated his behavior, which was never directly discussed in the family. Instead, everyone participated in a cycle of denial, pretending that dysfunctional and hurtful things weren't happening, even lying at times to cover up her father's often inappropriate behavior.

Whenever Devin tried to express any unpleasant feelings to or share uncomfortable observations with either of her parents, she was reprimanded for not being able to take a joke or told to keep quiet like a "good" girl. She quickly learned that there were some things that shouldn't or couldn't be said to others. Afraid of feelings or thoughts that could be perceived as "bad," she continued to look to her parents to inform her how she should act and feel. She developed a harsh inner critic that, fueled by the rigid sense of morality she grew up with, constantly judged her thoughts and desires and sometimes expressed itself outwardly in the form of self-deprecating jokes or self-critical put-downs.

As Devin was growing up, her ego story became "I have to be good to be loved." Defensive of her "good" person image, she avoided interacting with anyone who challenged it. She judged herself harshly every time she thought or felt negatively about someone or something. She regularly felt guilty or punished herself whenever she wanted to act in ways that felt natural or instinctive but that contradicted what she thought was appropriate according to her conditioned values. Because she believed that she was never good enough or smart enough to make decisions on her own, she often overexplained or defended herself on the rare occasions when her words or actions ran contrary to the opinions or desires of others.

Now in her forties and married with two children, Devin remains deferential to others, believing she's too unworthy to trust herself to meet her own needs, let alone navigate the complexities of her life or relationships. Consistently playing the role of the Hero Worshiper, she continues to idealize others around her, just as she did her parents, while overlooking signs of issues or flaws in those she loves. Although many in her hometown know her husband is having extramarital affairs, Devin continues to ignore the rumors and evidence, driven by her ego to avoid all painful experiences. Denying the reality allows her to focus on what a good father she thinks her husband is to their young children, so she's started to avoid family and friends who think or say otherwise. As reports of her husband's infidelity have increased, so have Devin's attempts to control her family's picture-perfect appearance. Distrusting her intuition that has urged her to address the issues in her marriage, she rejects anyone who suggests the reality of her husband's infidelity, fighting to retain a false sense of safety in her idealized life.

EMPOWERMENT CONSCIOUSNESS

No matter what our conditioned self believes, the greater the awareness we have about our ego story and the more distance we create between ourselves and these narratives, the more accurately we can see the things happening within and around us. Other people may continue to behave in the same ways, but when we're able to witness our ego, we'll be able to spend less time in the grips of its fear-based reactivity. We can begin to question the automatic assumptions that continue to drive us to behave in conditioned ways when we develop what I call *empowerment consciousness*.

With empowerment consciousness, we develop the ability to witness our ego's instinctual thoughts, challenge the belief that we're not worthy, and make new choices about how we want to act that will eventually help us to create a new, more empowering belief. Empowerment consciousness helps us recognize the times when our ego story is causing us to have reactions that are based on our past experiences, not grounded in our present reality. When we're able to realize that we're experiencing these ego-driven thoughts and feelings, we can let them pass and choose to assign new meanings to what we're currently experiencing. Though there are many others, here are two examples of new ways to think about our current experiences:

- The only reason I feel like I have to drop everything right now and save my loved one from their crisis is to try to make myself feel worthy. I don't have to sacrifice my own needs and am worthy even if I can't support my loved one right now.

- My ego story wants me to believe that my colleague is being critical of me, and I want to open myself up to the possibility that they're actually being considerate and caring rather than critical. Because I was routinely criticized as a child, my subconscious is trying to protect my hurt inner child and keep me safe by making me lash out. I can now make the choice to act differently.

PRACTICING EMPOWERMENT CONSCIOUSNESS

While our ego stories will be unique to each of us and many of us will have more than one, the steps below will help you witness and separate yourself from your ego's reactive cycles.

1. **Witness your ego story.** Becoming aware of the stories or narratives you have about yourself enables you to recognize the times when you're letting your ego story run the show by making assumptions and becoming reactive with others as a result.
2. **Question your thoughts.** When you know you're in an ego-conscious state with others, take a time-out to examine your thoughts and feelings. Do they really represent your reality, or is your ego story distorting what you think and feel? For example, if your partner hasn't texted you back for several hours, and you spiral into thinking that they don't care about you, you can question the validity of those thoughts and consider other possibilities for their lack of response that have nothing to do with your worth.
3. **Reparent your hurt inner child.** Your ego story was created by your subconscious to help you cope with the unmet needs that caused you to believe that you're not worthy. Reparent your hurt inner child by telling yourself that you're safe now and are worthy in every way. Remember, if your nervous system is in an active stress response, it'll be important for you to reparent yourself by continuing to practice daily the acts of self-care we talked about in chapter 5 to create nervous wellness and soothe your nervous system dysregulation.

4. **Rewire your ego story with affirmations.** Believing that you're worthy when you've thought otherwise for years isn't easy, as this belief is physically programmed into your mind and body. Affirmations, which are positive mantras about ourselves or experiences, can help rewire your neural networks, even if you don't believe them at first. Telling yourself that you're safe and worthy fires different neurons in your brain that, over time, can become new neural networks that are easy and instinctual for your brain to follow. Examples of possible affirmations include:
   - I am safe and loved regardless of how I feel.
   - I am able to take care of myself even if I need support at times.
   - I am worthy of love and connection.
   - I am an intentional creator of all my life experiences.
   - I am lovable exactly as I am.
   - I am worthy exactly as I am.
   - I am safe and secure in my relationship with myself and others.
   - I am most powerful when I cocreate with others around me.
   - I am connected to my emotional world and able to safely express myself.
   - I am an active participant in how I create and respond to my life experiences.

The more we use affirmations to rewire our beliefs, the more empowered we'll feel to *be* our authentic Self with and the more confident and grounded we'll feel within our relationships. Over time, as we consistently practice mind consciousness and become conscious of our subconscious, we give ourselves the opportunity to decide how we relate to and connect with others rather than reacting instinctually from a place of pain and hurt. We give ourselves the opportunity to respond from our heart, our internal reservoir of love and compassion, using practices we'll explore in the next chapter.

7

UNLOCKING THE POWER OF YOUR HEART

Follow your heart, not your head.

You've probably heard this advice before, maybe even hundreds of times, and I'm going to guess that as a reader of this book, you likely agree with it. But have you ever taken the time to consider whether you actually *do* follow your heart? Many of us believe that we do, but most of us—including me for much of my life—tend to follow our thoughts. We spend most of our time paying attention to our thinking mind, not to our physical heart exploring the deeper desires, dreams, and wants that live there. We make our decisions with our "logical, rational" brain, overlooking the pull we may feel in our gut or the flutter in our heart that is telling us something different.

While our thinking mind is described as "logical" and "rational," our choices are often not reasonable at all. When we let our conditioning drive our actions, we remain disconnected from our inner wisdom. Unable to access our intuition, we end up overthinking our way through life, endlessly weighing our choices, sometimes too paralyzed to make any decision at all. Detached from our heart's inner compass, we're more easily influenced by external messages from the media, our peers, and other outside influences. We keep repeating the same solutions to familiar issues, unable to see new possibilities or break out of our old dysfunctional habits. Unable to determine what we really want and need, we end up feeling dissatis-fied, disillusioned, or confused about how to navigate our relation-ships and surroundings.

To reconnect with your innate inner guidance, you'll need to learn how to tune in to the deeper wisdom that resides in your heart. Your heart isn't just an organ that pumps blood throughout your body. Your physical heart—the one beating inside your chest right now—is also where your intuition lives. It's the most energetically powerful organ in the human body, emitting an electric field that extends well beyond your physcial being. Your heart transmits the individual energy that makes each of you unique—what I call our soul or essence. If you want to make choices in your relationships that align with your soul or authentic Self, you'll need to be connected with your heart.

Many people view their heart as the physical center of themselves, where they would point if someone asked them to identify their core. Most of us also believe that our heart is the hub of our emotions. Around the world and throughout human history, the heart has been synonymous with love, along with identity, intention, and intuition. In English alone, dozens of idioms describe the heart as the center of our emotional and intuitive self, with phrases like "the heart of the matter," "with all my heart," "from the bottom of my heart," "follow your heart," and "heartfelt emotions."

The historical and cultural emphasis on the heart is not arbitrary. Over the past several decades, research has shown that the heart is more powerful than we ever thought. We now know that our heart communicates with our brain, transmitting nerve impulses, hor-mones, pressure waves, and electromagnetic energy that impact how our nervous system functions. Our heart's signals are so strong, in fact, that other people and animals can feel our energy. If I were to place an electrode in a cup of water a few feet away from you, I would be able to observe your heartbeat in the gentle movement of the liquid.

If you don't understand what it means to be connected to your heart, I can relate. For years, I didn't, either. When yoga instructors or other healers talked about dropping into their heart space to make decisions and find peace or clarity, I didn't really get it. It wasn't until I took a trip to Bali—or, more accurately, stayed overnight in the middle of the Balinese jungle—that I began to understand what it means to be connected with my heart and why it's so important.

After I completed my doctorate, my parents gifted me some money (financial rewards for academic achievements were a common display of love in my family). Lolly and I decided to spend it on a shoestring vacation in Bali, driving around the island on a moped and staying in inexpensive guesthouses. Toward the end of the trip, we splurged to stay at a popular retreat center not far from where we were staying in Ubud, an inland part of the island surrounded by rice paddies, ravines, and temples. The facility was serenely beautiful, with windows that opened up onto fields so green they looked blue. During our first day there, Lolly and I visited the reading room, and each of us selected a book. Drawn to it by its cover and title, I picked up Gregg Braden's *The Divine Matrix: Bridging Time, Space, Miracles, and Belief.*

In the book, Braden, a well-known spiritualist, uses science to support the presence of an energy web that connects all humankind. Within minutes, I was captivated by his concepts. I devoured page after page while lying on a daybed as the wind carried in the soft scent of hibiscus and the chirp of birds through a set of open doors. Two days later, when we checked out, I had already finished the book.

After we returned home, I ordered several more books related to the ideas I had learned from Braden. Somewhere during that deep dive, I was introduced to the idea of heart-brain coherence. Heart-brain coherence, more simply known as heart coherence, is a scientifically quantifiable, psychophysiological state that occurs when our heart and brain operate efficiently together and our heart sends energetically rhythmic or coherent messages to our brain and vice versa. I hadn't heard of it. Immediately, I wanted to learn as much as I could, and I began my journey toward *heart consciousness*.

Heart consciousness is the term I use to describe a state of heart-based awareness in which we are open to receiving messages from our heart and making decisions based on its intelligence. When we're heart conscious, we're able to tap into our true passions and purpose and express our unique energy to others, spending more time being lead by our true interests and desires. When we listen to our heart, we're more authentically connected to ourselves and more open and available to authentically connect with others. Our grounded presence can help create safety with others, as our nervous system sends soothing signals to those around us, helping them feel physically calm, too (we'll talk more about this process of co-regulation in the next chapter). Ultimately, cultivating heart consciousness can help us better attune to our heart's intuition to guide us toward more-aligned choices for ourselves and within our relationships, despite the unknown of our future.

AT THE HEART OF THE MATTER: HEART COHERENCE

Though many people aren't familiar with the idea of heart coherence, the concept has been studied for decades and used in medicine to help people transform their physical and emotional well-being. Scientific research has shown that heart coherence can help prevent or treat a number of physical conditions, including heart disorders, diabetes, chronic fatigue, chronic pain, high blood pressure, autoimmune disorders, and fibromyalgia.[31] According to studies, heart coherence can also help people better cope with or recover from anxiety, depression, PTSD, ADHD, drug and alcohol addiction, anger issues, and eating disorders, in addition to helping them boost their memory and cognitive performance.[32]

Heart coherence occurs when our brain, heart, and emotions are aligned and our heart and brain are able to work efficiently together in energetic coordination. Said more simply, it's a state of physical and emotional connection with our heart that allows us to act according to its messages. It's a state of synchronicity and balance between the communication among our body's major physiological control centers, including our cardiovascular, nervous, hormonal, and immune systems. This internal choreography allows our autonomic nervous system to switch easily between the sympathetic and parasympathetic states, activating a stress response when necessary, then returning quickly to the peaceful calm of homeostasis. Heart coherence reduces our mental dialogue, enhancing our mental clarity and our ability to attune to our intuition.

Scientists measure heart coherence by evaluating the physical signals our heart sends our brain. With heart coherence, our heart sends our brain smooth S-shaped pressure waves, nerve impulses, hormones, neurotransmitters, and electromagnetic energy, all of which lower our perceived stress and increase our stress resiliency, or the amount of tension or unpleasant emotions we can tolerate. These harmonious signals can even lower the stress of those around us, giving meaning and possibility to the idea that we as individuals are capable of changing the world around us.

HEART-RHYTHM PATTERNS

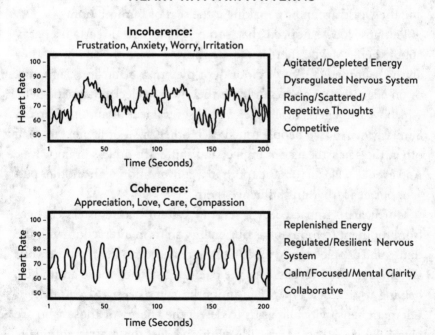

Our heart actually has its own "little brain," as scientists call it, which includes around forty thousand neurons.[33] Like our brain, our heart can store both short- and long-term memories, which explains why some heart transplant patients are able to recall memories of their donor's lives and even take on their donor's personality traits.[34]

Our heart is the most energetically powerful organ in our body, emitting an electrical energy field sixty times as strong as the one produced by our brain and an electromagnetic field that's one hundred times as strong.[35] The heart's electromagnetic energy can be detected everywhere on our skin's surface, up to five feet away from us, and by those physically near us, impacting their brain wave activity.[36] Using electrical and electromagnetic fields in addition to hormones and other sensory signals, our heart constantly sends information to us and those around us while at the same time receiving, encoding, and learning information from our environment.[37] In fact, it's our heart, not our brain, that interprets the electromagnetic signals from others and the world around us, making it the seat of our intuition.

Perhaps you've noticed that some people have a certain energy about them. Maybe they exude a lightness, warmth, or joy, or they always seem sad, heavy, or gloomy, or they may be anxious, agitated, or on edge. What you're sensing is their heart's electromagnetic field, which we can energetically feel within several feet of another person. Similarly, when two people touch each other or sit or lie next to each other, their heartbeats can impact and shift each other's brain waves. And even if we're across the room in a conversation with another person, our heart rhythms influence them.[38]

Our heart is impacted by a sensory system that registers changes from moment to moment as our energy shifts in interaction with the things and people around us. When we're heart coherent, our nervous system is open or receptive to the energetic state of those around us, helping us access a type of intuition known as *energetic sensitivity*.[39] Energetic sensitivity allows us to detect the energy of those who are physically closest to us or with whom we feel the most emotionally familiar. You likely felt this intuition the last time you were able to sense when a loved one was upset or bothered by something without speaking with them directly. Or you were able to notice a lightness or charge when near someone who just experienced something joyful, before you knew anything about what had occurred.

Our heart senses another type of intuition, known as nonlocal intuition or intuition at a distance. This type of intuition can help us sense the state of people and events that are outside our immediate proximity or are even happening at the moment. Though these experiences can be easily dismissed as "woo-woo," nonlocal intuition has solid scientific proof. Research shows that our hearts can actually predict events *before* they occur, with one study finding that people's physical hearts react to upsetting pictures before they see the images with their eyes.[40] These findings have been replicated cross-culturally using various stimuli.[41]

You may have experienced nonlocal intuition yourself if you have ever thought of someone and immediately received a text or call from that person, or if you ever knew what a loved one was thinking before they spoke out to you. Other examples include parents who have sensed that something's happened to their children who were not in their physical proximity, as well as entrepreneurs who have sensed their way to making successful business decisions.[42]

In addition to nonlocal intuition, our heart has intuitive powers that scientists admit they can't fully quantify. Despite this fact—or perhaps because of it—it's becoming clear to researchers that our heart is "coupled to a field of information that is not bound by the classical limits of time and space" while also containing something otherworldly or a "deeper part of one's self."[43]

We can only access this informational field when we're in a safe and socially connected state of ventral vagal parasympathetic activation, which we talked about in chapter 3. When we're in this state, our body can quiet the static caused by our thoughts so that we can actually hear our heart's intuitive pings. Think about the open, light, or airy way your heart or chest might feel when you're relaxed, calm, and peaceful. Compare this with the closed, heavy, or constricted sensations you may notice when you're feeling scared, stressed, or worried. This is your intuition talking to you.

When our heart and brain are energetically and emotionally aligned we're better able to feel our heart's sensations and can begin to understand its messages. If our heart feels centered, calm, and expansive when we're considering an action within our relationships, it's likely a safe or aligned choice for us in that moment. If our heart feels constricted, shut down, or fearful, on the other hand, our intended action may not be the safest or most aligned choice for us in that moment.

Over time, we can all come to recognize those tugs on the back of our mind, moments of deep knowing, gut feelings, unexpected inner voices, images or visions, or flutters in our heart. When we're open to feeling our heart and receiving its messages, we may notice our awareness open in other ways, too. We may begin to notice those other moments of insight or clarity that occur when an idea or solution bursts into our consciousness, interrupting our mind's repetitive thoughts. Or detect those gentle nudges urging us to move our beloved mug before it falls off the counter, to grab an umbrella in time for an unexpected rainstorm, or to take a different route home from work to find a kitten that needs to be rescued. All of those are examples of our intuition speaking to us.

Being connected to our heart and being in a state of coherence enables us to access our inherent creativity and more easily enter a "flow state," becoming totally immersed in a project, hobby, conversation, or whatever's happening in the moment.[44] Those expansive moments of easeful attention and connection can help us identify and pursue our true passion and purpose.

The problem for most of us is that we spend very little, if any, time connected to our hearts and in a state of heart coherence. When we're constantly overwhelmed by either our external environment because of chaotic or unsafe living conditions or by our internal environment because of worrying or upsetting thoughts or emotions, our body is overstimulated and overstressed, keeping us disconnected from our hearts and in an incoherent state. In those moments, our brain and heart will scramble the messages passing between them and from the world around us, and we won't be able to access our intuition, assess situations clearly or accurately, or be open or curious about others. Our heart may be sending us messages, but we won't be able to hear them because our brain will override its signals. When it is out of sync with our heart, our brain may see only conflict, finding and highlighting the separateness or differences in the people we love the most. Thankfully, though, there are ways we can clear the static that prevents us from embodying the eternal presence of love.

We can all begin to enjoy moments of heart coherence and tap into our intuition, helping us develop trust and security in the face of our inevitably uncertain future. Though remember, creating heart coherence isn't going to end all our stress and anxiety; that isn't humanly possible; stressful and upsetting situations are part of life. But cultivating heart coherence can enhance our ability to bring our nervous system back to safety after tense or uncomfortable experiences or emotions. Our increased stress resilience helps us to tolerate a wider range of situations without becoming overwhelmed with stress and stuck in a nervous system response as a result. If we can't regulate or calm ourselves down when we're stressed or upset, our brain will continue to send fear-based messages, and we won't ever be able to feel safe enough in our body to connect with or listen to our heart.

HEALING YOUR RELATIONSHIPS WITH HEART COHERENCE

When our heart and brain work together harmoniously and efficiently, we can sense our environment more accurately and make decisions that allow us to maintain our connections to others. We can think more clearly and better deal with the emotional stress of life.

Though our nervous system is wired to respond to threats, our heart is able to create compassionate connections. Tolerating stress and emotional hardship without becoming dysregulated, overwhelmed, or shut down helps us respond to others in calmer and loving ways. We'll still feel stressed or upset in our lives or relationships at times, of course, but we'll also be able to stay open to and curious about another's perspectives and experiences. We'll be able to create space within our relationships to explore and connect to different and unique individuals. At the same time, we'll be able to set and hold clear boundaries so that we don't feel depleted or resentful of those differences, increasing our ability to show up as the loving, compassionate person we are capable of being.

Creating this life- and relationship-changing state of heart coherence starts with dedicating small moments during the day to focus on embodying what researchers call *core heart feelings*, or positive emotions like appreciation, gratitude, compassion, care, and love. Experiencing these positive emotions can harmonize our heart's rhythms, shifting them from jagged or irregular patterns into smooth, "sinelike waves," and can also reduce the activity of our sympathetic nervous system while increasing the activity of our parasympathetic.[45]

Practicing gratitude, in particular, can help us feel more grounded in the current moment rather than stuck reliving the difficulties of our past or worrying about our future. Gratitude grounds us in an awareness of what *is* present in the here-and-now, giving us the opportunity to accept our current reality and helping to shift us out of the state of energetic resistance in which many of us regularly find ourselves. To quickly experience the impact of gratitude for yourself, take a moment to notice how your body's energy feels the next time you find yourself thinking that you "have to" or "should" do something, whether it's calling back a loved one or brushing your teeth before bed. Then take a moment to shift your thoughts to ones that extend gratitude for the opportunity to complete whatever action it is you need to do. In other words, change your mental language from "I have to do *X*" or "I should do *Y*" to "I can choose to do *X*," noticing how your body's energy changes in response to this mental shift. It can be helpful to build on this practice by adding in another moment to consider your purpose or intention behind whatever your action or choice. Using the above examples, this can look like taking a moment to remind yourself, "I can choose to call back my loved one because it helps us feel connected to each other, and that's important to me" or "I can choose to brush my teeth because my body's wellness is important to me."

Reconnecting with and activating your heart in these small ways every day, as I hope you're beginning to see, is foundationally important to creating the space and opportunity you need to express yourself authentically and give others the space and opportunity to do the same. This authentic emotional expression is what creates the possibility for us to be truly known by and connected with others, enabling them to feel safe enough for them to be known by and connected with us. Truly knowing someone or attuning to them with both our heart and brain helps us feel from *their* emotional viewpoint; this is the basis of authentic, empathetic connection.

THE SECRETS HIDDEN IN YOUR HEARTBEAT

Our heartbeat is the rhythm of our life, a force that can be felt throughout our entire body and the first vital sign doctors check to discern the living from the dead. But our heartbeat isn't only a marker of our physical existence; it's our heart's "intelligent language," used to communicate our emotional experiences to our brain, our body, and the world around us. Every time our heart beats, it sends neural impulses that alter our brain's electrical activity, especially in the areas related to emotions. Our heartbeat can even change the electrical activity in the brains of those around us, including animals as well as people.[46]

Our heart's language is specific to each of us. Contrary to common belief, our heart doesn't beat like a metronome, ticking away in a precise, equal rhythm. Instead, it beats at varying amplitudes and intervals from second to second, with shorter or longer intervals between beats. This is known as heart rate variability (HRV), a measurement of the moment-to-moment fluctuations in our heart rate that we can't feel because they're so minuscule. It is controlled by our autonomic nervous system, which also operates our sympathetic and parasympathetic branches and the fight, flight, freeze or shutdown, and fawn stress responses.

The more variation our heart has between beats, the higher our HRV. The less variation between beats, the lower our HRV. When we have high HRV, we're better able to tolerate stress, because our heart can quickly recover or return to its regular rhythm after a stressful experience. When we have low HRV, on the other hand, we respond to stress less effectively as our heart struggles to recover, often remaining elevated long after the stressful experience ends.

You may have experienced the impact of your HRV the last time a car sped past you while you were walking down the street. If you have high HRV, your heart likely raced for a second, giving you the energy to jump out of the way if necessary. Soon after, though, it slowed, helping you settle back into feeling calm and safe again. If you have low HRV, your heart likely raced and stayed elevated, unable to calm and causing you to stay on edge for longer than necessary.

In general, having high HRV is associated with increased physical health, emotional well-being, behavioral resiliency, and emotional regulation. High HRV allows our nervous system to spend more time in a ventral vagal state, improving our heart coherence and our ability to be open to connecting and cooperating with those around us.

Low HRV reduces our ability to cope with stressful situations and up-setting emotions, no matter how much we'd like to deal with them calmly or effectively. We may feel chronically impatient, agitated, or on edge, ex-perience waves of deep pain, and act irrationally by hurting ourselves or others or by turning to drugs, alcohol, food, sex, or other substances or dysfunctional behavioral habits in an attempt to self-soothe. In a constant state of survival, we become self-centered to our own being, unable to attune to another person or see or feel things from their perspective.

In our relationships, the difference between high and low HRV can mean reacting calmly and responsively when a loved one comes home agitated or fighting, or taking their upset personally, fully absorbing their transferred emotional state. With higher HRV, we're better able to give them the space or time to self-regulate if needed or we can attune to and co-regulate with them. If we're the one who comes home stressed, we can more quickly and effectively regulate ourselves by taking a few moments alone or by directly letting them know the support we want or need, whether its space, time, or an empathetic ear.

HRV SELF-ASSESSMENT

Take a look at the following questions and select the answers that most consistently resonate with your experiences.

Do you feel out of control, overwhelmed, or explosively reactive when you're upset with others?
1. Never
2. Sometimes
3. Often

Do you feel unable to relax or feel at ease with others?
1. Never
2. Sometimes
3. Often

Do you feel too scared, uncomfortable, or unsafe to be physically close to or to physically connect with others?
1. Never
2. Sometimes
3. Often

Do you feel too scared, uncomfortable, or unsafe to be emotionally vulnerable with or close to others?
1. Never
2. Sometimes
3. Often

Do you feel too scared, uncomfortable, or unsafe to give or receive love, often resisting others' attempts to connect emotionally or show love to you?
1. Never
2. Sometimes
3. Often

Do you feel unable to relax or feel at ease by yourself or become uncomfortable during moments of silence or solitude, like during meditation or when you're alone?

1. Never
2. Sometimes
3. Often

Add up your answers. The higher your score, the lower your HRV and the more incoherent your heart may be. Continue to extend compassion to yourself whatever your score and consider using this exercise as an opportunity to begin creating change in your body, mind, and heart, change that is possible every moment of every day. Wherever you are on your healing journey, increasing your HRV and heart coherence by developing body and mind consciousness can help you begin to shift out of your conditioned patterns of reactivity, find peace, and better attune to your heart's messages.

MY JOURNEY TO
HEART CONSCIOUSNESS

Like many of you, I didn't grow up with emotionally attuned parents, which caused me to fearfully disconnect from my heart. Both my parents were second-generation immigrants who grew up in physically and emotionally underresourced environments. Because my mom had largely been ignored by her own father and mother, she remained emotionally underdeveloped as an adult and unable to cope with stress to allow herself the opportunity to authentically connect with others. When my sister experienced a series of health crises as a young child, my parents were overwhelmed and undersupported, especially after their extended family began to distance themselves, either unsure of how to offer support or unwilling to do so. My mother started to shut down emotionally in order to survive the near-constant stress she faced and developed chronic pain and health issues herself. Without the ability to regulate her emotions, she began an endless journey to find ways to relieve her ever-increasing pain.

By the time I was born, both my parents were in their midforties and had been living for decades in bodies that were stuck in a fear-based state of nervous system dysregulation. Driven by deep-rooted fear and prioritizing their own survival, they were unable to truly empathize with me or my emotional world. Without anyone to help me navigate what was happening inside and around me, I grew up feeling constantly unsafe, too. Regularly overwhelmed and dysregulated, I could rarely access the parasympathetic ventral vagal state that we need to feel grounded and peacefully connected to our body and within relationships.

I became the living embodiment of our family's intergenerationally and epigenetically passed on belief—that the world was scary and lonely place—which came directly from my parents' and now my own lived experiences. In her early twenties and soon after she left home, my mom learned that her father had died suddenly of a heart attack. That abrupt loss activated her deep-rooted abandonment wound and increased her sense of disconnection from others. Years later, when returning from their honeymoon, my parents saw a car flipping over several times in a serious accident—an image that terrified her and hunted our family's car rides for years. My dad had been painfully teased as a child and after becoming the victim of identity fraud later in life, he began to assume that everyone was out to swindle or deceive him.

My own experiences reinforced my parents' expressed worries. Growing up in an area of Philadelphia that wasn't always safe, I was often awoken by sirens from emergency vehicles responding to crimes and other accidents. In fact, the day I came home from the hospital as a baby, the garage of our city home caught fire after my older brother accidentally struck a spark while restoring an old vehicle. On more than one occasion, I woke up to learn that our family car had been stolen out of the driveway. And, after my next-door neighbor's house was robbed while she was gardening in her backyard, my parents only increased the frequency with which they reminded me that I was never truly safe, even when inside my own home.

Over time, I rarely felt safe in my body and in the world around me. With what felt like a constant threat of the illness, loss, or death of those on whom I was dependent for survival, I frequently lay in bed at night with fear and feelings of constriction in my chest. Over time, my body began to adopt a hunched-over posture during the day, protecting my vulnerable heart, despite regular reminders by my mom to stand up straight. Before too long, I embodied the LePera family mantra that there was always something to worry about, as I physically looked to be carrying the weight of the world on my shoulders. Soon, like both my parents', my body began to function mostly in survival mode. Constricted by fear and always bracing for the worst, I couldn't connect with my heart, even if I had known and wanted to. I simply didn't feel safe being seen or experienced by others, causing me to appear quiet and painfully shy to most of the outside world, hiding under tables when strangers visited or behind my mom's leg when out in public. To ease my deep-rooted fears, I continued to habitually suck my thumb (as I had in the womb) and bit my nails down to a painful length, despite being regularly teased by my family for doing so.

Throughout my teenage years and into my twenties, my body continued to prioritize my survival over all else. Disconnected from my body and physical heart, I was disconnected from my intuition. After decades of looking to others, I couldn't make even the smallest decisions in life, like deciding what to eat for lunch or how to fill a free hour of alone time. For so long, I had relied on others for cues as to what was expected of me. I had learned to depend on the validation I received as I tirelessly attempted to avoid disappointing others at all costs. Instinctually believing that my worth was based on how others experienced me, I continued to betray my authentic wants and needs in order to meet the imagined and often unrealistic expectations I placed on myself. Before long, my neurobiologically conditioned role of the Overachiever came so easily that it felt natural, as though it were part of my personality to act in ways that eroded my self-trust and self-esteem. I even obsessed over my performance while doing "enjoyable" things, like an art project, journaling, or picking out my outfit, judging myself for my paint choices, penmanship, or clothes.

At the same time, I genuinely believed that I was following my intuition as I avoided things that made me feel physically uncomfortable. Something else I had learned from my mom, who had come to believe that physical discomfort always signaled that something was wrong. For years, whenever I felt physically uncomfortable, even while exercising or stretching, I assumed that it meant I should stop. It wasn't until much later in life that I discovered that I almost always felt physically uncomfortable, with near-constant muscle tension and other troublesome sensations related to my body's chronic stress and nervous system dysregulation. When my heart rate and blood flow increased while I was more intensely exercising, I felt fearful, not empowered, because those sensations were similar to the ones I felt when I had a panic attack—and why, over time, I typically ended up avoiding most forms of even helpful rigorous aerobic exercise. I stopped doing anything that I wasn't immediately good at because I couldn't tolerate the emotional discomfort and frustration that often occurs while learning new things. Though she was well-meaning, my mom's choice to allow me to avoid uncomfortable activities only enabled me to come up with excuses instead of assisting me to build a much needed tolerance for stress and discomfort.

As I continued to see myself more clearly, I started to realize that I wasn't necessarily the kind, considerate person I had intuitively believed myself to be, always caring so much about what others thought. After I learned about the power of the human heart, I started to realize that I could never be truly compassionate if I remained closed off from my heart and continued to make choices based on my personal survival. Though, for me, connecting with others on an emotional level felt so unfamiliar and unsafe that I kept my heart cautiously locked away.

Being disconnected from my heart cut me off from my personal hobbies, interests, and even a fulfilling professional path. Though I'd always been a driven person—I knew from a young age that I wanted to be a psychologist—I felt passionless and purposeless. In my twenties, I read a book by Dr. Wayne Dyer, a fellow therapist, in which he described finding his passion and purpose in writing and teaching. When my partner, Lolly, told me that she frequently felt a passionate spark of curiosity and interest regarding certain topics or experiences, I began to think that maybe I hadn't been born with the "passion gene," if such a thing existed.

Now I can see that I was so detached from my heart that I was actually shut down to what truly lit me up. When I look back at my childhood, I can feel the spark of passion in a little girl who really enjoyed her dance classes, even though I had quit them, feeling uncomfortable in my body while realizing that I got more validation from other activities. I now see myself, as I see all of us, as a being filled with limitless creativity and a unique purpose who loves to share my thoughts and ideas with those around me. I'm filled with the same spark of passionate creation that makes each of us glow internally.

After my trip to Bali with Lolly, I knew that I had to reconnect with my heart. To do so, I would have to begin to regulate my nervous system; otherwise, I'd be too shut down to connect with anything inside me or anyone around me. Using many of the practices we've already covered, I started to soothe my nervous system, helping me feel physically safer. I started to witness my ego story, seeing when and how it colored my emotional experiences and caused my brain to override my heart's messages. I started to pay conscious attention when I felt compelled to make a decision based on what I thought other people wanted or needed from me. I even turned off the alerts on my phone so that I was less readily available to others or external obligations in general and more available to myself. If someone left me a message and I noticed myself feeling pressured to return the call immediately, I paused to connect with my heart. Doing so helped me shift out of my people-pleasing mode and gave me space to assess what I really wanted or needed in the moment. If I was stressed or overwhelmed, I reminded myself that I didn't have to return their call that minute; I gave myself permission to say no, take time and space, check in with and regulate myself, and choose when and how to respond. Becoming more conscious and intentional in choosing when and how I would show up for others, I was no longer driven to act in certain ways to maintain my relationships. And, if and when I felt guilty about those new choices, which is natural when we create new boundaries or dynamics within our relationships, I reminded myself that making sure I'm meeting my own needs is the most loving thing I could do for another person.

Recognizing how little tolerance I had for physical stress and emotional discomfort, I began to intentionally expose myself to slightly uncomfortable conditions like doing cold therapy. I started to take quick cold showers or submerge my hands in ice water for a few minutes at a time. When my body resisted the discomfort by constricting my muscles, I breathed slowly and deeply into the tension, teaching my body to feel safe through the stress. With consistent practice over time, I helped train my nervous system to recover more quickly from stress by widening my window of tolerance for both physical and emotional discomfort.

By that time, I had noticed how much I avoided being alone with myself. During my twenties, I had spent little time alone, having lived in crowded cities, with an active social life. I obsessively scheduled how I would spend my free time, keeping myself busy making plans with others. I easily remember the first time I went out to lunch by myself and worked through many different uncomfortable feelings. As I continued to increase my tolerance of discomfort through the daily choices I was making, I made it a priority to begin to carve out moments to sit still, alone.

At first that stillness was hard to tolerate, as it may also be for you: when we're in survival mode, we feel driven to keep moving as our body's fight-or-flight response activates—and if we can't move, we may freeze or shut down, detaching from our physical body so that we don't feel anything at all.

But if we can learn to take the time and consciously practice sitting still when we're *not* stressed, we'll become better at feeling our emotions rather than fighting, fleeing from, freezing or shutting down to them. Connecting in stillness with our body's sensations, though perhaps uncomfortable at first, trains our brain to sync with our heart. To rebuild my own heart-brain connection, I made time every day for months to sit still with myself and explore to what my heart was saying, setting a timer on my phone for five minutes and sometimes doing the heart-conscious meditation you'll learn about on page 196.

Over time, I began to see patterns in my heart's messages. Certain choices and relationships made my heart feel open and expansive, while others caused it to feel closed and constricted. When I spent time with certain friends, I realized that my heart didn't feel light and open, so I started to limit the time I put into sustaining those connections. At the same time, I began to hear the difficult messages my heart was sending me about my then wife, which eventually helped me make the tough decision to end our marriage.

I quickly started to notice how little I could tolerate moments of silence with others. In social situations, I'd jump in immediately to fill dead air, sharing surface-level observations or stories. For a long time, that habit had been my way of evading the discomfort I felt while at the same time allowing me to entertain others so they would enjoy their time with me. Becoming more comfortable in my own stillness and silence ended up helping me become more comfortable in stillness and silence with others. Instead of jumping in to fill a pause in a conversation, I practiced allowing myself the time to consider if there was something I really wanted to share, then taking the opportunity to speak from my heart and share deeper emotional experiences rather than entertaining distractions. Today, I continue this practice weekly when I record podcasts, resisting the urge to fill a moment of silence by shifting into "teaching mode," even though there are admittedly still times when the fear and shame of sharing my more vulnerable personal journey quicken my heart and cause tension in my muscles.

Becoming more connected to my heart changed my professional life as much as it did my personal one. Instead of continuing to see clients clinically, I realized that my real passion was to teach others how to create change and empower themselves on their own healing journeys. I decided to launch my Instagram account, which I initially created as a space to share my personal journey more authentically with others. Being vulnerable on social media wasn't easy at first, and I can remember many moments when I had to work through my long-lived, often intense discomfort of being seen, especially when learning a new skill, like speaking on camera. Gradually, I'm becoming better able to embrace the process of learning new things. By working through my resistance and choosing my new career path to help guide others, I now feel more professionally passionate and fulfilled than ever before. I enter my flow state more easily, with the environment around me falling out of focus when I start to write, teach, or speak, inspired instead by the deepest sense of inner knowing.

Today, I continue to use my FSJ every morning to remind myself of my daily intention to stay connected to my heart by affirming or writing the following: *"I am grounded in peace and loving awareness. My soul is aligned with my intentions and daily choices. Today, I choose to embody love."* I then spend a few more moments in silent reflection while I read from a spiritual or meditation book. I continue to check in with my heart intentionally and frequently throughout the day to embody gratitude, compassion, or love, accessing a state of heart coherence. There are still occasions, of course, when I feel overwhelmed or stressed and my nervous system becomes dysregulated—and that's to be expected since I'm human. In those moments, I practice calming my body so that I can reconnect with my heart again. When I do so, I feel more at peace and better able to express myself in both my career and my relationships. I feel safer and more secure when I'm away from my partners, knowing that we're still connected and I'm still loved. And I'm more frequently able to be vulnerable with them, too, sharing what's in my mind as well as in my heart. I'm finally able to relieve that age-old feeling of being alone in a crowded room.

HASSAN'S JOURNEY TO HEART CONSCIOUSNESS

When Hassan started seeing me as a client, he was anxiously trying to complete a postbaccalaureate in premedicine so that he could apply to medical school, even though he'd struggled to finish his undergraduate degree in biology. The oldest son of first-generation Indian Americans, he'd grown up with parents who had directed everything he was to do, including his future career, telling him that he *had* to become a doctor to bring pride and financial security to his family.

In addition to feeling daily anxiety over his professional path, Hassan struggled with his identity as a gay man. He felt deeply insecure being openly gay and hid the few short-lived same-sex relationships he had, even from those closest to him. He regularly felt depressed, hopeless, and numb, as though he were simply going through the motions of life. Though he desperately wanted a partner (and career) he loved, he was so detached from his heart, as well as from his body, that he had no idea how to connect with himself, let alone with another person.

Just as in my experience, Hassan's disconnection from his heart began in childhood. When he was young, his parents were critical of any interests or desires that differed from what they deemed acceptable. He loved making art, drawing in his room, and walking in the woods—not playing outside with friends or reading about biology. When his parents discovered that he was spending a lot of time drawing instead of studying, they accused him of being unmotivated and procrastinating, sometimes even punishing him for wasting hours on what they believed to be a futile hobby. In response, he started to hide his drawing books and not tell his parents about his walks in the woods, eventually hiding the other parts of himself he was afraid they'd shame. The older he got and the more pressure they placed on him, the more he tried to keep himself small and out of the way, hoping to avoid being noticed for his "flaws."

Over time, Hassan started to embody the Underachiever conditioned self, making himself invisible in his attempt to avoid criticism. Facing a consistent threat of judgment, his nervous system gradually began to shut down, creating the emotional numbness, emptiness, disconnection, and depression he regularly experienced.

Shortly after his tenth birthday, Hassan became consciously aware that he was gay. He didn't dare tell his family out of fear that they wouldn't accept him, which caused him to become even more secretive, always shrinking away or trying to remain in the background of family events.

Feeling shameful about every aspect of his identity, he started to show even less of himself, believing that who he was at his core—artistic, shy, woodsy, introspective, gay—wasn't good enough. Protecting himself from the deep-rooted shame he felt about his identity, he became more and more disconnected from himself and his feelings.

Although he was intelligent and a quick learner, Hassan was never able to fully apply himself in school, crippled by feelings of unworthiness, low self-esteem, and self-restraining habits that made him feel safest around his parents. He graduated from high school as a C student, unable to get into the college his parents had wanted him to attend. Going to a state school, Hassan struggled through biology—the major his parents had directed him toward—and was miserable. He had few friends and even fewer romantic partners. The relationships he did have were superficial, as he subconsciously refused to open himself up to others out of fear that they'd see all his flaws and imperfections. He pushed friends and partners away with self-deprecating humor, making himself the butt of jokes to appease the internal voice of criticism that he had developed during his earliest experiences with his parents.

When Hassan first began his healing journey, he felt depressed, unfulfilled, and hopeless, struggling through an intense degree program that he felt compelled to pursue for reasons he couldn't understand. He was so low-energy that he came across as cold or indifferent, not the sensitive and passionate young man who had existed before years of conditioning that eroded his self-worth.

After Hassan learned about polyvagal theory and the different nervous system states, he began to see how shut down he was. He started to wonder whether his depressive symptoms—apathy, lethargy, low mood—were the physiological signs of parasympathetic dominance caused by a slow heart rate, shallow breathing, sluggish digestion, and low energy production. To stimulate his nervous system, he began to experiment with Wim Hof breathing, cold showers, and vigorous exercise, running sprints at a nearby track. Those activities helped shift his nervous system out of parasympathetic dorsal dominance, boosting his energy and making him feel more awake, motivated, and present.

As he started to feel more alive again, his nervous system began to respond to stressful situations with more flexibility, initiating a fight-or-flight response when appropriate before returning to peace and calm. He began to feel safer in his body, which gave him the ability to witness his ego story—the one telling him to remain isolated and invisible, fearful that exposing his "flaws" would make him unworthy of connection and love. As he grew more confident in himself and his choices, he reminded himself that he was worthy and lovable for being exactly who he was.

With his newly developing body and mind consciousness, Hassan started to take moments throughout his day, especially when faced with an important decision, to pause and check in with his heart. He also consistently set aside just five minutes every day to sit in stillness and try to reconnect with his different physical sensations, paying attention to the area around his heart space. During that time, he would practice embodying feelings of care, compassion, and gratitude for himself or his loved ones (we'll discuss how to do this in a moment).

With time, Hassan noticed that his heart was sending him messages all the time. As he continued to practice heart consciousness, he was able to recognize and accept that he wasn't interested in studying medicine or becoming a doctor—no wonder the biology and premed courses had been so difficult! What lit him up instead was art and design, and for the first time since he was a little boy, he felt excited about something as he started researching jobs in graphic design. He began to rethink how he spent his free time, pulling away from the hobbies he thought he should pursue, like watching sports and going out to gay clubs, to focus on what he really enjoyed, including visiting museums and spending time in nature.

Reconnecting with his heart and intuition helped Hassan realize that he craved a deeper bond with his partners, parents, and friends. More physically comfortable in his body and less dependent on his ego story, he gradually felt safe enough to be vulnerable with them, sharing more of his authentic Self. When he did, he was surprised to discover that no one actually abandoned him. With his growing sense of confidence, he was able to ask for support from his loved ones and allow himself to begin to accept the love and care they had to offer. He was compassionate and patient with himself as he gradually started to open his heart. And over time, he actually even to become more comfortable opening himself up to finding and connecting with others in relationships that better aligned with his true nature.

YOUR JOURNEY TO HEART CONSCIOUSNESS

Developing heart consciousness takes time. It's not something you can accomplish by following a quick checklist. Everyone's journey is different, though everyone will have to regulate your nervous system first. Otherwise, your nervous system will remain in a stressed state and you won't be able to sync your brain with your heart, no matter what you do. All of the practices we explored in chapter 5 will help you begin to regulate your nervous system, increasing your HRV and heart coherence. Any other self-care practice that you enjoy, whether it's journaling, doing yoga, or taking a warm bath in candlelight, can also help you better manage stress, boost your HRV, and reconnect with your heart.

To develop heart consciousness, you'll need to learn how to sit still with yourself so you can listen to your heart. I know from personal experience how difficult it can be to relax into stillness, sit with yourself to connect with your heart, and channel feelings like appreciation and gratitude, especially when you feel sad, upset, or lonely. For years, my body struggled to rest or relax most of the time, let alone embody core heart feelings; I often felt physically and emotionally incapable of doing so. If you feel the same way, there's nothing wrong with you, and you're not broken. Creating safety for your nervous system will help you access these core heart emotions and the more time you spend practicing, the more frequently you'll be able to experience them.

Awaken Your Heart Exercise

The following exercise will help you reconnect with your heart's energy so you can strengthen the pathway of communication between your heart and brain so you can attune to its intuitive signals. It's helpful to practice this heart-activating exercise daily or as consistently as possible, even (and especially) when you feel stressed. Because many of you may understandably find it difficult to extend core heart feelings to those with whom we have had a difficult experience or relationship, it'll be helpful to have patience with yourself along the way. The more consistently you practice, the more connected with your heart you'll feel, regardless of your circumstances.

1. Find a place to lie down or sit comfortably for a few moments. If you feel safe doing so, you may choose to close your eyes.

2. Take a few slow, deep breaths. As you feel your body begin to settle, take a moment to allow your shoulders to relax, with your shoulder blades rolled down your back. Let your arms hang by your sides, with your palms facing in front of you. Allow your chest and heart to open.

3. Begin to turn your attention to the area around your heart, breathing fully and deeply into your chest space; it may be helpful to imagine a golden or yellow light shining out from your heart. If you feel comfortable or called to do so, you may even choose to place a hand over your heart to feel its powerful beat.

4. Spend the next few moments calling to mind someone or something in your life that creates a feeling of unconditional love (whether it's a person, pet, experience, or anything else) as you invite a feeling of compassion and love to come into your heart.

5. When you feel yourself beginning to embody compassion and love, explore and note how its healing energy feels within

you. Practice coming back to this place as many times as you can throughout your day and extending this feeling outward to your loved ones, and the world around you, reminding yourself that love is your true nature.

There is a guided version of this practice available at:

INTUITION CHECK-IN

The more consistently you practice connecting with your heart, the more likely you will be able to hear the intuitive messages from your authentic Self. The following exercise can help you create a habit of pausing to connect with your heart, giving you the space to begin to attune to its signals. Consistently connecting with your heart will help you tap into and use your inner wisdom to better understand and guide your choices throughout the day.

- Pause for a moment and begin to breathe slowly and fully into your heart space, placing your hands on your chest if it feels safe and helpful to do so.
- Start to focus your attention on the area of your heart as you actively listen and ask yourself, "What is my heart saying to me?" Practice remaining open and curious to whatever it is you notice and keeping your attention focused on your body without trying to force or apply words or logic to describe what you are feeling.
- If you have a specific question or are looking for guidance about making a certain decision, take a few moments to imagine each of the different possibilities or outcomes and ask yourself, "How does my heart feel about this possibility or outcome? Does my

heart feel expansive, light, and airy, indicating a 'yes' to this possibility or outcome? Or does my heart feel constricted, tight, and fearful, indicating a 'no' to this possibility or outcome?"

- You may find it helpful to take a few moments after this practice to journal your thoughts and feelings without judging your answers, noting whatever came into your awareness.

Heart-Conscious Listening Exercise

The more you can attune to your heart, the more connected you'll be to your inner guidance when you are interacting with others or within your relationships. Listening with your heart means you're truly present to hear and connect with what someone is saying without thinking about how you'll respond or being distracted by something else entirely. Begin to pay attention to how often you actively listen to others when they are communicating with noting the steps below:

- Begin to consistently check in and witness your listening habits throughout the day.

- Notice how often you get lost in your own thoughts when someone is speaking to you. When you non-judgmentally notice yourself becoming distracted by the thoughts in your mind, practice turning your attention back to your heart, maybe even placing a hand on your chest to help shift your focus back to your body.

- Breathing slowly and fully from your heart space, practice fully listening to the words and experiences of another person while noticing any shifts or changes in the sensations in your heart.

*   *   *

As you begin your journey, remember that developing a consistent practice of heart consciousness can take time—weeks, months, or even years, depending on how disconnected you are now and how consistently you practice these tools. You also likely won't be able to remain in heart consciousness or heart coherence consistently for the rest of your life; connecting with and following your heart is a moment-to-moment journey that changes depending on what's happening around you and within your body. Though the more consistently you're able to create the safety you need to reconnect with your heart, the more often you'll be able to hear its messages and make choices in your life and relationships that are guided by intuition, compassion, and love. It is only when we are connected to our own heart that we can authentically connect with another's. And it is only when we are connected to our own heart that we can truly *be the love we seek*, through a practice called co-regulation we'll talk about next.

8

BECOMING THE LOVE YOU SEEK

It's happening over and over again. Alejandra thought. For the last year, anytime she brought up the topic of moving in with her partner, Luca, he changed the subject or reached for his phone, making excuses about a work email or last-minute text he had forgotten to send. His avoidant behavior continued to hurt her, but after four years together, it didn't surprise her: It was Luca's MO to avoid difficult conversations, deflecting or distracting when things got too close. He behaved the same way when she shared her feelings with him, and she could see how much he struggled to communicate his own feelings, especially if they were upsetting. When he felt irritated or sad, rather than expressing what was wrong, he'd usually make passive-aggressive or snarky comments instead.

Though Alejandra loved Luca, his unwillingness to share his emotions, talk about their relationship, or explore difficult topics created a push-pull dynamic between them, with Alejandra always pushing Luca to engage or share, which only caused him to pull away further. When she had first brought up the topic of marriage with him, stating that she wanted it for herself without any direct reference to him, he had immediately changed the subject to a divorced coworker who was now dating much younger women, causing Alejandra to storm out of the restaurant. Maybe, just maybe, she could understand if she had talked about marriage after only six months together, but the conversation had taken place after they'd been dating for more than two years. *Two years!* she thought. They fought the rest of the night, and the incident created tension between them and touchiness that remained around the entire subject of marriage.

The couple stayed stuck in that cycle for several years, until Alejandra began to regulate her nervous system and break the dysfunctional habits that stemmed its dysregulation. She started to notice how threatened she felt when Luca changed the subject or mentally checked out when she broached any topic related to their relationship or shared her feelings about what was happening between the two of them. Over time, she learned to practice taking slow, deep breaths and feeling her feet firmly grounded on the floor or her body supported by the earth under her. If she struggled to calm herself in Luca's presence, she'd excuse herself to use the bathroom until she felt grounded enough to reengage, limiting the times she stormed out of his presence or lobbed hurtful accusations at him.

The more compassion Alejandra developed for herself during those difficult moments, the more understanding and compassion she had for others, including Luca. In learning how her childhood trauma continued to activate emotionally immature coping strategies in herself, she began to see how Luca's upbringing had made upsetting feelings and conversations not only difficult but also frightening for him.

Luca grew up with an academically gifted older brother and a younger sister who was a violin prodigy. As the middle child without an immediately obvious talent, he was both overlooked and criticized by his parents, who often asked him, "Why don't you do well in school like your brother? Don't you want to be good at something like your sister?" Luca often felt ignored, discounted, and ultimately unworthy at his core.

Overwhelmed by feelings his parents didn't help him navigate, Luca started to distract himself in any way he could. At a young age he discovered alcohol, which helped ease the deep pain he felt, especially after he was sexually abused while hanging out with a group of older kids. Despite his increasing need for support, he avoided spending time at home, where he felt the worst about himself around his parents and "perfect" siblings. He started regularly staying out late with friends, partying, and getting into trouble. When his parents tried to talk with him about his low grades or seeming lack of motivation, he tuned them out by turning up the music in his room or made excuses about being hungry or having a headache. In his heart, he wasn't a deflector or a liar, but his inner child was so hurt that he was willing to do anything to avoid confrontation, criticism, and, ultimately, more humiliation. Feeling unsafe with most types of physical and emotional closeness, he kept his relationships casual to avoid feeling too exposed and activating the deep-rooted shame he inevitably felt as intimacy began to develop.

When Alejandra realized all the ways in which Luca's past trauma was driving his current behavior, she began to empathize with him rather than getting angry, upset, or hurt when he distracted or deflected during hard moments. She saw that it wasn't that he didn't care about her or their future together, as she had previously believed, but that his nervous system was activated, causing him to feel physically threatened and unsafe. He never learned how to navigate or tolerate tough emotions or difficult conversations and was often in Distractor Mode, one of the four common stress responses we explored in chapter 3. Distracting himself was how he had coped with his body's threat-based state ever since he had been a little boy, and his reaction to Alejandra in such moments had little to do with her and more to do with how his nervous system was wired.

With a growing compassion for Luca, Alejandra was able to use a different approach to these activating interactions. The solution wasn't to stop having difficult conversations with him; it was important that she express her feelings and desires. But she now knew that timing was everything when she brought up a threatening subject; if Luca's nervous system was already activated because he'd had a long day, hadn't slept well the night before, or had recently spoken to or seen his family, he'd likely shut down altogether if she tried to have a conversation that he'd perceive as stressful.

At the same time, no amount of strategic timing could prevent Luca from feeling uncomfortable when the conversation became challenging and from trying to distract himself to avoid physical and emotional discomfort it caused him. Now Alejandra didn't take his reaction personally. Instead, she brought her nervous system back to safety if she felt activated by his reaction, trying to remain calm while having difficult conversations with him.

Practicing nervous system regulation in real time enabled Alejandra to help them both have tough talks and deeper conversations: she began to co-regulate with Luca, using the safety of her nervous system to help his nervous system relax into safety without saying a word. This is possible because co-regulation, which has been studied for decades by psychologists and developmental specialists, occurs largely through the unseen signals that our body sends those around us.

In moments of acute stress, Alejandra started to attune to Luca when she knew his nervous system was activated. Safely grounded in her body and its calm energy, she could feel his energy shift and notice when he was physically tense, visibly fidgeting, or had turned away from her, all indicators of the beginning of his stress response. In those moments, she would pause and check in with him to see if he had noticed his energy shift, too. If he seemed somewhat open and receptive to sharing, she might even ask how their conversation was making him feel.

At first, Luca struggled to answer those questions, but over time, Alejandra's ability to help him feel safer allowed him to begin to open up to her. Instead of believing that she was always angry or irritated with him, he started to feel as though she, too, was softening and was even able to understand and be with him in his discomfort. Co-regulating in this way helped both of them create the safety they each individually needed to explore their emotions together and defuse the threat Luca often inherently felt in their conversations.

As time went on, Alejandra began to suggest ways that they could work together to help bring Luca's body back to safety. During one conversation when he was particularly open and receptive, she suggested that they practice breathwork together by taking five slow, deep belly breaths. Other times, they hugged or put their hands on each other's heart until they both felt more relaxed. If he began to feel overwhelmed or uncomfortable during those practices, she would suggest that they take a break until they both felt comfortable to begin again.

By practicing co-regulation and beginning to deepen their conversations and increase the security of their connection, Alejandra and Luca were eventually able to create a timeline to move in together that felt safe and doable to each. They set boundaries in advance of living together, which helped them both feel more comfortable with the prospect. Alejandra supported Luca going out every Friday with his friends, since socializing was still a big part of his life, while Luca reserved Saturdays for date nights with her. They compromised that one room in their new place would be entirely his, where he could be as messy as he wanted without her attention or criticism. Five years later, Alejandra and Luca are still living together, sharing deeper conversations and an authentic connection, as they continue to co-create safety when needed.

Co-regulation, as we'll see in this chapter, won't solve all your relationship problems. And it won't help you pry open an emotionally shutdown person; that person has to take responsibility and make a conscious choice to show up differently in the relationship in order to create true and lasting change. But when two people are willing to do a little work together, this practice can significantly shift their relationship dynamics, even those that may have been stuck or dysfunctional for years.

Let's take a deeper dive.

THE POWER OF CO-REGULATION

Humans are relational beings. It's part of our evolutionary nature to relate to and connect with other people. We're part of a complex, communal ecosystem in which we're physically, emotionally, and neurobiologically reliant on one another. Our social brain is both dependent on and wired by other people in more ways than most of us realize. Throughout our life, the people around us, especially those with whom we spend the most time, impact the health of our nervous system and vice versa.

When two people are in proximity, their bodies communicate directly and continuously with each other, even though they remain physically separated by skin and air. Known as the *social synapse*, this communication is similar to the way our brain cells "speak" to one another, which is called the *neural synapse*. In the case of the neural synapse, our neurons send electrical and chemical messages through the gaps between them.

While social interactions include "seen" signals, like words, facial expressions, and sounds, the majority of the way we communicate with one another is through unseen signals that are electrical, biochemical, hormonal, energetic, and emotional in nature, all occurring outside our conscious awareness. Even if we're not talking, looking, or directly interacting with someone else, our bodies constantly emit hormones, pheromones, electromagnetic energy, and neural impulses that impact each individual's state of nervous system regulation.

You've likely detected these unseen signals if you've ever walked into a room and sensed that something was off or wrong with someone else, even if they didn't explicitly say or do anything to suggest it. You picked up on their nervous system energy and other biochemical and hormonal signals. Or maybe you've turned around after feeling someone else's watchful gaze or attentional presence, only to catch them looking your way, a phenomenon verified by research.[47] These unseen signals play a role in creating our instinctual feelings or those that we sense without rational cause.

Many of us react to others based on seen signals—that is, what someone else directly says or does. But we'd be able to reduce far more conflict within our relationships if we started paying attention to their unseen signals as well.

Unseen signals have helped us as humans stay safe for eons, enabling our ancient ancestors to communicate danger to others in the same family or group without having to speak, yell, or make visible or audible gestures that could attract the attention of predators or warring parties. In modern times, unseen signals still serve the same purpose, alerting those around us that danger is imminent or nearby when we don't feel safe enough to communicate that information directly. Remember, our hearts emit powerful unseen electromagnetic signals that can transmit messages of safety, so much so that playing a parent's recorded heartbeat to their baby can reduce the baby's crying by 40 to 50 percent.[48]

Though unseen signals are evolutionarily advantageous, they don't always work in our favor when it comes to our relationships. If our nervous system is stuck in a stress response and our heart is emitting stressful or incoherent energy, our body will communicate stress, tension, and danger to those around us, even if the only threat is our stressed body. Whatever the cause, those around us will receive and absorb our stress signals, causing them to feel physically unsafe and possibly activating their own stress response. Then, as in a game of table tennis, we'll keep lobbying danger signals back and forth, ratcheting up the collective stress level.

Here's the thing: love has to feel safe in order for us to be open to receiving it. But the reality for many of us is that the only version of "love" we experienced as children did not consistently *feel* safe. Because trauma bonds are neurobiologically conditioned and familiar, we continue to seek safety in habitual patterns, regardless of how unsafe they continue to make us and those around us feel. With few of us ever feeling peaceful and at ease, we stay stuck in cycles of stress reactivity, often acting like cornered animals with each other, creating or escalating conflict rather than joining together in truly loving and collaborative relationships.

We can, however, begin to harness the power of co-regulation, the interpersonal and physiological process of using the state of our nervous system to connect and shift the physiological state of another's nervous system. Simply put, we can use our body's calm and relaxing energy to help the bodies around us to feel more calm and relaxed in our presence.

Let's say you're out for a celebratory dinner with your sibling after you just got a promotion when you make a comment that your meal was cold or bland. Your sibling, who picked the restaurant and has been looking forward to taking you out, suddenly feels that you're criticizing their choice and, fearing that you will be upset the rest of the dinner, starts to act in ways that could end up ruining the night. They freeze up and become quiet, distracted, and uninterested in their food (a common sign of the freeze or shutdown response is loss of appetite because of our slowed digestion).

Though you may not feel that their reaction is justified or even that big a deal, it doesn't matter to your body; your nervous system will sense their stress, possibly activating your own stress response. You may go into fight mode and get angry at them for "overreacting," snapping at them to stop being so sensitive. Or you may go into fawn mode and start asking every several minutes if everything is okay, offering to share your dinner, or bringing up subjects that usually excite them. No matter how your nervous system reacts, your body and theirs will continue to volley stress signals back and forth, increasing the overwhelm for both of you, causing your sibling to shut down and withdraw even more and you to dial up your yelling or appeasing. Pretty soon, dinner is unbearable and your night out together is actually ruined.

Practicing body consciousness and co-regulation could have helped you recognize what was happening in real time and possibly change the outcome of the evening. When you first noticed that you were activated at the restaurant—your jaw started to clench, your breath quickened, or your heart began to pound, indicating a fight-or-flight response—you could have taken a few slow, deep belly breaths, turned your attention to the feeling of your feet supported by the floor under the table, and told yourself that you were safe. You could have reminded yourself that your sibling's learned perfectionism has nothing to do with you and is a stored trauma response and coping strategy developed as their best attempt to stay safe in your overly critical family environment.

By helping yourself feel physically and emotionally safe, you no longer have to become overwhelmed by your sibling's stress and can avoid your habitual tendency to snap at them or hound them about what's wrong. Instead, you change the climate of unseen stress signals reverberating around the table, creating physical and emotional safety for you both. Although there are other verbal and physical ways to co-regulate in such a situation (we'll talk about these later in the chapter), the work described here is all nonverbal.

Don's experience offers another example of how co-regulation can work. After beginning to work from home during the covid pandemic, Don adopted a new meditation routine. Every day during his lunch hour, he meditated for ten minutes usually alone in his bedroom. One afternoon, though, he decided to meditate in the living room where his toddler son was playing. For the rest of the day and evening, he noticed that his son was calmer and had fewer tantrums. That was when Don decided to experiment and meditate every afternoon near his son, which produced the same results fairly consistently as the boy's body absorbed his father's peaceful, calm nervous system energy. When Don added a second short meditation practice before his son's bedtime, the boy had an easier time falling asleep. If meditation isn't part of your routine, we can co-regulate with others when engaging in other forms of regulatory behaviors, like gentle stretching, rhythmic swaying, or joyful dancing with them.

It can be particularly helpful to practice intentional co-regulation whenever there's conflict or tension in a relationship. One partner can suggest to take a pause from the conversation to create safety by doing breathwork together or holding each other until they're both relaxed. If hugging feels too intimate or uncomfortable, you can hold hands, sit next to each other in silence, or gaze into each other's eyes.

For many people, touch and direct eye contact can feel unsafe, so it's helpful to experiment to find what's most comfortable for you and your loved ones. We'll continue to explore more ways to co-regulate with others at the end of this chapter.

CO-REGULATION BEGINS IN CHILDHOOD

As infants and young children, we experienced soothing co-regulation if our parent-figures regularly smiled, gave us loving looks, used calming voices, hugged or cuddled us, and were consistently in a parasympathetic state when they interacted with us. When we became stressed or distressed and our nervous system was activated into fight, flight, or freeze or shutdown mode, our parent-figures (often unknowingly) used the safety of their own nervous system to bring ours back to a calmer, more receptive state.

If we experienced consistent moments of soothing co-regulation, we learned over time that we could trust our parent-figures, predicting and relying on their ability to provide us comfort and support. Physiologically, research shows that infants who receive this attunement and emotional security from their mothers have increased vagal tone for up to five years afterward (mothers who co-regulate with their children have better vagal tone, too)[49] and young children have lower coristol levels.[50]

Of course, no parent can be present and attuned to us all the time. Studies show that if our parent-figures co-regulated with us for just 30 percent of the occasions when we needed them, we grew up somewhat regulated or securely attached.[51] If they were unable to soothe us during an upsetting experience, initiating a repair process (something we'll talk more about in the next chapter) after they themselves were regulated increased our chances for a secure attachment. But very few of us received these consistent, soothing co-regulation or needed moments of repair.

Most of us instead grew up without an emotionally attuned parent, and as a result, we never learned to feel truly safe or secure in our body or relationships. Though many of us may have received loving looks and occasional hugs from Mom or Dad, if those looks and hugs went away when there was conflict or other overwhelming emotions in the home, we likely didn't receive comfort or support when we needed it most. That created fear, confusion, and emotional inconsistency or insecurity for us as children, and, as a result, we never learned how to regulate our own emotions. Today, as adults, we're likely still emotionally underdeveloped and unable to self-regulate, often reacting to current conflicts, stress, or other emotional upset in the same ways we did as children. Some of us try to avoid conflict and discomfort altogether, sometimes "ghosting" others to flee from any possible upsetting interactions rather than communicating directly. Others sulk and stomp away from conversations when we don't get our way or fall silent, completely ignoring those around us.

Even the most well-meaning parent-figures who desperately wanted to help us weren't able to actually soothe us unless their bodies first felt safe to them. When I was young, my mom was rarely able to soothe me because she never felt safe in her pain-ridden body. Instead, I absorbed her dysregulation and cycled through my own nervous system stress responses. Any slight discomfort would immediately throw me into fight-or-flight mode. Without the emotional resilience or tools to cope with this constant physical agitation, I grew up running around the house and "bouncing off the walls," as my mom described it, trying to discharge my overwhelming energetic discomfort. Looking back, I think that my agitated energy, coupled with the lack of healthy coping tools in my family, was a big reason why I was funneled into countless after-school programs and activities, which were a socially approved, even celebrated outlet for my pent-up energy.

When I wasn't busy and going seven days a week, as my mom characterized it, I would complain about how bored I was and nag others to play with me. I said it so often that it became a family joke. Sadly for me, none of us knew that for my dysregulated body, "I'm bored" really meant "I'm feeling uncomfortable on my own right now and need to feel connection or support."

As a child, I could easily erupt in anger and start yelling viciously, usually at my mom over some disappointed expectation, like an imperfection in the ponytail she combed into my hair while I got ready for school. "I hate you!" I would scream. Without a calming presence available, my emotions were often out of control, so much so that one morning I accidentally broke my little toe while storming down the hallway after seeing myself in the mirror.

Sometimes I even acted out in the presence of apparent support. During one softball game, while I was pitching a particularly difficult inning, my mom tried to shout helpful advice from the sidelines where she always sat. Unable to tolerate the discomfort I felt at being seen while underperforming, I shot her a deadly glare from the middle of the pitching mound, not caring who saw me, even though nearly everyone watching the game did. In that moment, I felt so threatened by and ashamed of my visible imperfections, I didn't care how I appeared to anyone else. I was dysregulated and emotionally pushing my mom away from me to try to manage the overwhelming shame I was feeling.

Over time, my stress and related emotional dysregulation became so consistent that my nervous system eventually shifted into shutdown mode, making it almost impossible for me to connect with or co-regulate with anyone else. By the time I became an adult, I routinely exceeded my body's internal resources and increased its *allostatic load*, or the cumulative effects of chronic stress. Unable to relax by myself or co-regulate with others, I rarely slept and suffered chronic digestive issues that only further depleted my physical and emotional resources. As my stress cycles continued and increased in frequency, I relied on my learned childhood coping strategies, distracting myself by staying constantly busy and eventually by using substances to try to manage my feelings and numb my deep-rooted pain.

After becoming aware of my body's conditioned habits, I started to regulate my nervous system. Gradually, I had to teach myself not only to feel safe within my own body but to feel safe enough to open myself up to co-regulating with others. I practiced consciousness check-ins (see page 58) by assessing my body's stress levels throughout the day, especially if I noticed a shift or change in my heart rate, breathing, or muscle tension. I started to recognize when my body was reacting to perceived stress in either my external or internal world, giving me the space and opportunity to make new choices about how I coped with it.

When I noticed that I felt internally agitated, which would normally have caused me to emotionally erupt, say mean things, or distract myself, I paused to check in with my body instead of allowing my autopilot brain to determine my next action. If I noticed myself pushing people away or being emotionally cold or distant with them, I created the space to connect with them instead of isolating myself, if I had the energetic resources. And, if I didn't have the energetic resources, I directly communicated as much and acknowledged my need for time and space before reconnecting. Whenever I noticed this hyper-independence reflected in my mind, noticing thoughts like *I don't need them* or *I can and will take care of myself*, I paused to remind myself that I do want to be open to receive support and connection from others.

Pausing doesn't always prevent me from doing what I feel compelled or habituated to do, but it does give me the opportunity to make a different decision. In the moments when I return to old habits, I give myself the gift of grace and loving compassion, reminding myself that every new moment offers me a new opportunity to practice *being* the love I seek.

HOW TO KNOW WHEN OTHERS ARE ACTIVATED

Fight, flight, freeze or shutdown, and fawn modes produce similar outward behaviors. If you're able to recognize when you're in one of these stress responses, you'll likely also be able to tell when someone else is. In chapter 3, we talked about the stress modes associated with the four stress responses: Eruptor for fight, Distractor for flight, Detacher for freeze or shutdown, and Pleaser for fawn. Anyone can shift into Eruptor, Distractor, Detacher, or Pleaser mode some, most, or all the time, depending on whom they're with and what's happening around or within them.

To help you identify which nervous system state others may be in, take some time to answer the following questions. If you believe that a particular response best describes your loved one, consider how often (and when) they react this way, which can provide clues to help you recognize when the person shifts into a threat-based state in the future. If you find it helpful, write down your answers in a separate notebook or journal.

Eruptor mode (fight response). An Eruptor focuses most of their attention outward. They may scream, yell, storm out, throw things, or slam doors. They may also attempt to dominate or control the conversation by overpowering others or the room with the volume or content of their speech. They may appear calm on the outside but be seething on the inside, wavering on the verge of eruption. When you're around an Eruptor, you may feel scared or as though you're walking on eggs, waiting for the next outburst.

How often (and when) do I feel as though I might say or do the wrong thing, shifting my loved one's mood almost instantly?

_____

_____

How often (and when) do I feel as though my loved one's anger or upset takes up all the emotional energy in the room?

_____

_____

How often (and when) do I hold back on sharing my feelings, beliefs, or opinions for fear of how my loved one will react?

_____

_____

Distractor mode (flight response). A Distractor focuses most of their attention on anything other than difficult or upsetting experiences happening around them. They may be a workaholic, have an endless to-do list, obsessively use technology or watch TV, numb themselves with substances, or keep themselves constantly busy. Sometimes, a Distractor is a Super Mom, Super Boss, or Super Partner—the one who keeps everything running but is otherwise emotionally absent. When you're around a Distractor, you may feel disconnected or ignored (unless you're actively engaged in the same distraction, e.g., work, alcohol, chores, and so on).

How often (and when) does my loved one tend to be busy, going from one thing to the next?

_____

_____

How often (and when) do I want to connect with my loved one but end up feeling a lack of attention or presence from them when we're together?

_____

_____

How often (and when) does my loved one spend their free time playing video games, scrolling on social media, or focusing on another activity that keeps their attention glued to an external source and away from our interactions?

_____

_____

Detacher mode (freeze or shutdown response). A Detacher focuses most of their attention inward. They're not actively erupting or distracting; instead, they don't appear to be feeling or be connected to much of anything. Though the response can be difficult to identify since a Detacher is often physically present and can even appear to be actively engaged, they're emotionally empty, distant, or aloof. When you're around a Detacher, you may feel distant or shut out, no matter what you do or say and may also feel consistently rejected when you attempt to emotionally connect.

How often (and when) do I find myself pleading for my loved one to tell me what they're thinking or feeling?

_____

_____

How often (and when) do I feel emotionally disconnected from or shut out by my loved one?

_____

_____

How often (and when) do I feel rejected or criticized when sharing new interests or experiences with my loved one?

_____

_____

Pleaser mode (fawn response). A Pleaser focuses most of their attention on trying to make others happy. They're always anticipating what someone might want, attempting to meet others' needs, showing up in service of others, or actively avoiding conflict. A Pleaser doesn't often know or say what they want and remains deferential to other people's opinions. When you're around a Pleaser, you may feel overwhelmed, emotionally suffocated, or resentful.

How often (and when) do I witness my loved one doing things because their family or friends are telling them they need to do so?

_____

_____

How often (and when) does my loved one come to me to seek something (validation, emotional support, soothing contact), and how often do I feel comfortable or safe seeking the same from my loved one?

_____

_____

How often (and when) do I witness that my loved one says or does something in order to keep the peace or keep other people happy, often resulting in more conflict in the long run?

_____

_____

Being able to notice when our loved ones are dysregulated can help us bring them back to safety by using the co-regulation tools below. The practice can also help us depersonalize their behaviors, knowing that their reactions are a reflection of their felt lack of safety rather than a reaction to us.

LEARNING TO CO-REGULATE

Just because we didn't experience consistently soothing co-regulation as children doesn't mean we can't learn to practice it as adults. To start, it's helpful to know when our nervous system is dysregulated. If we don't feel safe, we won't be able to help anyone else feel safe, no matter what we do. Instead, we'll have the opposite effect, sending them messages of stress and danger, whether through unseen signals or seen ones, like angry looks or hurtful or passive-aggressive comments.

When we recognize that our nervous system is activated, we can help our loved ones feel safe by removing ourselves from their presence. If we have to or want to be around them, we can make a conscious effort to bring our nervous system back to safety by practicing the self-soothing techniques covered in earlier chapters, including intentional breathing, grounding, and reminding ourselves that their behavior may be based in their past trauma, not present reality. We can also, of course, always ask them to help us co-regulate if they are grounded and safe in their own body.

As we continue to regulate our own nervous systems, we'll become less likely to get stuck in a stress response. Like we've already explored, we can begin by prioritizing nutrient-rich foods while limiting inflammatory ones; moving our body regularly in ways that nourish us; getting enough good-quality sleep; increasing our capacity to tolerate physical and emotional discomfort; witnessing our ego stories of unworthiness; and connecting with our heart whenever possible. These choices help increase our stress resiliency, giving us the ability to tolerate a greater degree of upsetting or uncomfortable experiences without becoming overly activated and reactive or distracting from and avoiding them entirely. The more stress we can learn to tolerate, the less likely we are to project our anger or blame onto others, feel ashamed of our reactions, or suppress our Self expression.

In my own life, I had to learn how to tolerate the fear and discomfort I felt when I was physically distant or perceived myself to be emotionally distant from a loved one, especially in my romantic relationships. If I sensed a break in my connection to a partner or perceived that they were upset with me, I assumed I was likely to blame, a presumption that caused my body to tense up and my ego story of how unconsidered I was to flood my mind. Physically and emotionally, I was taken back to the young girl who had been emotionally abandoned by her mother. Without the words to describe the memory, my body enacted my deep pain in uncomfortable embodied sensations and behavioral reactions.

As I became a conscious witness to these sensations and reactions, I started to teach myself that not all distance in relationships is bad.

In fact, some distance is necessary to create relational balance. Every human being needs time and space in solitude away from others to recharge and replenish their individual energy stores, even if only for a few moments at a time.

Starved for emotional connection, I noticed a related pattern of forcing myself to be receptive to others whenever they were available for or desiring connection and shaming myself for the moments when I didn't feel open or available, for whatever reason. I am now learning to allow myself these moments of desired space to enjoy *being* in my own presence by listening to calming music through headphones, driving myself to the lake for a few hours, or even taking a solo staycation at a nearby hotel. I'm learning ways that I can support myself emotionally, too, even if it's just by going on a walk or taking a bath when I feel internal agitation (those moments when I'd proclaim "I'm bored" from years ago) instead of looking to others to blame or expecting them to help me feel better. I can now see these moments for what they are, an indicator that I may need some time alone to soothe and reconnect with myself before I can more fully connect with those around me.

Soothing ourselves, or finding our way back to safety, whether alone or by co-regulating with another person, is foundational to the embodiment of true compassion. Whenever we feel unsafe or threatened, we become hyper-focused on ourselves, seeing experiences only from our own perspective and as they relate to our immediate survival. As a result, we can end up acting in ways that hurt those around us. The same is true of those we love, and if we can learn to have grace and compassion for ourselves, we can extend it even to those that have hurt us. The harmful things they reactively do when they feel scared, stressed, overwhelmed, or angry don't reflect who they truly are, either.

Compassion is an embodied response that's dependent on nervous system regulation and safety. To feel true compassion for others and to want to support them in their suffering, we must first be able to feel or attune to their suffering. To emotionally attune to others, we have to be able to climb out of our own body's survival state so that we can see the experience from their perspective. We can do this only when our body feels safe enough to allow our mind to shift its attentional focus away from our own experiences. Extending compassion and patience to ourselves while we develop this new practice of embodying safety is especially important for those of us for whom safety itself is an unfamiliar experience. As with anything unfamiliar, both our body and our mind will try to resist these new experiences and attempt to return to their familiar, more stressful habits as we venture into the threatening unknown.

Embodying safety and compassion is particularly helpful in moments of active stress or conflict. If we can stay calm and grounded within our body, we're better able to depersonalize other's stress reaction, understanding it as the threat-based adaptation it is. As a result, we're less likely to scream back, force them to connect, or shake them out of it, knowing that these types of behaviors will likely only escalate their internal stress level and we'll be more likely to respond compassionately.

How can we create safety when someone else is upset? We have three options when we know someone's nervous system is activated in a stress response:

1. **We can hold space for them** while consciously reframing our experience of the situation so that we don't take their mood, words, or reactions personally. Understanding they're in a stress response often allows us to remain compassionate and responsive to their pain. We're less likely to become reactive ourselves and more likely to be able to join them in their emotional experience.

2. **We can remove ourselves from their presence** until they're regulated. This is often the best approach for someone in Eruptor mode. To remove yourself without being condescending or dismissive, you can say, "I need to take a break from this interaction or experience right now." Though doing so may further aggravate someone in Eruptor mode, especially if they're already activated, it's critical to communicate to them that maintaining your own safety is a priority for you. And remember, if you ever begin to

feel that you're in physical, emotional, or sexual danger, it is important to call emergency services.

3. **We can co-regulate** using the techniques already explored and those that you'll learn more about now.

ACTIVELY CO-REGULATING WITH OTHERS

Our ability to co-regulate with others on an ongoing basis is the foundation of emotional safety and security within our relationships. If we were modeled emotional reactivity or disconnection in childhood, we may find it difficult to remain connected to others during times of disagreement or perceived conflict. But we can develop this "felt" emotional trust over time by consistently repairing or returning to emotional safety and connection after conflict occurs. This return to a safe and secure connection is foundationally important, especially for children, who are often left confused, alone, and overwhelmed by reactive or explosive emotions, like being yelled at or given the silent treatment when a parent is upset.

While much of co-regulation happens largely through our body's unseen signals and our own nervous system safety, we can begin to intentionally choose to actively co-regulate with others by hugging, holding hands, exchanging loving looks, sitting close-by in shared silence, or practicing the heart-centered exercise on page 220.

If you choose to co-regulate with another person, it's important to anticipate some possible resistance, especially if they're unfamiliar with the concept. To introduce the practice, it's helpful to have a conversation with your loved one when they're not actively upset, asking if they'd be willing to practice during future times of conflict or stress. Below are some basic facts about this practice, which you can share with your loved one to help them understand the power and potential of co-regulation.

FIVE FACTS ABOUT CO-REGULATION

- Our body is wired to connect with others.
- Co-regulation is a process that helps provide us with the safety we need to feel open to connect.
- Our body's nervous system communicates with other people's nervous systems through electrical, hormonal, and energetic signals that we can't see.
- When we struggle to soothe our emotions (or regulate our nervous systems), we can use the peace and calm of another's body to help us calm down.
- We can start to use various tools and practices to feel safer with and more connected to each other right now.

Heart-Centered Co-regulation Exercise

Below is an easy exercise to help you practice co-regulation with a loved one. When you begin this practice it can be helpful if one of you is in a calm or parasympathetic state.

1. Sit across from each other and place a hand on each other's heart or chest area. You'll feel each other's chest rising and falling, allowing you to synchronize your breath.

2. Breathe slowly and deeply.

3. Begin to visualize your nervous system sending signals of peace and calm to your loved one. And then visualize your nervous system receiving your loved one's peace and calm.

This exercise is especially useful to do before potentially difficult conversations or stressful experiences because it increases our feelings of connection and can help rebalance our relationship's collective energy.

CO-REGULATION MENU

The following is a list of some more things you can do to co-regulate with a loved one during times of stress or conflict.

- Smile or send calming glances to each other, increasing the signals of safety and helping activate the ventral vagal state of everyone around you.
- Practice breathing slowly and deeply in sync with each other while sitting facing each other or with your backs together.
- Lovingly touch or cuddle with each other to activate the "love" hormone oxytocin while increasing feelings of trust and connectedness.
- Look or comfortably gaze into each other's eyes.
- Ask a loved one to play with your hair or calmly stroke their hair to soothe and connect.
- Hug each other to increase oxytocin and help relax any tension in your muscles.
- Kiss each other to increase oxytocin and decrease cortisol levels.
- Go for a walk with each other, focusing on syncing your pace and movement rather than on having an active conversation; this can help reduce stress and promote relational connection and communication.

If you are alone or unable to co-regulate with another person, you can imagine a moment of connection with them, which will also increase oxytocin and feelings of safety. You can even connect with an animal's regulated nervous system to help you find safety in your own body. Petting, brushing, or even lying next to a relaxed pet can help you achieve the same calming effects.

★ ★ ★

As we've been exploring together, it is only when we understand the influence our nervous system has on those around us that we can take steps to create true safety and security within our relationships. Embodying a sense of safety enables us to better navigate conflict with others, often without saying a word, and can help us become more collaborative partners. By extending safety to others through the process of co-regulation we can begin to shift our interactions and dynamics with another, even during moments of stress, hardship, or disagreement. As we reconnect with the compassion that lives in our heart, we empower ourselves to begin to break dysfunctional patterns in any of our relationships.

9

EMPOWERING YOUR RELATIONSHIPS

In the introduction, you read about the five love languages, created by Dr. Gary Chapman in the early 1990s. He theorizes that each of us has a preferred way of receiving affection that, when communicated to our loved ones, can create or sustain the love we seek. According to Dr. Chapman, our five love languages are:

- **Words of affirmation.** We want verbal affirmation or praise from our loved one.
- **Quality time.** We want to spend frequent, preplanned, or mindful time with our loved one.
- **Receiving gifts.** We want our loved one to give us visible or quantifiable symbols of love.
- **Acts of service.** We want our loved one to perform chores or other favors for us.
- **Physical touch.** We want our loved one to show us affection through physical touch or other intimate acts.

This life-changing concept helps many of us recognize that we each have separate, often distinct preferences. Some of us have even used these categories to directly communicate our emotional preferences within our relationships and transform our interpersonal experiences.

Recognizing the uniqueness in our experiences, preferences, and perspectives opens us up to infinite possibilities in self-expression and emotional connection. But there's a big difference between communicating our emotional preferences to others and expecting them to meet our needs in a specific way.

When we ask our loved ones to change their natural way of expressing themelves, we can close ourselves off to other kinds of emotional expression and opportunities for connection. When we overlook what comes naturally to those we love, we inadvertently limit the space we provide others to *be* themselves.

Complicating things, the ways we've all learned to feel valued or loved by others are based on our past conditioning and experiences. When we limit ourselves to these familiar displays of affection, we're often simply asking our loved ones to re-create our earliest relationships, or what love feels like to us. Expecting others to treat us in these familiar ways, we risk re-creating our childhood dysfunctional dynamics.

For years, I believed that I was loved only if my romantic partner performed acts of service for me, like washing the dishes, doing the laundry, or cleaning the house. When they didn't show up for me in this specific way, my abandonment-based ego narratives colored my experiences, leaving me feeling unconsidered, uncared for, and ultimately unloved. Those feelings were based not in my current relational reality but in my childhood wounding. When I was growing up, the primary way my mom showed me affection was by cooking, serving my favorite meals, doing my laundry, and cleaning up after me. Otherwise, unless I was outwardly succeeding in school or sports, she was often distracted by the pain and overwhelming emotions that were accumulating in her body or consumed by worrisome thoughts that were racing through her mind.

As an adult, when I didn't receive the same type of attention from others, I was taken back to those early memories that still live in my body and mind. When Lolly and I first started dating, I felt hurt and ignored when she didn't make me dinner, do the dishes, or help with my laundry. Though she constantly told me how much she cared for me and showed me affection in other ways, I regularly started fights or acted passive-aggressively if I came home and my dinner wasn't made, the house was messy, or laundry was piling up around the apartment. Not only did this create conflict in our relationship, it activated Lolly: when she was young, her mom exploded every time she saw that Lolly had left dishes in the living room or had not straightened up after herself.

As was the case in my relationships, asking someone to change what is comfortable to them can increase conflict, build resentment, and even spark deep-rooted feelings of unworthiness that prevent us from creating or sustaining a deeper connection. Our request to receive love in a certain way may be well-meaning, but it can drive two people further apart.

The reality is we need to feel safe in our body and open to our heart before we can be open to receiving *any* type of love, no matter how we or others express it. If our dysregulated nervous system and related ego stories are keeping us disconnected from our heart, it doesn't matter what our loved ones say or do; we may continue to reject any of their attempts to show us love or connection. If our heart is closed to protect us from possible pain, our connections and relationships will continue to erode. And relying on others to adapt their natural ways of expression to meet our needs can plant a seed of resentment and create dysfunctional cycles of conflict within our relationships that will only continue to weaken our bonds.

To do our part to create this relational safety, we can practice *empowerment consciousness* by taking responsibility to make sure our needs are being met in our relationships. When we consistently create nervous system wellness through daily acts of self-care, we can more easily relax into our natural state of being, or our authentic Self, while giving others the space to do the same. Practicing empowerment consciousness, we don't "need" our loved ones to show up or express affection in a specific way; we can take responsibility for our own safety by making sure we're meeting our needs and by asking for additional support when we want or need it.

Requesting support from others can look like texting to see if a friend has the time and energy to listen while you share your feelings, asking them to spend time with you in quiet, or offering reassurance to each other when needed. It can look like asking a family member to watch your kid(s) for a few hours when they're available so that you can take a long bath, catch up on your sleep, or run personal errands. It can look like seeking feedback from a trusted colleague to read your report before you submit it to your boss. Or it can look like posting on social media or in a virtual community to connect with others facing similar issues, helping you feel less alone with your struggles. Asking for support in these ways isn't always easy, especially if we were unsupported in our childhood. Below are some suggestions that may help you begin to more safely and effectively communicate to others when you need additional support.

In this chapter, you'll also learn how to build empowerment consciousness using the *five steps to empower your relationships*, my approach to healing conflict within our relationships, both romantic and platonic, without sparking conflict, creating resentment, or attempting to change others.

INTERDEPENDENCE

Before we dive more deeply into empowerment consciousness, let's talk about the concept of *interdependence*. Interdependence occurs when separate entities, whether people, plants, animals, companies, or countries, retain their individual identities while sharing a connection. In human relationships, interdependence exists when we depend on others for safety and support while sustaining our integrity and worth as separate and distinct individuals.

To create interdependent relationships, we must first build a foundation of safety and security that allows each individual the space to express their unique skills and passions. When we feel truly safe to express our creativity and bring our unique skills to our relationships, we remain great on our own but become even better together. It's like that sports team where each player is given the time, respect, and freedom to train for their individual position while bringing their full and best effort to group workouts and games.

We function interdependently within our relationships when we're able to connect or join cooperatively together as complete, whole individuals. And, as we've been learning, we're best able to connect to our authentic Self when we consistently:

- Regulate our nervous system especially in times of stress or conflict so that we can feel more physically and emotionally safe and secure
- Witness the impact of the different ego stories that often create moments of reactivity and nervous system dysregulation
- Connect with our heart so that we can make more authentically aligned choices and feel more grounded in those decisions

True interdependence—what I call *separate togetherness*—allows for harmony and collaboration among group members. Whether we're a group of two or twenty, we consider the different needs and best interests of each individual in our group, as well as the needs and best interests of the group itself.[52] When we trust the security of our connection to the *"we,"* we create the space necessary to see things from multiple perspectives so that we can attune to and support others. Considering our group's best interests not only boosts our own well-being by increasing our production of the hormone dopamine, it also increases our motivation and feelings of reward.[53]

Interdependence doesn't always come naturally. Because many of us were raised by emotionally underdeveloped parents, we grew up not feeling safe and secure enough to take the space we needed to curiously explore and know ourselves as separate, whole individuals. Instead, we continue to engage in familiar patterns of self-betrayal often playing conditioned roles instead of living as our authentic Self. Locked in survival mode, we unconsciously prioritize our own thoughts, feelings, and perspectives. But we have to be able to attune to another person's perspective if we want to exist in a compassionate relationship. And to be able to attune to another person, we have to be able to climb out of our body's survival state so that we even see their perspective.

Though our sense of self-worth was impacted by our conditioning, we can learn to cultivate and increase our self-connection and self-love using the practices outlined throughout this book, regardless of our relationship status. To rebuild our self-worth and cultivate self-love, many of us will need to learn how to set boundaries with others so that we can begin to give ourselves the time, space, and resources we need to explore our thoughts, feelings, and interests. The more we create the space to attune to our inner worlds, the better we'll be at noticing when we need to change the way we show up in our relationships. We can begin to identify our limits by pausing and noticing when certain relationships or experiences consistently create stress or emotional upset. It is when we witness and acknowledge our own limits that we can begin to take responsibility for our separate energetic space, or, simply, our individual Self.

As you can likely imagine, heart coherence is necessary if we want to be able to create this interdepence within our relationships. When we're heart coherent, we're open to creating a lasting and loving connection with another person. We're emotionally resilient and mature making us better able to hold space for another's unique self-expression so we can attune, co-regulate, and join in cooperation and co-creation with them. And, we're better able to tolerate the misunderstandings that will naturally occur when navigating life with others, allowing space for our inherent differences and individuality.

EMPOWERMENT CONSCIOUSNESS

We gain true interdependence when practice *empowerment consciousness*, a state that enables us to honor the inherent and beautiful aspects of our loved ones that make them special and unique. We can remain open and curious about our differences, attempting to understand their unique perspectives. We can let go of the idea that we need to receive affection in a certain way to feel loved or chosen and instead can begin to identify and celebrate all the other ways our loved ones value and love us that are more natural to them.

When we're empowered, we no longer expect others to read our minds or intuitively know how we feel in order to meet our emotional needs for us. We recognize that it's not anyone else's responsibility to make us feel better or take away our sadness, loneliness, irritation, desperation, or any other painful emotions. Instead, we can communicate and directly ask for comfort or support in a way that feels safe and comfortable for everyone involved. We're emotionally resilient and able to both self-regulate and co-regulate with others.

Because I was raised by dysregulated, emotionally underdeveloped, and unavailable parents, as many of you also were, I've always had a difficult time asking others for comfort or support and still struggle with it at times. Wanting support makes me feel too vulnerable, as though I'm underperforming in my relationships and activates my deep-rooted feelings of unworthiness. Relatedly, I can become annoyed when I see my loved ones directly asking for the support or comfort they need. I cringe when they request a quick foot rub. I glare when they tell me they're going to tuck themselves away in a back bedroom for the day to enjoy some alone time. Now I can see that my feeling of annoyance indicates the discomfort I still feel when expressing my own needs, often feeling too uncomfortable to take the time or space I may need or too vulnerable to directly ask for the support or connection I may want. While I may think that I am upset with them, I am really upset with myself for my own acts of self-betrayal and related neglected needs. Now, my reaction suggests to me that my resources may be running low and that I, too, may benefit from some self-care or supportive connection.

Reading this, I imagine some of you are feeling fearful or worried that your loved ones may be genuinely unable or unwilling to give you the support you ask for. Even in these moments when we're feeling hopeless or powerless, when we're empowered and connected with our heart, we can tap into our intuition and trust our choices if we do decide to leave a relationship or commit to doing our part in making it a more mutually supportive space. We can do our part by intentionally working to change the dynamics of the relationship by seeing a friend less frequently, choosing to live or sleep separately from a romantic partner, or taking time and space for ourselves more frequently so that we're able to be more open and supportive within the relationship.

Asking for support can be challenging for many of us, especially for those who's parent-figures weren't able to ask for what they needed or enabled others' dysfunctional habits. Driven by what we saw and experienced in our earliest relationships, we may continue to embody the same dysfunctional habits today. Those of us who routinely feel compelled to step in to help a friend in their latest self-created crisis, make excuses to cover up a partner's lies, or placate a parent in order to avoid an explosive reaction are enabling others to continue their patterns of harmful or self-destructive behaviors. Though we may think we're acting compassionately or even supportively, we're really allowing ourselves and others to stay stuck in dysfunctional cycles, often at both of our physical or emotional expenses.

When we're empowered, we don't let others treat us any way they choose. We feel safe and secure enough to leave the room or take the space we need without worrying about whether it will cause a break in our connection. We trust the security of our bond, knowing that the relationship can and will survive natural conflict. And if the conflict or relationship itself ever becomes threatening, we trust our ability to remove ourselves and find our way to safety, even when it means involving social services or law enforcement. Though we are personally never responsible for abusive or violating behaviors, it is our responsibility to identify when our limits have been crossed and seek safety accordingly.

Our goal with empowerment consciousness is to learn to support the uniqueness in others and their different ways of being while taking time to ensure that our own boundaries aren't overstepped or we're not contributing to others' harmful behaviors. The next time a loved one calls or texts in need of emotional support and you're going through something stressful or difficult yourself, remember to pause before immediately offering your support. Sometimes the most loving thing you may be able to do is use your remaining resources to support your own emotional needs, which can go a long way to preventing future resentment within your relationship.

I hope it is becoming clear to you that it is only when we become present to our own needs that we can be present to the needs of our relationships. We can start to communicate our natural need for our own self-care to others by saying something as simple as "I would love to be able to support you right now, but I am going through something myself, so I have few emotional resources available. I'll check in with you in a few hours/days, when I can be more fully present and able to be there for you."

Remember this the next time you witness yourself becoming dysregulated by a text you receive from a friend, for example, about how your relationship is impacting them or a partner discloses their infidelity in a past relationship—you can pause before reacting, whether you feel upset with their actions or overwhelmed by your emotions. By taking a pause, you can then recognize the vulnerability it may have taken for your loved one to share the information while also recognizing the emotional impact it has on you. To avoid future upset, the most loving thing you may be able to do for both of you is give yourself the time to process and figure out how *you* feel before responding. You can communicate this need for time and space by saying something as simple as "I appreciate your sharing [insert something personal about their share] and can imagine that it may not have been easy for you to do so. I am having something come up for me that I'll need some time to process and would be grateful to have the opportunity to share it with you later, if you're open to it."

Despite what your conditioned mind may tell you, you don't need to have a "valid" or "warranted" reason to take time or space for yourself, whether pausing before you respond or pursuing your own creativity, passions, or purpose. Wanting to remain in a balanced, productive, or creative space within yourself will only help you better show up to connect with and support others within your relationships. I try to practice this by holding space for myself not only when others are in a good mood but also when a loved one is upset, stressed, or shut down for whatever reason. Remaining grounded in my own emotional space is not selfish but actually enables me to offer them more compassionate and empathetic support within our relationship.

Focusing on building and maintaining a healthy, interdependent emotional connection will inevitably decrease resentment within our relationships. We will feel more secure in our connections and expand our ability to feel loved beyond more limited gestures of affection. And we will create lasting change by making new choices whenever we notice we're reenacting the conditioned habits of our past.

ARE YOUR RELATIONSHIPS EMPOWERED OR DISEMPOWERED?

Take a look at the disempowered versus empowered relationship chart on the next page as you spend time witnessing yourself and interactions with others. This exploratory exercise can help you identify habitual patterns in your various relationships.

HOW TO COMMUNICATE YOUR EMOTIONAL NEEDS

Just because we shouldn't exclusively depend on others to meet our needs or to take away our painful emotions doesn't mean we shouldn't acknowledge and communicate our needs and ask for emotional support when necessary. Becoming more consciously aware of our emotional needs allows us to build a feeling of ownership over our life experiences. This empowered state helps us realize that we have more agency in life and decreases our tendency to blame others or our life circumstances. As we take responsibility for and share our various emotional experiences, we do our part to cultivate emotional intimacy. And when we, and others, feel safe, valued, and loved within our relationships, we're able to vulnerably ask for the support and reassurance we need.

As you become more aware of the different ways some (or all) of your needs are not being met in your different relationships, it will be helpful to take a moment to explore the questions on page 234.

DISEMPOWERED RELATIONSHIP	EMPOWERED RELATIONSHIP
We rely on each other to make us happy and to meet most, if not all, of the other person's needs and wants without directly communicating what they are.	We are each responsible for our own happiness and practice regular acts of self-care to ensure that our needs are met, directly communicating what we need and want.
We don't set or uphold boundaries, often ignoring or enabling unacceptable or dysfunctional behaviors (sometimes seeing them as punishment or something we deserve).	We are autonomous, respecting boundaries and saying no without emotional reactivity (e.g., rage, exploding, shutting down, or icing) or feeling pressured, guilted, or forced into anything.
We have difficulty expressing our emotions and become reactive or harmful in disagreement, conflict, or upset, or, we avoid our emotions entirely.	We welcome authentic emotional expression, creating a safe space to share our feelings and taking space, when necessary, to pause before reconnecting.
We regularly talk over, interrupt, or blame each other or the external world for our thoughts and feelings, making things solely about us and our experiences and worry mostly about our own best interests, rarely, if ever, engaging in repair.	We regularly practice heart-centered listening so we can emotionally attune and shift our perspective to develop a "felt" sense of the other person's experience and act as a team to find a workable solution.
We hold on to grudges or resentment from past experiences and often engage in communications or behaviors that shame each other.	We forgive ourselves and each other, regularly seeing the good in us both and trusting that we are both doing the best we can.
We regularly put the other person's needs or wants before our own or take responsibility for their behavior, often experiencing feelings of anger or resentment as a result. We may lack appreciation or blame each other (e.g., "If you didn't X, I wouldn't have Y" or "You made me do X").	We give each other space and support to meet our individual wants and needs (personal responsibility) and allow for mutual growth and evolution (relational responsibility).
We often find ourselves stuck in survival mode or crisis management and are unable to take moments alone or prioritize our individual interests, hobbies, or passions.	We are committed to creating unstructured time to allow for play and activities that bring joy both inside and outside the relationship, including time and space to pursue solitude and individual interests, hobbies, or passions.

Have I directly told my loved one(s) what I need/want or what I don't need/don't want? Many of us are able to voice the issues we have with our loved ones or repeat the things we don't want. But to make sure our needs can be met, it's helpful to voice what we *specifically* want or need, which increases clarity, fosters a collaborative environment, and puts us on the same page with those around us. Instead of saying "You don't care about me when you're away," we could ask, "Can you text me before you go to bed so we can catch up about our day? That would help me feel more connected to you while you're away." Or before we yell, "You never listen to me!" we can calmly request, "Can we have a conversation where neither of us is distracted by our phone? This will help me be able to get all of my thoughts and feelings out."

How can I meet this need/desire on my own if my loved one is unable or unwilling to do so? If you're unsure how to answer this question, that's okay; be patient and compassionate with yourself. Continue to take time and space to self-reflect and curiously explore yourself using the exercises throughout this book. Remember, even in emotionally attuned partnerships, there is a give-and-take in the availability of supportive resources, and it's normal and even necessary to take turns playing a supportive role based on the energetic resources available to each of you. Because no one person can meet all of our needs all the time, it may also be helpful to find supportive relationships or communities outside our primary partnership.

For many of us, communicating our emotions is challenging, even in our long-standing relationships. We're so desperate to be loved by others and scared of "losing" them that we don't ask for support or set needed boundaries. This is especially true if our feelings were ignored or dismissed in childhood. And, when we believe our ego stories that we're unworthy of having our needs met, we continue to suppress or deny them. But if we pretend to be "independent" and "strong" all the time or act as though we never get upset or need support (as I used to do), we can't develop the security and connection we need to survive and thrive.

If we don't communicate our feelings and set boundaries, we can't expect to feel safe, valued, or loved within our relationships. To begin to communicate more effectively to others, we can:

1. **Consider the timing.** If our loved ones are distracted, defensive, depressed, hurt, jealous, insecure, or reacting from their own stored trauma, they won't be able to hear our needs, no matter how effectively or directly we communicate them. And we have to feel safe in our own body to even be able to clearly and effectively share our needs. Unfortunately, many of us attempt to communicate our needs when we feel upset, are in the middle of a heated conversation, or are being ignored by someone who is reactive, distracted, or dissociated. In these instances, it's likely no one feels safe. Make sure that both you and your loved one feel calm, grounded, and present when you decide to share your needs.

2. **Communicate your intention.** Many of us don't specify or explicitly say why we're sharing our wants and needs with someone else, whether it's because we want to feel safer in their company or more securely connected within the relationship. Before having a conversation about your desires, think about the reason you're sharing them, even if it's simply because you want to improve your relationship. When we give the "why" behind our communication, we increase the likelihood that others will be able to see and understand our perspective.

3. **Choose your words wisely.** When we share our emotional needs with others, we want to avoid criticizing, blaming, or using "you"-based language (focus on using "I" statements instead). It's helpful to avoid "all-or-never" language like "You always say X, Y, or Z"; "You never do A, B, or C." This kind of all-or-nothing thinking

activates our ego and the ego of our loved one so that we both end up feeling threatened, focused on our individual differences, and unable to clearly see the other's perspective or even the conflict itself. This naturally impacts our ability to communicate productively and approach the problem or issue collaboratively with both of our best interests in mind.

Here are examples of language you can use to communicate your emotional needs more clearly and effectively to another person.

- "I've had a rough day and need some support. Do you have the space and energy to listen to me now or sometime in the next few hours?"
- "I'm having a hard time finding a solution for this work issue and would love to get your perspective. Can I share what's going on with you and ask for your advice?"
- "I'm feeling sad and need some support. Would you be willing to sit next to me for a few minutes?"
- "I'm feeling disconnected and would like to connect with you. Would you be willing to spend a few hours doing [insert activity] with me?"
- "I'm feeling overwhelmed by caring for Mom (or Dad, my child, my partner, etc.) and need some time by myself. Can you come over and sit with them for a few hours so I can take that space?"
- "At night, I can get anxious or restless. I need to spend a half hour or so doing [insert activity] to wind down. Can you give me that space?"
- "I need to be able to vent sometimes without you trying to fix my issue. Can you work on listening without giving me advice or telling me what I should do? I feel supported this way."
- "When I come home, I notice it's difficult for me to connect right away. I need it to be okay that I take some space and time to adapt to being home before we connect. Can you give me [insert how long you'd like] to spend by myself before we hang out?"
- "I'm uncomfortable when you share certain details of our relationship with others, especially your family. I need some things to

be between us. Can we talk about the boundaries with our family that would help us both feel most comfortable?"

- "I'm uncomfortable sharing intimate details about my personal relationship around our other colleagues at our work's lunch table. Can we talk about the boundaries with our colleagues that would help us both feel more comfortable?"
- "Conflict meant complete destruction or disconnection for me growing up so I need reassurance after a conflict to feel safe. Can you remind me that you still love me even when you're upset?"
- "When you mock or tease me when we're out socially, it hurts my feelings. You may not be aware of this, and I need you to understand how I feel."
- "Being spontaneous doesn't come natural to me like it does to you. I appreciate that about you and need it to be understood that planning helps me feel safer."
- "I see how much you love doing [insert activity]. I honestly don't love it like you do, and while I support you continuing to enjoy your passions, I won't be joining you as frequently."
- "When we go to visit my family, I need emotional support. You can support me by checking in with me and asking how I'm feeling, giving me a hug, or [insert any other action that would feel supportive]."

When we build empowerment consciousness, we can even start to recognize when someone else needs our support. We can often sense when our loved ones are irritated or overstimulated and offer them support with their problems or share our perspective with them. When we compassionately share our experience in those dysregulated moments we can sometimes even gently encourage our loved ones to take the time or space they need to more fully regulate themselves. When we're aware of what's happening inside us, we're better able to hold space for the various, changing needs of those around us. And as we grow more and more confident in our self-worth and gain more security within our relationships, we're better able to honor what others need without perceiving their preferences as an indication of our worthlessness.

OVERCOMING DISEMPOWERING BELIEFS
ABOUT YOUR RELATIONSHIPS

Taking responsibility for our needs and building empowerment consciousness enables us to be the change we want to see in our relationships as we make them more sustainable and loving. When we focus on the ways we'd like others to be different, we create a dependency on external circumstances and deny the truth and power we all have to transform our experiences. Affirmations can be a useful tool to help change and eventually reprogram our mindset.

Below are listed examples of disempowering beliefs and the associated affirmations you can use to reconnect with your inherent power to create change in any relationship. At the end of this list, you'll find tips to help you create your own affirmations best suited to your individual experiences.

Old belief: My partner is the problem, and they really need to fix their issues.

Empowered affirmation: Relationships are co-created and both of us play a role. As I become more conscious of this, I have an opportunity to make choices to create healthier relationships.

Old belief: My ex is a liar, cheater, narcissist, and complete psycho.

Empowered affirmation: The dynamics of my earliest attachment with my parent-figure or other childhood trauma were re-enacted in a relationship that was insecure, unstable, or chaotic.

Old belief: My friend is always taking advantage of me.

Empowered affirmation: It is my responsibility to set and maintain the boundaries I need.

Old belief: My loved one says they're not interested in doing the work necessary to make our relationship healthier.

Empowered affirmation: This is useful information about where they are and I can now choose whether or not I can accept this.

Old belief: My mom/dad/sister/brother is constantly denying my reality (otherwise known as gaslighting).

Empowered affirmation: The way my mom/dad/sister/brother communicates with me is a powerful indicator of their emotional development, and I can now choose how I want to engage with them.

Old belief: My friend says one thing and does another, which leaves me feeling hurt and manipulated.

Empowered affirmation: I am conscious of my friend's actions, and I can make choices based on those actions, not just on their words.

Old belief: My mom always brings me into the family drama.

Empowered affirmation: I can now choose how I spend my time and energy and communicate my boundaries clearly to others, even my mom.

You can begin to change the disempowering relational beliefs you witness in yourself by changing the language of your thoughts. To do so, practice removing your focus from what you believe the other person has caused you to feel. Then take some time to explore one way that you can begin to change your circumstances and related emotions by showing up differently.

FIVE STEPS TO TAKE TO EMPOWER
YOUR RELATIONSHIPS

At this point in our journey, we've covered the steps necessary to understand our dysfunctional relationship habits and start to create deeper, sustainable, more authentic bonds with others. At the same time, I know we've discussed a lot of things that may feel challenging or uncomfortable, and it's normal to feel a little overwhelmed by all the new information and tools.

To make this work more approachable, here is all we've discussed so far organized into five pillars or steps. This process will help you become more aware of yourself, your safety, and the safety of all of those around you.

FIVE STEPS TO EMPOWER
YOUR RELATIONSHIPS

1. Embody your Self.
2. Create and share your nervous system safety.
3. Compassionately witness your conditioned Self.
4. Reconnect with your authentic Self.
5. Cultivate empowerment consciousness.

Though we've covered all these concepts in previous chapters, here's how to actually put them all into practice.

1. **Embody your Self.** Our first step is to realize that our relationships with others are impacted by more than what we think, say, and do or by what others think, say, and do. Because we interact with others as our embodied Self, or our body, mind, and soul, we have to meet our physical, mental, and spiritual needs before we can show up as our whole Self.
2. **Create and share your nervous system safety.** The state of our nervous system affects our thoughts, words, and actions. If our ner-

vous system is stuck in a stress response, as most of ours are, we'll think, do, and say things that create or escalate conflict with others. Our nervous system will communicate our threat state to those around us, amping up the collective stress level. When we become aware of our nervous system stress, we can choose to bring our body back to safety or wait to interact until we're calm and grounded again or we can safely co-regulate with others.

3. **Compassionately witness your conditioned Self.** We all have a conditioned Self, created by the roles we learned to play in our earliest relationships or, simply, how we learned to feel safe, valued, and loved as children. When we play these roles as adults, we subconsciously expect others to meet our needs and play their part in our childhood re-enactments. It's only when we witness our conditioning, that we can begin to make new choices that better align with what we truly want and need.

4. **Reconnect with your authentic Self.** When we consistently commit to these first three practices, we naturally begin to live in integrity and make choices that are aligned with our authentic Self. We're able to express our genuine thoughts and emotions, share our deeper passions and purpose, trust the decisions we make, and feel more whole and complete in ourselves and around others. This, in turn, enables us to connect more authentically with those in our lives.

5. **Cultivate empowerment consciousness.** When we're empowered to take responsibility for creating the safety we need to authentically express ourselves or *be* who we are; we gift others with the opportunity to do the same. When we're authentically connected to our heart, we can tap into our deep wisdom and intuition, learning to regain and rebuild trust in our instincts. Reconnected with our own source energy, we can truly *become* the love we seek.

Empowerment Consciousness Self-Exploration:
Journal Prompts

The following questions can help you identify areas in which you already feel empowered and interdependent in your relationships and areas in which you may want to work to develop more relational empowerment and interdependence. Spend time thinking about each of your relationships, writing down your thoughts and feelings in a separate notebook or journal if helpful.

How do I feel when I'm in this individual's presence? How do I feel before and after I spend time with them?

_____

_____

What do I like about this individual? What do I dislike about them or perceive as possible red flags?

_____

_____

Are they honest and consistent in their communication (i.e. they do what they say)? Are they dishonest and inconsistent in their communication (i.e., they say one thing and do another)?

_____

_____

Is there space in our relationship for emotional expression and attunement? That is, are my feelings heard and understood?

_____

_____

Do they listen to requests and respect boundaries?

_____

_____

Do they clearly ask for what they need?

_____

_____

Do they understand and take responsibility for their roles and emotions within the relationship?

_____

_____

Do we want the same things, and do our values align?

_____

_____

Am I open to this kind of relationship at this time?

_____

_____

Does our dynamic feel healthy, and is this something I want to continue to pursue as it is? What do I need to change about our dynamic in order for it to feel healthy and be something I want to continue to pursue?

_____

_____

It's completely normal if you feel uncomfortable or disheartened about some of your responses to these questions. It's helpful to view your answers as an opportunity or a starting point to identify and clarify areas that you'd like to address. Understanding what isn't working can often help you to begin to find your way toward what will work, even if that means changing the dynamics of your current relationship or venturing into the unknown, alone. Remember, leaving a relationship when it's no longer aligned or you feel complete and have grown all you can is different from leaving to try to find something better, which many of us, including myself, have done in the past. Be patient and give yourself time and space to grieve any changes or losses in any of your relationships, even those you've chosen to initiate for yourself.

As you explore your current circumstances or begin to create new ones, continuing to extend yourself grace and compassion and reminding yourself that each of us is a work in progress, doing the best we can. The fact that you are this far along in the work is an incredible sign of your desire and commitment to create change for yourself and your relationships.

HOW TO HAVE A DIFFICULT CONVERSATION

As you've already learned, taking a moment to pause and connect with your heart can help you move toward a more connected and collaborative space of heart coherence. Before you enter what could be an upsetting interaction or conversation, place your hands on your heart and take a few slow, deep breaths as you remind yourself what is truly important to you about this person or relationship. It could be as simple as calling to mind something you like or appreciate about who they are and how they show up in your relationship. Spend as long a time here as you'd like before beginning the interaction or conversation, noticing if your experience or outlook changes in any way. Pay particular attention to both the differences in how you approach the interaction and how the other person responds to any shifts in your energy.

Those of you who want to begin to address more difficult topics or realities may find the following guidance helpful.

- Ask to have explicit and open conversations with others that directly address the source of conflict or issue. Attempt to break habits that may cause you to avoid or deflect difficult topics.
- Practice validating others' thoughts, feelings, and perspectives, even if you disagree. You don't have to agree with someone or feel the same way they do to attempt to understand or validate and accept how they feel. To demonstrate that you're trying to understand them, you can say, "I understand this really hurt you" or "I can see how you could feel that way."
- Break the natural habit of trying to make sense of another's thoughts, feelings, or intentions or assume what they may be. Instead, practice asking questions and listening from a place of curiosity and connection to your heart space, allowing them to speak without speaking over or interrupting them.
- Own your role in your shared experiences, be open and humble, and apologize or take responsibility when you hurt someone.
- Practice trying to compromise and navigate conflicts as a team to come up with mutually workable solutions. Break any habits you may have of focusing only on yourself and your own best interests (when it's safe and appropriate to do so).

- Try to stick to the current issue or topic, and break any habit you may have of bringing up the past or using absolutist statements like "You always do *X*" or "You never do *Y*."
- Affirm your love and connection to your loved one during conflict, reminding yourself that it can be stressful and overwhelming for both of you, even if your loved one appears distracted or detached. If you can't do so during a conflict, affirm your connection when you're both calm, letting them know that you love them, appreciate them, and remain committed to the relationship. (This is particularly important for those who grew up in a home where conflict meant big blowups or the loss of love, like the silent treatment.)

HOW TO REPAIR A CONNECTION
AFTER A CONFLICT

Conflicts are a natural part of navigating life with someone else who inevitably has different ideas, feelings, perspectives, and past experiences. Learning how to acknowledge our individual roles in conflict, including the impact of our emotional reactivity, helps increase our security and trust in a relationship. Emotionally healthy couples repair their relationship after disagreements or disconnection instead of ignoring their issues or pretending the conflict didn't happen. Practice using the tips in the list below to help you repair your relationship or reconnect after heated or disconnected moments in your relationship.

- **Check in with your nervous system to make sure you're regulated.** You want your body to be in a calm and grounded state when you apologize or attempt to repair the disconnection. If you're stressed or upset, you won't be able to think or speak clearly or hold space for the other person's feelings.
- **Be specific.** Name the behavior, its impact (be curious and ask if unsure), and your role in it. For example: "The other night when

I made that joke in front of our friends, I was trying to be funny and am really sorry I hurt you." Or, "I'm wondering how you felt when I made that joke in front of our friends the other night?"

- **Listen without being defensive.** This will be difficult if you came from a home where people deflected or invalidated one another's feelings. Remember, you may not agree with what the other person is saying, but practice allowing them to share their experiences anyway.

- **Focus on the other person's feelings, not yours.** If you, like me, were raised by emotionally underdeveloped parents, you'll notice the urge to center the conversation around how you feel. Try to shift out of this habit, since true and meaningful apologies are centered around others' feelings, not our own.

- **State what you'll do differently in the future.** Identify your role or responsibility in creating change or decreasing the likelihood that it happens again. For example: "When I'm tired or irritable, I'm going to work on taking space and being aware of what activates me because it's not okay to snap at you." I've had to say this often myself!

- **Practice forgiving yourself.** Remember, we all hurt people throughout our life; it's part of being a human being. After you apologize, remember to practice self-care, extending yourself grace and compassion and reminding yourself that you are doing the best you can and take a moment to celebrate yourself for taking accountability. Practice redirecting your attention away from any self-shaming or critical thoughts.

★   ★   ★

Naturally, most of us want to feel loved in the same ways we learned to feel loved as children. For most of us, these ways are anchored in trauma and what we needed to do to feel safe, valued, and loved in our childhood environment. As we become more aware of the expectations we place on others and take responsibility for our unmet childhood needs, we become intentional creators of our experiences with others instead of allowing our past trauma to drive and dictate how we interact with them. When we're empowered in our interactions and relationships, we're able to connect more authentically with the people with whom we share space and time. We're also better able to connect with the energetic power of the natural world in which we live, a life-changing power you'll learn more about in the next chapter.

10

RECONNECTING WITH THE COLLECTIVE

The summer of 1993 was both sweltering and deadly in Washington, DC. At the time, the city had one of the highest crime rates in the country and was experiencing the kind of temperatures that send even the most ardent of heat seekers into air-conditioned cool. Despite the heat and the violence, four thousand people chose to descend on the city to sit in silence and meditate with one intent in mind: to lower the crime rate by focusing their mental energy on spreading peace and safety to others.

It worked. At the height of the two-month experiment, violent crimes in DC dropped by 23 percent.[54] Prior to the study, led by the quantum physicist John Hagelin, Washington, DC's, police chief had told reporters that only twenty inches of snow during the summer would cause as noticeable a fall in crime.[55]

What happened that summer wasn't a one-off incident. Decades of research provide evidence that when groups of people focus their attention on promoting peace, harmony, health, or well-being, they achieve their intended outcome in quantifiable ways. Another notable study found that during the Israel-Lebanon war in 1983, deaths dropped by 76 percent as a result of a heart-centered daily group meditation.[56] Everyday stress like crime, traffic accidents, and fires also decreased in the surrounding area.

The "field effects of consciousness," as Hagelin termed it, go beyond meditation: Any practice that creates physiological safety in our nervous system and coherence between our heart and brain can impact the overall well-being of others. More surprisingly, when we band together to focus our mental energy on specific feelings, intentions, or outcomes, it can spread those feelings, intentions, or outcomes to people around the world, not just to those in our town, city, or even country. This is known as *nonlocal consciousness*.

Some of the strongest research into nonlocal consciousness has been conducted with prayer or other intention-setting practices. Cardiologists at Duke University found that when people of various faiths from around the world prayed for 150 cardiac patients by name, those patients fared 50 to 100 percent better than those who didn't receive any prayer, even though the patients and those who were praying for them were separated by hundreds or even thousands of miles.[57] Another study of nearly a thousand cardiac patients reached similar results, showing that those who were prayed for nonlocally had healthier outcomes than those who weren't.[58] As researchers point out, their results don't prove that God exists or that He/She/They answer prayers but that collective consciousness is extremely powerful.[59]

Though the term has various meanings, I define *collective consciousness* as the combined state of energy in a group of people, whether that group is our family, circle of friends, work office, sports team, university, company, corporation, town, city, or country. There is also *global consciousness*, or the mass energetic state of everyone on Earth who is alive at any given time.

Our collective consciousness can be calm, collaborative, productive, and harmonious—or stressed, agitated, fearful, and chaotic. If you've ever thought that everyone you encountered one day seemed a little on edge or that the energy of your office, community, or even the entire planet was off, you were likely feeling the effects of the collective or global consciousness.

What determines collective consciousness? We all do, based on how physiologically safe we each individually feel in our nervous system and whether we're in a coherent state. This is because everyone's individual safety and heart coherence affect those of everyone else in our group and around the world, as if we are all playing one giant game of dominos.

With 8 billion hearts and nervous systems communicating with one another all the time, unseen signals are constantly boomeranging around the world, faster and more effectively than any wireless network. Whether we're aware of it or not, we all affect one another in a continual feedback loop.

For more proof of our collective and global consciousness, it's interesting to look at research conducted by the Global Consciousness Project (GCP). This international collaboration of scientists analyzed the effects of hundreds of events, including the death of Princess Diana and the September 11th attacks on the World Trade Center, that have activated a worldwide emotional reaction or outpouring. Over the past few decades, the GCP has found that these globally impactful events alter the output of random number generators—quantum-based devices often used in research—in a statistically significant way that cannot be explained by chance. This has led the scientists to conclude that it is our collective energy shifts the outputs.[60] Though the GCP has been criticized by some for being biased, the project has analyzed the quantum output of more than five hundred worldwide events to date, enabling its scientists to argue that their results cannot be misinterpreted.[61]

There's no denying that we as human beings are interconnected in a state of collective or global consciousness. We're all made of the same natural elements, share the same space here on Earth, and pass nervous system energy back and forth to one another every second of every day. We may spend most of our attention and energy interacting with those in our immediate environments, but we're also connected to wider groups, networks, systems, and humanity as a whole. And because we're connected, we as individuals can begin to use the peaceful state of our own body to impact the bodies of those around us.

YOUR HEART IMPACTS OTHERS

In chapter 8, we learned about co-regulation and some of the ways in which we can use the safety of our nervous system to help our loved ones feel safe and open to connecting with us on a deeper level. Now we're going to explore how we can use co-regulation to communicate safety not only to those in our immediate proximity but also to those in our groups and communities and even people we don't directly interact with or even know. What I'm referring to is a phenomenon known as *social coherence*, which occurs when our state of heart coherence spreads to others in our wider groups, networks, and systems.

On the simplest level, social coherence occurs because kindness is contagious—literally. When we embody core heart feelings like compassion, appreciation, acceptance, tolerance, patience, forgiveness, and love, we radiate these feelings through seen behavior, including our words, actions, vocal tone, and facial expressions, in addition to unseen signals, like the energy we emit from our nervous system and heart. This spread of social coherence is a form of *entrainment*, which occurs when cooperative rhythms are generated between individuals. Anytime we interact with others, whether they're near or far, our individual system will actively coordinate with their energetic communications. This energetic entrainment joins the *"me"* of us as individuals into a *"we"* in a relationship with another.

This synchronization of human energetic communication has been documented by a phenomenon known as *emotional contagion*. You already read about the meditation studies at the beginning of the chapter, that illustrate the widespread impact that a small percentage of peaceful individuals can cause. Emotional contagion is the spread of emotions between and among individuals. Emotions spread because we subconsciously mimic the behaviors of others, as our brain activates *mirror neurons*, cells that fire when we witness another person's actions.[62] Mirror neurons help us attune to or feel the emotional state of the other person, which can spread emotional energy and deepen our bond with them.[63]

Lots of research has been conducted on emotional contagion, in part because businesses and corporations have used the findings to influence consumer decisions and purchases, as well as employee satisfaction and loyalty.[64] By eliciting certain emotions through ads and marketing, businesses have learned how to influence consumers' purchasing decisions. Though this can understandably be viewed as cause for concern, the research can help us comprehend why our individual safety matters so much to the collective consciousness.

A massive study of Facebook users found that when researchers manipulated their news feed to present more negative content, users created more negative posts and vice versa, generating more positive posts after seeing more positive content.[65] Another well-known study shows that people are more likely to be generous when they see other people acting generously and more likely to be stingy when seeing others do the same. Those who see generous behavior are also friendlier, more empathetic, and more supportive of strangers.[66]

The empowering message for us is that when we show up in a state of safe coherence, whether we're directly interacting with others or not, we have the power to spread social coherence to many other people, including those outside our immediate circles.

YOUR COHERENCE MAKES YOUR GROUPS MORE SUCCESSFUL

When we embody heart coherence, we help make our groups more harmonious, productive, effective, and ultimately successful. We're better able to pursue our unique skills, talents, and gifts and can more easily enter our flow state, increasing our personal productivity, creativity, and problem-solving ability. Being in our own flow state can even activate the same brain regions in those around us, helping them more easily get into their own flow.[67]

When we're incoherent, on the other hand, we're more likely to stay locked in stressful cycles, rife with competition, conflict, and inefficient functioning, according to research.[68] Only when we feel safe and social are we able to tolerate others' differences, and, as a result, feel less competitive and stressed. When we can see things from a more distanced perspective, we're better able to consider the group's best interests and negotiate for the greater good rather than being more focused on our individual desires or interests. Research on individual safety and heart coherence even shows that one person alone can reduce conflict among families, offices, organizations, sports teams, and larger entities.[69] And, the more synchronization in brain waves between a speaker and students in a school setting, the more effective the communication is, with higher levels of class engagement and improved social dynamics.

Sharing a sense of communal safety enables individuals to be more present to the current moment, which can open up new opportunities in their relationships to break repeated cycles. When we are fully in the moment, we are more likely to engage our creativity and imagination, allowing us to see and honor the creativity in those around us. Our safety and energy encourages others to share their unique skills, talents, and gifts with the group. This enables the group to then have multiple perspectives to consider when coming up with new and more innovative solutions to problems. In other words, social coherence enables everyone in the group to find their flow and specialize in what they do best, benefiting the group as a whole. Companies, hospitals, sports teams, and military units that have worked to develop social coherence have lower rates of physical and mental stress and/or improved communication, satisfaction, productivity, and problem-solving among their members, according to research.[70]

I've experienced the effects of social coherence in many of my own communities, including with the creation of The Holistic Psychologist. After I began my healing journey, I started to seek more authentic relationships with those with whom I shared interests or goals and could *be* myself. Understanding the importance of *being* myself in my relationships, I created the @the.holistic.psychologist Instagram account and started using the hashtag #selfhealers as a way to connect with other like-minded people who were on a similar healing journey. My hope was that, over time, I could create a socially coherent community in which collective safety would make the process of healing more accessible for everyone; to truly heal, we need to feel safe enough to express and share ourselves without focusing on our differences from others or fearing judgment by them.

Soon after launching the account and hashtag, people from around the world began to communicate, connect, and join with me, honoring our individual differences and journeys. Sensitive to the reality that many people don't have the resources to access the services they need, I made it one of my missions to ensure that the information and tools we shared on the free platform were available to all.

After the account had been live for several months, I started to receive more and more requests from followers to create a safe space outside the social media account. Inspired by these messages, I created SelfHealers Circle, a private community where members can share compassionate communication and self-exploration, both of which are essential to healing and social coherence. I'm continuously humbled when I hear the impact that this safe and supportive communal environment has had on member's individual healing journeys.

In addition to its benefits within our chosen communities, social coherence can change the dynamics of unorganized groups like the atmosphere we experience at restaurants, theaters, parties, and other social or public events or spaces. Let me give you an example.

You recently attended a group event with some colleagues but arrived a little later than most. When you walked into the room, you could feel that the collective energy was strained and uneasy; people didn't know one another, and the conversation seemed tentative. Because you felt particularly safe, coherent, and joyful that evening, you embodied your heart-coherent self: you smiled at everyone, channeled compassion and gratitude to those in the room, and were genuinely interested in hearing about other's experiences and stories. Shortly after you arrived, the dynamics of the event started to shift; others began to smile and speak more openly to those next to them. Their body language became more relaxed, and the room started to lighten with laughter and more fluid conversation.

Here's another example. Imagine a busy restaurant where a server shows up in a safe, grounded state. This socially coherent server holds compassion for any irritated or demanding patrons and can more authentically connect with those around them. They don't complain to other servers about how terrible their tables are, which prevents the other waitstaff from looking for similar or confirming experiences elsewhere. The safe server emits unseen signals of coherence, helping regulate others in the room. Patrons and staff who show up stressed, irritated, or upset may start to soften and smile. Soon after, the energy of the restaurant shifts to be friendlier and more harmonious. Feeling this energetic shift himself, the server continues to benefit from the aftereffects of his initiated compassion. We can all do this, too, whenever we choose to embody a more compassionate response in our own daily interactions.

This harmonious, socially coherent state has allowed humans to evolve and thrive as a species. Banding together in collaborative ways enables some of us to meet our fundamental needs for food, shelter, child care, and health care while others pursue art, music, technology, and other interests that bring them and others joy or make it easier for us to live longer or more fulfilling lives.

DEVELOPING SOCIAL COHERENCE

Creating sustained social coherence requires more than making sure we're not dysregulated at an individual level; we also need to be able to extend compassion, empathy, and even support to others. When we embody compassion we send regulating signals to those around us so that they're better able to feel safe, coherent, and more connected to the group. We're better able to empathize, or to be present with others in their emotional world by listening attentively as they share their experiences instead of becoming distracted by our thoughts or feelings about what is being shared. And we're able to ask questions to better understand the other person's perspective before making assumptions or disregarding their viewpoint.

As we develop social coherence, we're also better able to notice the times when we feel unsafe or combative, giving us the opportunity to calm and ground ourselves by taking space away from the group or reaching out to a trusted loved one for help or support to co-regulate. Once we return to a more open state, we can practice collaboration by honoring one another's differences while focusing on the group's shared goals. We're able to be curious about one another, even if we're at odds over certain issues, and find ways to move forward while re-taining our own sense of individual safety. With social coherence, we can stay an *I* even as we connect with others as a *we*.

To increase social coherence, it's helpful to notice or seek out others who allow us to feel safe and at ease. On the other hand, if we notice we struggle to feel comfortable or at ease around certain people, we can communicate our need to take space and choose to re-engage with them when we feel ready and able—not when we don't have the internal resources to needed to navigate the interaction. Though it's not possible to avoid all stressful or upsetting interactions or ex-periences, social coherence increases our ability to tolerate stress and other activating emotions. And when we cultivate a community where all members feel safe and at ease we can all develop deeper, more authentic connections. Finding and rooting yourself in just one community where you feel a sense of belonging or social coherence can help you build and sustain the safety you need to extend coher-ence to your wider world.

Social Coherence Checklist

The following checklist can help you assess your current state of social coherence. Be as honest and objective with yourself as possible. And, remember that to get to where we want to be, we first have to be realistic about where we are now. Consider the statements below and mark the response(s) that resonate most.

_____ I notice how I feel during and after consuming certain content (TV shows, podcasts, social media, etc.).

_____ I can identify which relationships, circumstances, or experiences make me feel lighter, hopeful, and more expansive or spacious and airy.

_____ I can identify which relationships, circumstances, or experiences make me feel unsafe, heavy, fearful, worried, constricted, or tense.

_____ I know when I'm overwhelmed and can ask for and receive or accept support.

_____ I feel securely connected to those around me and am able to authentically express myself to them.

_____ I can consider my own needs as well as the needs of the group or collective at large.

_____ I know which activities I like to do for fun and what brings me joy.

_____ I know what is important or meaningful to me and regularly make sure to embody these values and work toward these goals in my relationships.

_____ I know what inspires me or makes me feel uplifted.

_____ I can engage in active and open communication with others, allowing for a calm and curious exchange of thoughts and emotions.

_____ I work to resolve conflicts by trying to understand the lived experiences and perspectives of others.

_____ I celebrate my own successes as well as the successes of those around me.

The more statements you checked, the more likely you are to be moving toward social coherence and able to influence the experiences of those around you. As you continue your journey, you can revisit this checklist as a way to notice and celebrate your progress.

TAPPING INTO YOUR GLOBAL CONSCIOUSNESS

Our body is always gathering energetic information from our environment. When we're heart coherent, we're able to intuitively assess that information and feel shifts in the collective and global consciousness. The more connected we are with our heart, the better able we are to accurately sense and interpret what's happening in the world around us.

Everyone alive on Earth today impacts the global consciousness because each of our individual bodies emits energy. Similarly, the earth itself produces energy, in part through something called the Schumann resonances, which are low-frequency electromagnetic waves that exist between the earth and the ionosphere, the atmosphere's outer layer.[71] Schumann resonances are sometimes called the earth's "heartbeat." Centuries before scientists discovered and named this field of energy, ancient scholars and indigenous healers described this "web of creation," or a unifying energetic force that holds everything together. And, because humans are made up of the same four elements (hydrogen, nitrogen, oxygen, and carbon) that make up our universe, our physical bodies are easily impacted by changes in the natural world around us, including shifts in the earth's heartbeat.

The earth's natural Schumann resonance is 7.8 hertz (Hz), which is relaxing to the human body, whereas lower or higher levels can make us drowsy or send us into fight-or-flight, according to research.[72] Schumann resonances fluctuate based on ionospheric changes, and when they do, they affect our nervous system, dialing our collective stress level up or down, altering human health and behavior.[73] Increased solar and geomagnetic activity impacts our autonomic nervous system (ANS) by altering our melatonin and serotonin balance and blood pressure, along with our immune, reproductive, cardiac, and neurological processes. Some studies even show that our body can experience an "anticipatory reaction" two to three days before a geomagnetic event that alters our heart rate, heart rate variability, blood pressure, and skin conductance.[74]

Being exposed to Schumann resonances when they're relaxing—

or at the 7.8 Hz frequency—is extremely beneficial. One study found that participants who lived in a special underground bunker that screened out Schumann resonances for one month suffered from sleep problems, emotional distress, and migraine headaches.[75] Their health stabilized after they were reimmersed in the natural world. Other research has found that exposure to natural Schumann resonances helps us fall asleep faster and stay asleep through the night.[76] I know that I often experience this effect, sleeping better at night after I spend time in contact with nature during the day.

Just as the earth affects our energy and health, our global nervous system energy can change the planet's natural frequencies. Put more simply, we humans and Earth are in a continuous feedback loop.[77] Modern society may even be shifting Earth's natural energy with its production of *electrosmog*, or the man-made magnetic fields generated by modern technologies like Wi-Fi, TVs, microwaves, and GPS tracking devices. According to research, these low-level electromagnetic frequencies (EMFs) bump Earth's natural Schumann resonance from 7.8 Hz to levels that can raise global stress.[78]

Given the scientifically documented relationship between the earth's energy and our own, an inspiring new project called the Global Coherence Initiative (GCI) was launched to help create opportunities for individuals to impact the earth's energetic and geomagnetic fields by joining together in heart coherence. To measure the impact on global consciousness, researchers strategically installed a network of ultra-sensitive magnetic field detectors designed to measure the earth's magnetic resonances around the world. This research can offer a powerful reminder to each of us to do our own part to help decrease the presence and impact of our individual and global states of stress on our shared planet.

Becoming aware of both our global consciousness and the earth's energy can help us understand why we may feel anxious or stressed one day, even if nothing is upsetting us personally. When we experience these moments of anxiety for seemingly no reason, we can practice self-care or take steps to self- or co-regulate to soothe the effects that the global incoherence can have on our individual energy. We can be more empathetic to others during these times as well, realizing that they may feel more agitated, anxious, or upset due to energetic agitation in our global consciousness. When possible, some of us can decide to reschedule high-pressure meetings or difficult conversations for a more peaceful time.

SCHUMANN RESONANCE MENU

Below is a list of various ways we can reconnect with the earth's natural energy, its heartbeat. Consider regularly practicing the ones that appeal to you.

- Spend more time in nature by visiting a park, forest, beach, or other natural environment.
- Establish direct contact with the earth by walking on the ground in bare feet, taking a nap on the grass, slowing and deeply breathing in fresh air, or gazing at the stars.
- Limit the amount of time you spend with modern technology and your exposure to EMFs by using blue-light glasses or EMF blockers whenever possible.
- Listen to music that includes a Schumann resonance or frequency in the background during work or play (YouTube is a great place to find these recordings).

As with all of the tools you've learned throughout this book, the more consistently you practice, the more connected you will feel to the earth itself.

EXPAND YOUR AWARENESS

Like the earth, we too are made of energy. Practice the following exercises to help you become more aware of your energetic and interdependent relationship with nature. Choose one of the three sensory modalities listed—visual, audio, or energetic—and practice as consistently as possible.

Expand Your Awareness Exercises

Expanded vision. Focus your awareness on an object in your immediate field of vision, then gradually expand your awareness to include more of the objects to the left and right of it, and then any objects above or below it. The goal of this practice isn't to scan your environment but to gently expand your natural awareness to include more of your visual field.

Expanded hearing. If you feel safe enough, close your eyes. Focus your awareness on any sounds you hear in your immediate environment, then gradually expand your awareness to include fainter sounds and those coming from farther away. Again the goal isn't to strain your hearing but to gently expand your natural awareness to include more of your auditory field.

Expanded energetic awareness. Take three deep belly breaths, focusing your awareness on the rise and fall of your stomach with each inhalation and exhalation. Gently expand your awareness to include your entire body as it rises and falls with every breath. Gently expand your awareness again to include the space around you, which shifts with the flow of air from your body to your surroundings. Finally, gently expand your awareness one last time to include everything that flows in the space between you and the things around you, as well as between you and all that came before and will come after you.

The following exercise can help you expand your awareness to include the global consciousness, helping you tune in to your energetic nature.

1. Find a place in which to lie or sit comfortably for five to ten minutes. If you feel safe enough to do so, you may close your eyes.
2. Take two deep, slow breaths, feeling your body relax.
3. Spend a moment gently expanding your awareness to notice the

air itself and the different sensations as it caresses your skin, nourishes your lungs and body, and carries sounds to you.

4. Spend a moment gently expanding your awareness to notice the different thoughts in your mind without becoming distracted or focused on any one thought, allowing yourself to rest comfortably in this space of expanded awareness.

5. As you continue to rest in stillness, notice your body in space, gently expanding your awareness to:

- the space in front of you, noticing as far as you can sense
- the space behind you, noticing as far as you can sense
- the space to your left, noticing as far as you can sense
- the space to your right, noticing as far as you can sense
- the space above your head, noticing any sounds or movement above you as far as you can sense
- the space below you, noticing where your body touches the earth and any subtle vibrations you can sense.

6. Spend a moment gently expanding your awareness to notice the various sounds within and around you, paying attention to both any noise and the space between noises as you listen without paying attention to judgment or mental commentary. Allow yourself to rest comfortably in this expanded awareness.

7. Spend a moment expanding your awareness to notice the various smells or aromas around you, allowing yourself to rest comfortably in this expanded awareness.

8. Spend a moment expanding your awareness to notice the various memories from the past that may be coming to the present, allowing yourself to rest comfortably in this expanded awareness.

9. Spend a moment expanding your awareness to notice the various physical sensations in your living body in this moment, allowing yourself to rest comfortably in this expanded awareness.

10. Spend a moment gently expanding your awareness to notice

the vastness and interconnectedness of life itself, allowing yourself explore the boundless support present in every moment. Allowing yourself to rest comfortably in this expanded awareness.

These exercises will help attune your awareness as an energetic being interconnected with the natural world around you. Harnessing Earth's energy will help you create more energetic coherence in your brain and body that can then extend back outward, creating a more coherent collective consciousness. Embodying or living with more peace and compassion, we can each as an individual greatly impact all of humanity as we join together in the ultimate energetic collaboration— truly changing the world around us!

*   *   *

While we've reached the last few pages of this book, your journey doesn't end here. Your journey, I hope, will change as a result of this book. Life is a process of change, I've learned. For decades, I thought I'd inevitably reach a state of "achievement," "doneness," or "completion" where I'd be able to relax into unending peace, love, and connection. And I've since realized that there isn't any end or destination at which we arrive. We carry peace, love, and connection within us in every moment. And similar to nature and life itself, our being is always evolving, and embodying who we are is an ongoing process.

Our earliest environment shaped each of us into who we needed to be at the time in order to fit in and survive. We all continue to carry the accumulated stress of the generations who came before us, whose lack of knowledge and resources impacted our own bodies and minds, keeping us stuck in survival mode. Today, many of us can barely meet our own needs, and we don't feel safe in our bodies. Both prevent us from showing up as our authentic Self or connecting with another, no matter what we say, how much we try, or who's around.

Healing your most important relationship—the one you have with your Self—is the greatest way you can love others and find joy and ease in your relationships. Only once you feel safe and securely connected to who you are—body, mind, and soul—will you be able to build authentic connections with others and break the cycles that keep you locked in your past as well as the pasts of those who came before you.

When you feel safe and secure, you're better able to navigate the emotions that color your human experience and that hold valuable insight for your daily decisions. You're more attuned to the messages from your heart—your internal compass always beating inside you—that can direct you as you continue your journey into the unknown. And you're more frequently able to access the love and compassion that's always present in your heart and offer it to all your relationships, as well as to the world around you. Ultimately, when you're truly connected to your heart, you're better able to both perceive and receive the love that's present and available from others.

I continue the same journey alongside each of you. Every day, I set an intention to remain committed to my relationship with my Self so that I can continue to serve the people and community around me. To support this intention, I make daily choices to strengthen my connection to my heart and continue to learn what authentic love feels like in my own body and mind.

Love, as it turns out, doesn't come from anything or anyone outside us; it lives within each of us. When we reconnect with the infinite supply of kindness and compassion inside each of our hearts, we are guided by love.

And when we act in alignment with this loving guidance, we *become* love itself.

MY HEART'S UNEXPECTED TRUTH

I n one of your relationships over the years, you may have experienced a period of time when nearly every word, glance, or incident—no matter how seemingly minor—turned into an argument, hurt feeling, or hang-up. Maybe there was an underlying current of tension in all your interactions with that person, and although you may have gotten along at one time, little between you felt relaxed or loving anymore.

Several years ago, that situation existed among Lolly, Jenna, and me for a few months. The problem wasn't that we weren't committed to connecting with our heart, it was that we weren't actually listening to what our hearts were saying. For many of us, the heart's intuitive pings can be challenging to hear and even more challenging to heed; this is especially the case if our heart's messages are different from the conventions or expectations that we or society have put on ourselves. At the same time, if we don't live by our heart's truth, no matter how uncomfortable (or new) the messages may be at first, we may stay stuck in dysfunctional relationship cycles or be unable to relieve tension or resolve conflict with others. Though I knew all of that on an intellectual level, it took one memorable morning with Jenna before I truly understood it in a real way.

Jenna was the first person to join Lolly and me on our team at The Holistic Psychologist. If you read *How to Do the Work*, you may remember the story: The day we launched Self Healers Circle, our site's external server crashed, overwhelmed by the number of people trying to enroll in it. Lolly and I, eager to help those who wanted to join our community, spiraled into a panic as we tried to keep all the plates spinning. That was when Jenna, a long-time member of the community, followed her heart's intuitive ping and messaged to say that she saw and shared the same vision and was there to help. We read her message only seconds after she sent it, which was notable—and, as it would turn out, synchronistic—in a community of millions.

We talked by phone, and it became clear that Jenna shared our values, vision, and healing journey. She offered a professional partnership that Lolly and I didn't realize could be possible, and the three of us worked together virtually for several months before Jenna flew from California to Philadelphia, where Lolly and I were living at the time, to finally meet in person.

Very quickly, Jenna established herself as an essential member of our team, bringing communication and leadership that complemented the strengths Lolly and I had, enabling each of us to focus on specific areas of our fast-growing business. Our professional relationship blossomed swiftly and synergistically, and we became fast friends as well.

A few months after Jenna joined us, Lolly and I moved to Los Angeles, a transition that we had been considering for some time after feeling more aligned with both the weather and the opportunities offered there. Jenna, who had also relocated from the East Coast to California years before, moved to an apartment in Venice Beach within walking distance of our new place, and we continued to work closely together, now in person.

For the first year, the three of us worked smoothly and collaboratively as a team. On most days, Jenna would make the short walk to our apartment in the morning and we'd all have coffee together; then we'd work until lunch, eat together, and continue to work, often late into the night. As more people from around the world joined our SelfHealing movement, Jenna, Lolly, and I started spending even more time together, our "office" hours blurring into later nights, earlier mornings, dinners, and weekends together.

Pretty soon, the three of us had weekly rituals, like Taco Tuesday and Farmer's Market Friday, when we'd shop for produce and flowers in the open-air mall steps away from our front door. We started celebrating milestones together as a team, like when *How to Do the Work* hit the number one spot on the *New York Times* best-seller list and our membership community expanded to new reach around the world. We even began to celebrate birthdays and holidays together.

Over time, however, tension, irritability, and insecurity began to creep into our relationship, slowly and insidiously at first, like oil settling on water. We started arguing about small things, including silly stuff like someone forgetting to pick up an extra item at the grocery store or someone not using one specific word in a text. Though Jenna spent much of her time with us, she still had her own apartment a few blocks away. She'd often get sad at night after we finished work, wanting to be home but also not wanting to leave us. Lolly and I also felt conflicted, wanting her to stay but also unsure what to do with the sadness and guilt we'd sometimes feel after she did leave. The three of us began to cut one another off, act passive-aggressively, and take things personally. The more time we spent together, the more the tension grew and thickened, becoming so heavy that it felt palpable.

With care and compassion for one another, we realized that we were struggling to communicate as a team, both personally and professionally. All three of us were committed and willing to have difficult conversations, but no amount of loving confrontation or mature dialogue seemed to change the dynamics among us.

Then, one Friday morning, Jenna stopped by our apartment bright and early, around 6:00 a.m., and asked if she could talk to us each privately. She was on her way to see a friend in town for coffee at the farmer's market before Lolly and I were to meet them for our usual Friday-midmorning ritual.

The apartment that Lolly and I shared was fairly small, so Jenna and I found a quiet space in the back bedroom and closed the door. I sat on the bed and faced her as she sat across from me, making eye contact and taking a deep breath. I could tell she needed to share something that was weighing on her heart and mind: her face was flushed as she looked at me, choosing the words to speak. Seeing that she was on the verge of sharing something that appeared difficult to say, I gazed calmly at her. I intentionally connected to my heart while holding space, sitting in silence, and giving her the time to say whatever she wanted or needed to.

Jenna took a deep breath, put a hand on her heart, and began by acknowledging the escalating tension among us. She said she'd been spending time looking inward, connecting to her heart, and exploring her role in the rising tension, which was true to her character: Jenna has spent most her life intuitively and intentionally dropping into her heart, listening to its truth, and following its guidance. She also said that the work we were teaching in SelfHealers Circle that month—a course on Courageous Authenticity, which is about speaking and living by your heart's wisdom—had been inspired by her recent realization of her own heart's truth.

Courageously speaking from her heart, Jenna shared that she loved both Lolly and me as more than just friends or colleagues. She had romantic feelings for both of us, and although she had no idea how I'd feel or whether we'd be open to exploring a different kind of loving relationship with her, she wanted to honor her heart and explore its truth. She suggested that we take as much time as we needed to figure out how we felt and that no matter what each of our heart's said, she was committed to continuing our work together. If her feelings weren't reciprocated or an expanded relationship dynamic wasn't meant to be, she would accept that, and we could create boundaries moving forward to better define our professional relationship.

As I watched Jenna and listened to her speak, my heart began to race. A mix of nervousness and excitement flooded my body. At the same time, I felt a huge sense of relief, even though I couldn't discern whether it was relief for me, relief for Jenna, or relief for all three of us. What was clear to me at the time, though, was that Jenna had just identified the unspoken basis of our underlying conflict.

Still sitting on the bed, I didn't say anything to Jenna other than to thank her from my heart for sharing. I knew I needed time to process what she had told me before I responded; I also knew she wanted me to drop into and connect with my own heart's truth before I did.

She smiled lovingly, and we hugged before she left to meet her friend, which gave me the opportunity to take a moment to process our conversation. It also gave Lolly and me a chance to explore our individual responses to what Jenna had shared.

Lolly and I decided to go for a walk to a nearby coffee shop. Because Jenna had also spoken alone with Lolly, I didn't have to update her on what had happened. Instead, we looked at each other and each asked how the other felt. Our conversation didn't last long: We discovered quickly that we were both open to and curious about what Jenna had shared and were also willing to step into that curiosity. I knew that Lolly had always seen and wanted the best in and for me, and I felt the same way about her, helping us make a decision to grant that exploratory freedom to each other.

Looking back on the situation now, both Lolly and I can see the different ways in which we each ignored our heart's intuitive pings. I would feel a tightness in my heart when Jenna talked about dating other people, or Lolly would roll her eyes when Jenna mentioned seeing an ex, each of which was our own way of suppressing or overlooking our heart's messages. That morning, it became apparent to both of us that we hadn't been living by our heart's truth and that all three of us actually felt the same pull toward a possibility of expanded love. And although I didn't have an example of what a nonconventional relationship could look like, my heart was urging me to follow its pings. At that point in my journey, I knew I had to listen.

After Lolly and I left the coffee shop, we met Jenna and her friend at the farmer's market. We didn't say anything about what had just occurred; instead, we all wanted to take the time and space to reintegrate with one another without the pressure of communicating or talking about a decision. So we strolled, chatting and taking in the kaleidoscope of colors and aromas that filled the market, including those of fresh orchids, lilies, ripe melons, and peaches the color of a California sunset. To me that morning, the farmer's market seemed even more vibrant, more beautiful, more alive, effusive with the scent of fresh citrus, the abundance of freshly cut flowers, and the sense of expanded joy and restored harmony in the two most meaningful relationships in my life.

Jenna's decision to speak her heart's truth that Friday morning forever changed the dynamics among the three of us. The mutual tension, arguments, passive-aggressive comments, and hurt feelings dissipated almost immediately as our communication became more honest, efficient, and effortless. We became not just romantic partners but also better friends and even more productive colleagues. Emotionally, we evolved into a more fulfilling love that has allowed each of us to both honor and be valued for *being* who we are, as we grew our relationship and love together as a whole. I remain forever grateful to Jenna for her courageous authenticity and her ability to honor and to speak her heart's truth because her honesty allowed me to access my own.

In my whole life, I never thought that this would be where I'd land—in this expanded relationship—yet here I am. It surprised me, and I imagine part of you may feel surprised, too. And, please know, I am by no means suggesting that this is the path for you or your relationships.

I continue to share my journey with you to illustrate the toll that disconnection from your heart can take. And to show the power of connecting with and acting from your heart. Your heart will, of course, offer different whispers: a new home, a new city, or a new career or no career at all, as varied as we are as human beings. As I hope you know realize, your heart's messages are worth taking the time to hear, interpret, and heed. They are your own source of deeper guidance. Your heart is speaking to you right now, and its wisdom is limitless. The question is: Are you willing to listen?

Your human heart is incredibly powerful and capable of love in so many different and unique ways. Each of you has a heart that holds an infinite capacity for love, however that love looks for you.

To all of your hearts reading these words right now: You *already are* the love you seek.

ACKNOWLEDGMENTS

As with anything I ever create, I want to express my infinite gratitude for every one of you who felt inspired to pick up or share my work. It is as we become open and curious to each other's ideas and perspectives that we are given the opportunity to see ourselves and the world around us more clearly.

While I can't possibly name everyone who's impacted me thus far on my journey, I'm grateful for all the relationships that have or will crossed my path and allowed me to expand my own ability to know and love myself so that I may continue learn how to better know and love another.

To our global community of SelfHealers, thank you all for helping to support my own journey toward authentic Self-expression in this world. It is through my interactions with each of you that I see so much of myself and, as a result, feel less alone.

To my family, especially my dad and sister, who continue to allow me the space to prioritize my own healing and to rebuild a stronger foundation of more trusting and secure relationships—thank you both for your support in my process of becoming.

To my life partners, Jenna and Lolly, who continue to show me the most expanded love I have ever known. Lolly, I am eternally grateful for and ever inspired by your inherent ability to fully embrace yourself and your natural curiosity to understand other perspectives. Jenna, I am eternally grateful for and ever inspired by your inherent ability to be fully connected to your heart and your natural tendency to live a heart-led life.

To all the teachers who have passed on their wisdom and lived experience throughout the ages, may my own journey offer insight and value to our shared collective wisdom so that all who come next may be of benefit.

To all our ancestors, it is through my reconnection to all who have come before that I become more aware of my connection to all there is and all there will ever be. May each of you reading this begin to reconnect with your own infinite nature.

To my team—Brittany, Cristen, Furkan, Mike, MJ, and Tia— thank you for your daily work to embody these teachings and your collaborative efforts in service of our community.

To Dado, who has become an integral part and inspirational champion of all my creations, thank you for choosing to share your gifts to help spread such life-changing messages.

To Sarah Toland, whose open and curious desire to truly understand and translate this work helped to create this beautiful gift to the collective.

To the team at Harper Wave—Amanda, Emma, Karen, Julie, Yelena—who continue to see our vision and wholeheartedly support the creation of these works, and to the Harper Wave design team— Jo, Leah, and Suzy—whose dedicated efforts produced such beautiful artwork, and the production team whose tireless efforts made this book possible.

And finally, to all of you who will continue your own journey back to your heart's truth, who will collectively join our global movement to change the world around us, and who will inspire others to do the same.

NOTES

1. E. Ron de Kloet, Melly S. Oitzl, and Marian Joels, "Stress and Cognition: Are Corticosteroids Good or Bad Guys?," *Trends in Neurosciences* 22, no. 10 (1999): 422–26, https://doi:10.1016/s0166-2236(99)01438-1.

2. John Bowlby, "The Nature of the Child's Tie to His Mother," *International Journal of Psychoanalysis* 39, no. 5 (1958): 350–73.

3. Daniel Siegel, *The Developing Mind: How Relationships and the Brain Interact to Shape Who We Are*, 3rd ed. (New York: Guilford Press, 2020), 7.

4. Louise C. Hawkley and John T. Cacioppo, "Loneliness Matters: A Theoretical and Empirical Review of Consequences and Mechanisms," *Annals of Behavioral Medicine* 40, no. 2 (2010): 218–27, https://doi:10.1007/s12160-010-9210-8.

5. Siegel, *The Developing Mind*, 7.

6. "In Brief: The Science of Early Childhood Development," Center on the Developing Child, Harvard University, https://developingchild.harvard.edu/resources/inbrief-science-of-ecd/.

7. John Horgan, "What God, Quantum Mechanics and Consciousness Have in Common," *Scientific American*, April 14, 2021, https://www.scientificamerican.com/article/what-god-quantum-mechanics-and-consciousness-have-in-common/.

8. Siegel, *The Developing Mind*, 14.

9. Kory Taylor and Elizabeth B. Jones, *Adult Dehydration* (Treasure Island, FL: StatPearls Publishing, 2022), https://www.ncbi.nlm.nih.gov/books/NBK555956/.

10. Lisa Feldman Barrett, "The Theory of Constructed Emotion: An Active Inference Account of Interoception and Categorization," *Social Cognitive and Affective Neuroscience* 12, no. 1 (January 2017): 1–23, https://doi.org/10.1093/scan/nsw154.

11. Ali M. Alshami, "Pain: Is It All in the Brain or the Heart?," *Current Pain and Headache Reports* 23, no. 12 (November 2019), https://doi:10.1007/s11916-019-0827-4.

12. "A Deeper View of Intuition," HeartMath Institute, August 26, 2019, https://www.heartmath.org/articles-of-the-heart/a-deeper-view-of-intuition/.

13. Rollin McCraty, Mike Atkinson, and Raymond Trevor Bradley, "Electrophysiological Evidence of Intuition: Part 2. A System-wide Process?," *Journal of Alternative and Complementary Medicine* 10, no. 2 (April 2004): 325–36, https://doi:10.1089/107555304323062310.

14. Timothy T. Brown and Terry L. Jernigan, "Brain Development During the Preschool Years," *Neuropsychology Review* 22, no. 4 (2012): 313–33, https://doi:10.1007/s11065-012-9214-1.

15. Lena Lim and Chiea Chuen Khor. "Examining the Common and Specific Grey Mat-

ter Abnormalities in Childhood Maltreatment and Peer Victimization," *BJPsych Open* 8, no. 4 (July 12, 2022): e132, https://doi:10.1192/bjo.2022.531.

16. Marieke J. H. Begemann et al., "Childhood Trauma Is Associated with Reduced Frontal Gray Matter Volume: A Large Transdiagnostic Structural MRI Study," *Psychological Medicine* 53, no. 3 (June 2021): 1–9, https://doi:10.1017/S0033291721002087.

17. Zoya Marinova and Andreas Maercker, "Biological Correlates of Complex Posttraumatic Stress Disorder—State of Research and Future Directions," *European Journal of Psychotraumatology* 6, no. 1 (April 2015): 2591, https://doi:10.3402/ejpt.v6.25913.

18. Monique C. Pfaltz et al., "Are You Angry at Me? Negative Interpretations of Neutral Facial Expressions Are Linked to Child Maltreatment but Not to Posttraumatic Stress Disorder," *European Journal of Psychotraumatology* 10, no. 1 (November 2019): 1682929, https://doi:10.1080/20008198.2019.1682929.

19. Lisa Feldman Barrett, "The Theory of Constructed Emotion: An Active Inference Account of Interoception and Categorization," *Social Cognitive and Affective Neuroscience* 12, no. 1 (January 2017): 1–23, https://doi.org/10.1093/scan/nsw154.

20. Ibid.

21. David Q. Stoye et al., "Maternal Cortisol Is Associated with Neonatal Amygdala Microstructure and Connectivity in a Sexually Dimorphic Manner," eLife, November 24, 2020, e60729, https://doi:10.7554/eLife.60729.

22. Wendy Menigoz et al., "Integrative and Lifestyle Medicine Strategies Should Include Earthing (Grounding): Review of Research Evidence and Clinical Observations," *Explore* 16, no. 3 (May–June 2020): 152–60, https://doi.org/10.1016/j.explore.2019.10.005.

23. Ibid.

24. "The Connection Between Leaky Gut and Leaky Brain," Mindd Foundation, https://mindd.org/connection-leaky-gut-leaky-brain/.

25. Edward Reynolds, "Vitamin B_{12}, Folic Acid, and the Nervous System," *Lancet. Neurology* 5, no. 11 (November 2006): 949–60, https://doi:10.1016/S1474-4422(06)70598-1.

26. "Vitamin D and Your Health: Breaking Old Rules, Raising New Hopes," Harvard Health Publishing, September 13, 2021, https://www.health.harvard.edu/staying-healthy/vitamin-d-and-your-health-breaking-old-rules-raising-new-hopes.

27. Hércules Rezende Freitas et al., "Fatty Acids, Antioxidants and Physical Activity in Brain Aging," *Nutrients* 9, no. 11 (November 2017): 1263, https://doi:10.3390/nu9111263.

28. Giada De Palma et al., "Effects of a Gluten-Free Diet on Gut Microbiota and Immune Function in Healthy Adult Subjects," *British Journal of Nutrition* 102, no. 8 (2009): 1154–60, https://doi.org/10.1017/S0007114509371767.

29. Beate Wild et al., "Acupuncture in Persons with an Increased Stress Level—Results from a Randomized-Controlled Pilot Trial," *PLOS ONE* 15, no. 7 (July 2020): e0236004, https://doi:10.1371/journal.pone.0236004.

30. Sarah J. Schubert, Christopher W. Lee, and Peter D. Drummond, "Eye Movements Matter, But Why? Psychophysiological Correlates of EMDR Therapy to Treat Trauma in Timor-Leste," *Journal of EMDR Practice and Research* 10, no. 2 (2016): 70–81, https://doi.org/10.1891/1933-3196.10.2.70

31. "Health Outcome Studies," HeartMath Institute, https://www.heartmath.org/research/science-of-the-heart/health-outcome-studies/.

32. Ibid.

33. John Armour, "Intrinsic Cardiac Neurons," *Journal of Cardiovascular Electrophysiology* 2, no. 4 (August 1991): 331–41, https://doi.org/10.1111/j.1540-8167.1991.tb01330.x/.

34. Mitchell B. Liester, "Personality Changes Following Heart Transplantation: The Role of Cellular Memory," *Medical Hypotheses* 135 (2020): 109468, https://doi:10.1016/j.mehy.2019.109468.

35. "Energetic Communication," HeartMath Institute, https://www.heartmath.org/research/science-of-the-heart/energetic-communication/.

36. Ibid.

37. J. A. Armour, "Anatomy and Function of the Intrathoracic Neurons Regulating the Mammalian Heart," I. H. Zucker and J. P. Gilmore, eds. *Reflex Control of the Circulation* (Boca Raton, FL: CRC Press; 1991) 1–37.

38. Rollin McCraty, "The Social Heart: Energy Fields and Consciousness," Pathways to Family Wellness, https://pathwaystofamilywellness.org/new-edge-science/the-social-heart-energy-fields-and-consciousness.html.

39. Rollin McCraty and Maria Zayas, "Intuitive Intelligence, Self-Regulation, and Lifting Consciousness," *Global Advances in Health and Medicine* 3, no. 2 (2014): 56–65, https://doi:10.7453/gahmj.2014.013.

40. "A Deeper View of Intuition," HeartMath Institute, August 26, 2019, https://www.heartmath.org/articles-of-the-heart/a-deeper-view-of-intuition/.

41. Saeed Rezaei et al., "Nonlocal Intuition: Replication and Paired-Subjects Enhancement Effects," *Global Advances in Health and Medicine* 3, no. 2 (2014): 5–15, https://doi:10.7453/gahmj.2014.012.

42. "Intuition Research: Coherence and the Surprising Role of the Heart," HeartMath Institute, https://www.heartmath.org/research/science-of-the-heart/intuition-research/.

43. McCraty and Zayas, "Intuitive Intelligence."

44. "Coherence," HeartMath Institute, https://www.heartmath.org/research/science-of-the-heart/coherence/.

45. W. A. Tiller, Rollin McCraty, and M. Atkinson, "Cardiac Coherence: A New, Noninvasive Measure of Autonomic Nervous System Order," *Alternative Therapies in Health and Medicine* 2, no. 1 (February 1996): 52–65.

46. "Energetic Communication," HeartMath Institute.

47. Richard Wiseman and Marilyn Schlitz, "Experimenter Effects and the Remote Detection of Staring," *Journal of Parapsychology* 61, no. 3 (1997): 197–208, https://psycnet.apa.org/record/1998-02543-002.

48. Penney Peirce, *Frequency: The Power of Personal Vibration* (New York: Atria Books/Beyond Words, 2011).

49. Martha G. Welch et al., "Family Nurture Intervention in the NICU Increases Autonomic Regulation in Mothers and Children at 4–5 Years of Age: Follow-up Results from a Randomized Controlled Trial," *PLOS ONE* 15, no. 8 (August 2020): e0236930, https://doi:10.1371/journal.pone.0236930.

50. Madalynn Neu et al., "Effect of Holding on Co-Regulation in Preterm Infants: A Randomized Controlled Trial," *Early Human Development* 90, no. 3 (March 2014): 141–47, https://doi:10.1016/j.earlhumdev.2014.01.008.

51. "Children's Social and Emotional Development Starts with Co-regulation," National

Institute for Children's Health Quality, https://www.nichq.org/insight/childrens-social-and-emotional-development-starts-co-regulation.

52. Read Montague, *Your Brain Is (Almost) Perfect: How We Make Decisions* (New York: Plume, 2007).

53. Ibid.

54. John S. Hagelin et al., "Effects of Group Practice of the 'Transcendental Meditation' Program on Preventing Violent Crime in Washington, DC: Results of the National Demonstration Project, June–July 1993," *Social Indicators Research* 47, no. 2 (1999): 153–201, http://www.jstor.org/stable/27522387.

55. "Washington Meditation Project Reverses Violent Crime Trend by 23.3%," World Peace Group, https://www.worldpeacegroup.org/washington_crime_prevention_full_article.html.

56. "Lebanon Peace Project Reduces War Deaths by 76%," World Peace Group, https://www.worldpeacegroup.org/lebanon_peace_project_research.html.

57. "Prayer and Healing," Duke Today, November 30, 2001, https://today.duke.edu/2001/11/mm_prayerand.html.

58. William S. Harris et al., "A Randomized, Controlled Trial of the Effects of Remote, Intercessory Prayer on Outcomes in Patients Admitted to the Coronary Care Unit," *Archives of Internal Medicine* 159, no. 19 (October 1999): 2273–78, https://doi:10.1001/archinte.159.19.2273.

59. Larry Dossey, "Spirituality, Prayer, and Medicine: What Is the Fuss Really About?," *Virtual Mentor* 7, no. 5 (May 2005): 390–94, https://doi.org/10.1001/virtualmentor.2005.7.5.oped2-0505.

60. R. D. Nelson, "Multiple Field REG/RNG Recordings During a Global Event," *Electronic Journal for Anomalous Phenomena* 98, no. 3 (1977), https://noosphere.princeton.edu/ejap/diana/nelson_eJAP.htm.

61. Peter A. Bancel, "Searching for Global Consciousness: A 17-Year Exploration," *Explore* 13, no. 2 (2017): 94–101, https://doi:10.1016/j.explore.2016.12.003.

62. Eliska Prochazkova and Mariska E. Kret, "Connecting Minds and Sharing Emotions Through Mimicry: A Neurocognitive Model of Emotional Contagion," *Neuroscience and Biobehavioral Reviews* 80 (2017): 99–114, https://doi:10.1016/j.neubiorev.2017.05.013.

63. Carolina Herrando and Efthymios Constantinides, "Emotional Contagion: A Brief Overview and Future Directions," *Frontiers in Psychology* 12 (July 2021): article 712606, https://doi:10.3389/fpsyg.2021.712606.

64. Ibid.

65. Adam D. I. Kramer, Jamie E. Guillory, and Jeffrey T. Hancock, "Experimental Evidence of Massive-Scale Emotional Contagion Through Social Networks," *Psychological and Cognitive Sciences* 111, no. 24 (June 2014): 8788–90, https://doi:10.1073/pnas.1320040111.

66. Jamil Zaki, "Kindness Contagion," *Scientific American*, July 26, 2016, https://www.scientificamerican.com/article/kindness-contagion/.

67. Takayuki Nozawa et al., "Prefrontal Inter-Brain Synchronization Reflects Convergence and Divergence of Flow Dynamics in Collaborative Learning: A Pilot Study," *Frontiers in Neuroergonomics* 2 (2021): 19, https://doi.org/10.3389/fnrgo.2021.686596.

68. Heidi Hoel, Kate Sparks, and Cary L. Cooper, "The Cost of Violence/Stress at Work

and the Benefits of a Violence/Stress-Free Working Environment," Report Commissioned by the International Labour Organization, January 1, 2001, https://www.ilo.org/wcmsp5/groups/public/—ed_protect/—protrav/—safework/documents/publication/wcms_108532.pdf.

69. Rollin McCraty, "New Frontiers in Heart Rate Variability and Social Coherence Research: Techniques, Technologies, and Implications for Improving Group Dynamics and Outcome," *Frontiers in Public Health* 5 (October 2017): article 267, https://doi:10.3389/fpubh.2017.00267.

70. "Social Coherence: Outcome Studies in Organizations," HeartMath Institute, https://www.heartmath.org/research/science-of-the-heart/social-coherence/.

71. "Schumann Resonance," National Aeronautics and Space Administration, https://www.nasa.gov/mission_pages/sunearth/news/gallery/schumann-resonance.html.

72. "Schumann Resonances and Their Effect on Human Bioregulation," Bioregulatory Medicine Institute, February 7, 2020, https://www.biologicalmedicineinstitute.com/post/2019/09/20/schumann-resonances-and-their-effect-on-human-bioregulation.

73. Viktor Stolc et al., "The Impact of the Schumann Resonances on Human and Mammalian Physiology," white paper submitted to the NASA Biological and Physical Sciences Decadal Survey, October 31, 2021, http://surveygizmoresponseuploads.s3.amazonaws.com/fileuploads/623127/6378869/139-39805df8350d398db74a88610c37ca5e_STOLCVIKTOR_.pdf.

74. Rollin McCraty et al., "Synchronization of Human Autonomic Nervous System Rhythms with Geomagnetic Activity in Human Subjects," *International Journal of Environmental Research and Public Health* 14, no. 7 (July 2017): 770, https://doi:10.3390/ijerph14070770.

75. E. Jacobi, O. Richter, and Gertrud Krüskemper, "Simulated VLF-Fields as a Risk Factor of Thrombosis," *International Journal of Biometeorology* 25, no. 2 (1981): 133–42, https://doi.org/10.1007/BF02184461.

76. Yu-Shu Huang et al., "The Subjective and Objective Improvement of Non-invasive Treatment of Schumann Resonance in Insomnia—A Randomized and Double-Blinded Study," *Nature and Science of Sleep* 14 (June 2022): 1113–24, https://doi:10.2147/NSS.S346941.

77. "Global Coherence Research: The Science of Interconnectivity," HeartMath Institute, https://www.heartmath.org/gci/research/global-coherence/.

78. "Schumann Resonances and Their Effect on Human Bioregulation," Bioregulatory Medicine Institute.

INDEX

ABOUT THE AUTHOR

DR. NICOLE LEPERA is the author of the #1 *New York Times* bestselling book *How to Do the Work* and *How to Meet Your Self* and the creator of the #selfhealers movement, a community of people joining to take healing into their own hands. Dr. LePera received her BA in clinical psychology from Cornell University and her doctorate from The New School for Social Research. Dr. LePera has also studied at the Philadelphia School of Psychoanalysis and has worked with a wide spectrum of patients in a variety of capacities, including couples therapy and substance use treatment and support. Her teachings empower the individual to break free from intergenerational trauma and inherited beliefs to reconnect with their authentic Self and heal their relationships.